W9-ARZ-552

A Critical Dictionary
of Psychoanalysis

A Critical Dictionary of Psychoanalysis

CHARLES RYCROFT

1973

LITTLEFIELD, ADAMS & CO.

Totowa, New Jersey

Published 1973 by
LITTLEFIELD, ADAMS & CO.
by arrangement with Thomas Nelson and Sons Ltd.

Library of Congress Cataloging in Publication Data

Rycroft, Charles
    A Critical Dictionary of Psychoanalysis

    (A Littlefield, Adams Quality Paperback No. 270)
    Bibliography: p.
    1. Psychiatry—Dictionaries. 2. Psychoanalysis—
    Dictionaries. I. Title. [DNLM: 1. Psychoanalysis
    —Dictionary. WM13 R991c 1973]
[RC437.R9 1973]   616.8'917'03   73-14626
ISBN 0-8226-0270-9

Printed in the United States of America

Acknowledgements

I should like to express my gratitude to Mr James Mitchell for suggesting that I construct this dictionary and for his moral support while I was doing so, and to Mr Peter Ford for his labours in creating order out of an exceptionally chaotic manuscript.

CHARLES RYCROFT

AUTHOR'S NOTE

Cross-references are indicated by the use of small capitals. The abbreviation *C.O.D.* is used to refer to the *Concise Oxford Dictionary*, *O.E.D.* to the *Oxford English Dictionary*.

Introduction

Psychoanalysis remains a sufficiently controversial subject for it to be perhaps necessary to state explicitly that this book is not a dictionary of criticisms of psychoanalysis but a critical dictionary of psychoanalysis. Its aim is not to provide ammunition for those who, for whatever reason, wish to demolish psychoanalysis, but to help those who need or wish to inform themselves about it to do so intelligently and critically. To this end its entries consist not merely of formal dictionary definitions of technical terms used in the analytical literature, but also give some account of their origin, of their connexion with other terms and concepts used in analytical theory, and of the controversies relating to them that exist among analysts themselves. Extensive use has been made of cross-references which will, it is hoped, enable readers who look up one entry to discover the position it occupies within the total frame of reference of analytical theory.

Since the author is a practising psychoanalyst who was trained in the Freudian school, and since, furthermore, this dictionary has grown out of a notebook in which he recorded his puzzlement and doubts about certain aspects of Freudian theory, the term 'psychoanalysis' refers throughout, unless explicitly qualified, to Freudian psychoanalysis. This is not parochialism on the author's part but conformity to the usage generally current among those professionally involved in the field. For them the term 'psychoanalysis' refers specifically to the psychological theories and forms of treatment which derive directly from Freud and which are taught to students who seek training at any of the institutes affiliated to the International Psycho-Analytical Association. Other schools of thought, such as the Jungian, Adlerian, and existential, all of which are psychoanalytical in the popular sense, have their own distinguishing names and labels, the purpose of which is to ensure that their members are not mistaken for Freudians. Jungian analysts call themselves 'analytical psychologists' and their theory 'analytical psychology', Adlerians are 'individual psychologists', while existentialists talk of 'existential psychoanalysis'. These distinctions are a source of great confusion to the general public, which tends to be more impressed by the resemblances between the various psychotherapeutic schools than by their differences, and it is hoped that the relevant entries in this dictionary will do something to clarify matters.

For rather similar reasons I have included entries explaining the differing functions of psychiatrists, psychotherapists, psychoanalysts, and psychologists. These are words which cause considerable confusion to the laity, who frequently misuse them to the irritation of workers in the field who, like most professional people, dislike being incorrectly designated.

However, despite the fact that this dictionary contains fuller accounts of Freudian concepts than it does of those belonging to other schools, it is far from being exclusively Freudian. Its range is wider than, for instance, Laplanche and Pontalis's *Vocabulaire de la Psychoanalyse* (which is an introduction to psychoanalytical theory constructed in dictionary form), since it includes:

1. Definitions of psychiatric terms, particularly those used to describe symptoms and make diagnoses. These have been included for two reasons. Firstly, most psychoanalysts are doctors. The disorders they treat and write about are regarded both by society at large and by the medical profession in particular as 'illnesses', and as such they are subject to the same procedures of description in technical language and diagnostic labelling as are physical illnesses. As a result, much of the psychoanalytical literature uses the technical, medical, and psychiatric vocabulary with which its authors and the readers for whom it was originally intended are at home. Secondly, many of these psychiatric terms have of recent years passed into general currency, without, however, retaining their original, precise meanings. As a result readers who are familiar with the journalistic and literary connotations of words such as 'manic', 'depressive', 'schizophrenic', 'compulsive', 'ambivalent' are liable to get confused when they encounter them in the psychoanalytical literature, where they are almost always used to refer to specific clinical phenomena. Alternatively, and even worse, they may imagine that they are understanding what in fact they are not.

The same consideration applies, of course, to specifically

psychoanalytical terms which have passed into general currency. For instance, 'narcissism', a term which was invented by Havelock Ellis to describe a form of sexual perversion, was borrowed by Freud to describe a variety of phenomena concerned with the individual's relation to himself, and has since passed into everyday language as a derogatory term, which the *Concise Oxford Dictionary* defines as: 'n. (psycho-anal.) Tendency to self-worship; absorption in one's own personal perfections.' Anyone reading the technical psychoanalytical literature with this definition in mind will, however, soon be in difficulties, since he will encounter references to narcissistic wounds, traumata, identifications, depletions, supplies which clearly have little if anything to do with self-worship, and will find distinctions being made between primary and secondary narcissism, or between healthy and defensive narcissism, which are obviously entirely unrelated to moral judgements.

2. Definitions of a number of specifically medical terms, which, for the reasons given above, psychoanalysts use without explanation.

3. Definitions of Jungian terms. Since the author suffers from the not uncommon constitutional defect of being incapable of understanding Jung's writings, it seemed fairer to the reader, and to Jung, to take these from E. A. Bennet's *What Jung Really Said* than to vamp them himself. Bennet was a close friend of Jung and his book explains Jung's ideas clearly and simply – indeed so clearly and simply that it leaves the reader wondering why Jung has ever been regarded as mystical or obscure.

4. Definitions and descriptions of the basic existential concepts. These have been included for a number of reasons. Firstly, the writings of Sartre, R. D. Laing, and Rollo May have of recent years aroused considerable interest and discussion among both the general public and the psychotherapeutic professions. Secondly, many of the criticisms and doubts about the validity of a number of basic Freudian assumptions which have recently been voiced from within the Freudian fold are essentially existential in nature. I refer here specifically to the doubts which have been expressed by Szasz, Home, Lomas, myself, and others as to whether the causal-deterministic assumptions of Freudian theory are valid, i.e. whether it is really possible to maintain that

human behaviour has causes in the sense that physical phenomena do or that human personality can really be explained as the result of events that happened to it as a child. Thirdly, existential criticisms of Freudian psychoanalysis are, in general, well-informed and made by persons who understand the nature of psychotherapeutic relationships and take subjective phenomena and suffering seriously. As a result they constitute a greater challenge than do the criticisms of Eysenck and the behaviour therapists, which derive from a theoretical position – that provided by learning theory – which is concerned to remove the psyche from psychology and attempts to understand human nature by dehumanizing it.

5. Definitions of a number of biological concepts which are necessary for an understanding of Freud's views on instinct and evolution.

6. Definitions of a number of anthropological concepts which are necessary for an understanding of Freud's speculative excursions into this field.

Having given a brief account of the scope and aims of this dictionary, it is now necessary for me to describe some of the stumbling-blocks and pitfalls which beset the path of those who seek to discover what psychoanalysis is really all about. I must confess to a conviction that there is something daunting about the psychoanalytical literature and that many who venture to explore it get lost and confused – sometimes permanently. There are, I believe, three main reasons for this, which I shall discuss under the headings of linguistics, dissension, and sources:

Linguistics
I have already referred to one of the linguistic stumbling-blocks to gaining entry into the psychoanalytical literature. This is jargon, the existence of a technical language constructed by psychoanalysts for communication among themselves. Some people object on principle to analytical jargon, maintaining that it should be possible to write about human experience without using technical terms, but I doubt whether those who take this view really appreciate how remote from everyday experience some abnormal

mental states are. Nor are they taking into account the fact that sciences develop by classifying facts – a procedure which makes it necessary to attach definable labels to the classes so established – and by discovering latent connexions (between apparently unconnected facts) which also require exact labels. Diagnostic terms, such as 'obsessional neurosis' and 'schizophrenia', and descriptive terms, such as 'Isakower phenomenon' or 'depersonalization', arise from the need to classify facts, while the technical terms used by psychoanalysis to formulate its theories of infantile development arise from the need for concepts to explain the hidden, developmental connexion between childhood and maturity.

The misuse of jargon can, however, create pitfalls for the unwary, and indeed often does. One pitfall is created by the use of abstract explanatory concepts while describing facts, as occurs when analysts use technical terms while describing the data provided them by patients. Ideally case-histories are written in everyday language, theoretical concepts only being used during the ensuing discussion of the data, but all too often this ideal is not even aimed at, and the reader is only allowed to see the reported facts through a theoretical haze. As a result he is given no opportunity to consider the possibility that the facts presented to him might have been explained in some other way.

Another is the ease with which technical jargon can be used to construct theories which are tautologous, which are internally consistent and intellectually satisfying not because they really explain the facts but because the definitions of the technical terms involved interlock beautifully. To my mind, the fascination exerted on some analysts by Freud's cherished conception, the 'psychic apparatus', derives not from the accuracy with which it reflects the workings of the human mind but from the intellectual and aesthetic appeal of an internally consistent theory. Its bits fit together perfectly and would continue to do so even if it were proved to be nonsense.

Yet another pitfall is that created by the use of jargon to conceal ignorance. Learned words, particularly if derived from an ancient tongue, sound impressive and can be used to impress the innocent. Psychiatrists, following a long-established medical tradition, are more often guilty of this form of unconscious deception than are the analysts, the procedure or trick being to translate the patient's complaint into Greek and then assure him that his troubles are due to an illness with an outlandish and exotic name. The patient complains that he has lost his memory, so the physician tells him he is suffering from *amnesia*; the patient is frightened of open spaces and the physician tells him he has *agoraphobia*. And curiously enough both parties to the transaction feel better for it, the physician because he feels he has done something, the patient because his suffering has found a label which renders it less mysterious. Freud himself seems to have been remarkably free from the tendency to be duped by words, and one of the least-sung achievements of psychoanalysis has been to rescue psychiatry from a preoccupation with the art of diagnostic labelling by demonstrating that it is dynamic processes not states of mind that count.

Having circumvented jargon, the reader who is determined to come to grips with psychoanalysis next has to contend, if he is English, with the complications arising from the fact that most of the psychoanalytical literature was originally written, and even more of it originally thought out, in German. Unfortunately ideas cannot be transported bodily from one language to another simply by translating them word by word and the possibility has to be seriously envisaged that something significant happens to an idea or a theory when it is translated into another language. Like immigrants, ideas from a foreign tongue are only assimilated with difficulty, and by the time they have been naturalized they are likely to have changed. Geoffrey Gorer, in an essay entitled *Cultural Community and Cultural Diversity*, has pointed out that those four freedoms – freedom of speech, freedom of religion, freedom from want, and freedom from fear – of which we heard so much in the later days of the Second World War, do not in fact make sense in any language other than English, for the simple reason that no other language possesses a word analogous to our 'freedom', which can embrace both 'not being prevented from' and 'being protected from'. Similarly a number of psychoanalytical concepts do not travel well and create difficulties for readers who have to encounter them at second hand.

One of the key concepts of Freudian theory is '*Angst*', which all English translators render 'anxiety'. No one has suggested a better translation than this, but unfortunately the range of meanings covered by '*Angst*' and 'anxiety' are not identical. '*Angst*' seems to be inextricably involved with ideas of anguish, fear, and pain and not to be all that closely tied to the notion of futurity, while 'anxiety' is, as *Roget's Thesaurus* puts it, one of the 'prospective affections' and can even be used to refer to pleasurable anticipation – 'I'm anxious to see such and such a film.' As a result of this linguistic discrepancy between English and German, anxiety always features in the analytical literature as an unpleasant experience which the individual seeks to avoid or to rid himself of and never as an eager preparedness to embrace the future. It is also used, particularly in the form of 'primary anxiety', to refer to experiences which an English writer would be inclined to describe as fright or terror. One curious and unfortunate consequence of this equation of anxiety with *Angst* has been the dissemination of the idea that anxiety is always a neurotic symptom and that the ideal 'healthy', 'adjusted' person would be 'anxiety-free'. This idea belongs, however, more to popular psychiatric folk-lore of the American variety than to psychoanalytical theory.

But it is not only single words that cause difficulties. It is also linguistic structure and the habits of thought that are both engendered and reflected by it. Freud's writings are permeated by the idea of opposites in conflict with one another. Until the 1920s he based his theory of neurosis on the assumption that there were two groups of instincts – the sexual (reproductive) and ego (self-preservative) instincts – and maintained that the human predisposition to neurosis derived from the inherent tendency of these two opposed forces to come into conflict with one another. But, one may ask, why did Freud assume that there were two groups of instincts and not three or four, and why did he assume that they were opposed and not complementary to one another? Was it really because the clinical facts compelled him to make these assumptions, or was it perhaps because linguistic habits of thought impelled him to follow Hegel and Marx and to construct a dialectical theory which came naturally to him but which seems alien to those who have been nurtured on the English language and on English empiricism? One's suspicion that the latter explanation is correct, that Freud's preoccupation with opposites was culturally and linguistically predetermined, is increased and indeed confirmed by the fact that when, in the 1920s, Freud proposed an entirely new theory of instincts, this new theory was again one of two groups of instincts, the Life and Death instincts, which were again assumed to be inherently opposed to one another. This new theory was also frankly speculative and, as we now know, totally misguided, since it was based on a misunderstanding of the second law of thermodynamics and on unwarrantable deductions from the fact that organisms are poisoned by their own excreta.

As I mention at several points in the main text of this book, contemporary animal psychology recognizes at least seven instincts (or innate behaviour patterns) and sees no necessity to assume inherent opposition between any two groups of them – though it does, of course, maintain that on specific occasions any two or more may be in conflict with one another.

Another aspect of psychoanalytical theory which is, I suspect, essentially Germanic is its habit of explaining behaviour by reference to hypothetical forces such as 'Sex', 'Aggression', 'Love', and 'Hate', which are conceived to impel the individual by, as it were, pushing him along from behind. These concepts presumably arise in the first instance from the need to generalize experiences of loving, hating, and being aggressive, and in English their gerundive nature (i.e. the fact that they are nouns derived from verbs and refer to processes and actions and not to things) is indicated by the absence of a preceding article. In German, however, abstract nouns are frequently preceded by a definite article and are treated grammatically as things with properties. I have recently read an article by myself translated into German and it includes frequent references to 'the childhood', 'the consciousness', 'the psychoanalysis', 'the cosmology', etc., when I have been using these ideas generally and have not been referring to any particular person's childhood or cosmology. It seems to me that one of the effects of this grammatical reification of abstract nouns must be to encourage belief in the real existence of abstractions and the propensity to invoke them as explanatory agents, as essences or noumena actuating behaviour in a way that is reminiscent of the angels which medieval cosmology invoked to explain the movements of the planets. These angels enabled the problem of how inanimate objects could move to be solved by postulating the existence of living creatures who pushed them along. Rather similarly, Freud assumed that the human ego was a passive entity lacking energy or force of its own and therefore only capable of movement in so far as it was acted upon by forces external to itself, these forces being located either in the Id (Unconscious) or the environment. But the idea that each individual has an 'I', an ego, on which some other unconscious part of himself acts, is itself an artefact of language, which arises as a result of treating 'I' as first a noun and then as a concrete one; the facts of the matter are that we do things, but that on occasion our acts are not those we intended; e.g. we make slips of the tongue, or are forced to realize that our motives were other than we thought.

Another difficulty confronting English readers of the psychoanalytical literature derives from the fact that English differs from German in having in effect two vocabularies, one largely Anglo-Saxon in origin, which is used as the vehicle of ordinary social intercourse, and another largely derived from Latin and Greek, which is used for conceptual thinking. In German the word for referring to oneself is '*ich*' and that for conceptual thinking about the idea of oneself is '*das Ich*', but in English the equivalent terms are 'I' and 'ego'. As a result it is easy for an English reader of the psychoanalytical literature to lose sight of the fact that the ego, which is so often presented to him as though it were an impersonal structure with properties and characteristics and occasionally even a shape, is really nothing other than himself being thought of in conceptual terms.

The classic example of this particular difficulty is provided by the noun 'cathexis' and its companion verbs 'to cathect' and 'to decathect'. These words, which have mystified countless English-speaking students of psychoanalysis, were invented by Freud's English translators for the purpose of rendering his concept '*Besetzung*'. In German, '*Besetzung*' is an ordinary, everyday, homely word, related to '*setzen*', 'to place or set', and can be used to describe such activities as garrisoning a town, manning a ship, putting money on a horse, stocking a pond with fish – to cite only examples taken from a school dictionary. In psychoanalytical theory, however, it is used to describe one of Freud's most obscure and difficult concepts: the hypothesis that there exists some form of mental energy 'which possesses all the characteristics of a quantity (though we have no means of measuring it), which is capable of increase, diminution, displacement and discharge, and which is spread over the memory traces of ideas somewhat as an electric charge is spread over the surface of a body' – Freud

(1896). According to this hypothesis, ideas (i.e. mental images in the mind) are '*besetzt*', or invested, with some sort of mental energy, and psychological changes, such as shifts in interest or personal attachments, are accompanied by changes in the *Besetzung* attached to the ideas corresponding to the things or persons involved. This is not an easy concept to grasp, but in German the reader's difficulties must presumably be mitigated by the fact that the word '*Besetzung*' is a familiar one which inevitably conjures up images which help to explain its meaning in its novel context. In English, on the other hand, the word 'cathexis' evokes no such images and effectively dissociates the theoretical concept from the metaphors which could give it life and meaning. It also fails to remind the reader that there must be a person or agent lurking somewhere inside the machinery who is doing the cathecting and decathecting.

Freud, incidentally, was himself unhappy about the introduction of this neologism into English in 1922, but he must have become reconciled to it, since he later used it himself in German.*

Ego and cathexis are, apparently, not the only instances of psychoanalytical technical terms which sound more impersonal and abstract in English than they do in German. Indeed, according to Brandt (1961), the majority of them have suffered a regrettable sea-change in their passage from German to English, in some instances having lost an essential part of their meaning and in others having lost vital associative overtones. Whether Brandt is right about this I am not qualified to say, but certainly the argument that psychoanalysis is only comprehensible if read in the original German is a gambit not uncommonly used by continental analysts in controversy with English ones. If he is, it would, however, do much to explain the curious impression one sometimes gets that psychoanalysis has not got its feet on the ground and is not about people after all. In the main text of this work I have drawn attention to gross discrepancies between English and German connotations whenever I have been aware of them. It should perhaps be added that everyone agrees that James Strachey's translation of Freud is excellent and that it earned him the Schlegel-Tieck Prize for 1966.

* See Strachey's footnote on page 63 of the Standard Edition, vol. III.

Dissension

It is a notorious and melancholy fact that psychoanalysts lack the capacity to agree among themselves and that their professional organizations exhibit an apparently inherent tendency towards fission. Their disruptive controversies are typically not of the minor, technical kind which occur in every science and branch of medicine, but concern fundamental principles, even though they are often found to involve clashes of personality and temperament when viewed historically. The original dissensions between Freud, Jung, and Adler are by now past history and well known and perhaps even generally understood – on the basis that Freud believed in Eros and Reason, that Adler believed in power and self-assertion, and that Jung was a mystic – but the unsuspecting enquirer into contemporary psychoanalysis is likely to be led astray unless he realizes that radical differences of opinion exist within the Freudian fold itself and that these are of sufficient seriousness to be reflected in the structure of psychoanalytical institutions. In Great Britain, for instance, the theoretical differences between sub-schools have necessitated the establishing of conventions (the so-called 'Gentleman's Agreement') to prevent the British Psycho-Analytical Society ever being taken over by one of the three groups into which it is divided, and parts of its training scheme are run in duplicate. In a number of other countries, the absence of a native genius for compromise has led to complete fission with, usually, one of the resulting fragments resigning or being expelled from the International Psycho-Analytical Association.

This is not the place to discuss the historical and psychological reasons for these dissensions, but several entries in this dictionary are designed to explain the theoretical points at issue. See particularly CLASSICAL ANALYTICAL THEORY, CLASSICAL ANALYTICAL TECHNIQUE, EGO PSYCHOLOGY, INSTINCT THEORY AND OBJECT THEORY, KLEINIAN, FAIRBAIRN'S REVISED PSYCHOPATHOLOGY, PERSONOLOGY, and PROCESS THEORY. Their existence does, however, make it necessary for me to alert prospective readers of the psychoanalytical literature to a number of hazards of which he might otherwise be unaware.

Firstly, books and papers which appear to be merely contributions to the understanding of some particular psychological problem or illness and which read as though they were expressing

a generally accepted point of view, may in fact be highly controversial and propaganda in favour of the author's own theoretical
position. It would be invidious to cite examples of this, particularly as demonstrating the ability of a scientific theory to explain
specific phenomena is, of course, a legitimate way of advancing it.

Secondly, references to the 'classical' literature and quotations
from Freud's own writings which occur in papers written by
contemporary analysts are sometimes dictated not by scientific
good manners, which demand that an author should acknowledge
his sources, but by the writer's need to make covert appeals to
authority in order to legitimize the ancestry of his theories or to
ward off charges of unorthodoxy. The reasons for anyone wanting,
or feeling it necessary, to be devious in this way derive from two
sources: the early history of the psychoanalytical movement,
which has left it with traumatic, tribal memories of earlier, primal
secessions; and the fact that every analyst has been analysed during
his years of training by some other analyst senior to himself and
nearer to Freud. This feature of psychoanalytical training has led
to the development of a mystique analogous to that of the Apostolic
Succession, which compels contemporary analysts to trace their
lineage back to one or other of the founding fathers. Analysts are
in general extremely curious to discover by whom an unfamiliar
colleague was analysed and are often inclined to judge his worth
by his descent rather than by his own qualities. Future historians
of psychoanalysis will no doubt find it necessary to construct
pedigrees tracing the analytical lineage of third- and fourth-
generation analysts.

Since many people find these aspects of the psychoanalytical
literature rather shocking, it should perhaps be mentioned that
covert in-fighting and the citing of authorities to give a cloak of
academic respectability to new but unpopular ideas are phenomena
not unknown in other disciplines. Nor would it always be difficult
to construct academic family trees of discipleship.

Thirdly, although these internal dissensions and theoretical
divergences can be regarded as signs of vitality and as evidence
that psychoanalysis has not succumbed to the dogmatism of
which it is so often accused, they also make it difficult for the
uninitiated to know which books on psychoanalysis are definitive,
authoritative, and sound and which are controversial, unorthodox,
and uninformed – a difficulty which is enhanced by the fact that

psychoanalysis has its lunatic and quack fringes and that many unscrupulous writers have been prepared to cash in on the vogue for psychoanalysis and the ubiquity of neurotic suffering. I have, therefore, given bibliographical references throughout this dictionary which will, I hope, help readers to find their way either to the original sources or to clear and reliable expositions. The following notes may also be helpful as a guide to the various psychoanalytical schools:

1. Classical psychoanalysis was summarized by Freud himself in his last work, *An Outline of Psycho-Analysis* (1940).

2. Ego psychology received its initial impetus from Freud's *The Ego and the Id* (1923), and has since been elaborated by Anna Freud in her *The Ego and the Mechanisms of Defence* (1937) and by Heinz Hartmann in his *Ego Psychology and the Problem of Adaptation* (1937; English translation 1958).

3. Kleinian psychoanalysis: Mrs Klein's own writings are not for the uninitiated, but her views have been ably summarized by Hanna Segal in her *Introduction to the Work of Melanie Klein* (1964).

4. Object theory (object relations theory): Until recently this has been an entirely British school of thought. W. R. D. Fairbairn's *Psychoanalytic Studies of the Personality* (1952) provides the most lucid exposition, and H. Guntrip's *Personality Structure and Human Interaction* (1961) the most enthusiastic. D. W. Winnicott's *Collected Papers* (1958) and Marjorie Brierley's *Trends in Psycho-Analysis* (1951) are also essential reading for anyone who wishes to understand object theory and its connexions with classical psychoanalysis and ego psychology.

5. Existential psychoanalysis: Rollo May's *Psychology and the Human Dilemma* (1967) provides a clear account of the issues separating Freudian and existential psychoanalysis, but the writings of R. D. Laing make more lively reading.

6. Jungian psychoanalysis (analytical psychology): As I have already mentioned, Jung's point of view has been clearly summarized by E. A. Bennet in his *What Jung Really Said* (1966).

The various controversies and dissensions within the psychoanalytical movement obviously raise the possibility that this dictionary is itself propaganda in favour of some particular theoretical standpoint. It is therefore necessary for me to state my own position briefly and to make explicit the direction of any bias this dictionary may show. In two respects I have already done so. In earlier paragraphs I have made it clear that I ally myself with those analysts who have become sceptical about the validity of applying causal-deterministic principles derived from the physical sciences to the study of living beings who are capable of consciousness and of creative activity; and I have also expressed the opinion that Freud's instinct theory is incompatible with contemporary biological ideas about the nature of instinct. Here I must add that, for reasons which will become clearer during the next section of this Introduction, I believe psychoanalytical theory will eventually have to be re-formulated as a communication theory and that it will have to reflect conceptually the source of its own data. At present, psychoanalysis is formulated *as though* it was based on the objective and detached scrutiny of isolated examples of the species *Homo sapiens* by a totally uninvolved spectator, but in fact, or so it seems to me, its insights arise out of the relationship that develops when two people are gathered together in a psychotherapeutic setting. Of existing psycho-analytical theories, object-relations theory undoubtedly comes nearest to taking account of inter-personal communication, but since most of the data and insights which analysts have accumu-lated over the last seventy years have been recorded in the lan-guage invented by Freud and the first generation of his pupils, anyone who intends to practise psychotherapy of any kind, or who for any other reason is serious about acquiring an under-standing of psychoanalysis, remains under a moral obligation to learn that language too.

Sources

It remains for me to mention the last stumbling-block lying in the path of anyone who wishes to master the psychoanalytical litera-ture. This is the fact that the source and origin of psychoanalytical ideas lies in a process which it is not easy either to describe or imagine. This difficulty is indeed so great that many analysts, including Freud* himself, have taken the view that psycho-

---

* 'You can believe me when I tell you that we do not enjoy giving an impression of being members of a secret society and of practising a mystical science. Yet we have been obliged to recognize and express as our conviction that no one has a right to join in a discussion of psycho-analysis who has not had particular experiences which can only be ob-tained by being analysed oneself' – Freud (1933).

analysis is incomprehensible to anyone who has not themselves been analysed. Although this is an extreme position which, if taken seriously, would compel one to regard psychoanalysis as an esoteric cult with tenets only accessible to the initiated, it does none the less draw attention to an important fact about psychoanalysis: its data are derived not from the direct observation of human behaviour in everyday life, but from the analyst's experience of a particular kind of therapeutic relationship invented by Freud. When Freud stopped hypnotizing his patients and instead allowed, indeed encouraged, his patients to talk to him without let or hindrance, he initiated a new kind of human relationship and set in action a number of totally unexpected processes which psychoanalytical theory seeks to explain.

An obvious example of the dependence of psychoanalytical theory on the therapeutic relationship is provided by the concept of of transference. This concept seeks to explain a specific clinical observation, viz. that patients whose utterances are allowed to flow freely without being disciplined by reminders of the actual nature of the person they are talking to give unmistakable evidence that they regard him as though he were someone other than the person he is – and that typically this other person is one or other of the patient's parents. To account for this fact, Freud introduced the idea of transference, which enabled him to explain it by saying that his patients transferred on to him emotions, ideas, and expectations which belonged, in the first instance, to their relationship to their parents. Since, however, these emotions and expectations are typically of a kind that one would expect a child and not a grown-up to have, and since, in addition, they indicate a greater degree of preoccupation with their parents than adult patients readily admit to, the concept of transference leads inevitably to three other basic analytic concepts: those of fixation, resistance, and the existence of unconscious mental processes, by means of which transference can be explained as the result of unconscious fixation on significant objects in the patient's childhood.

This example of transference is a particularly telling one since, as we know from his writings, Freud initially regarded it as a disturbing factor which interfered with what he at first thought was the essential analytical process – that of reviving repressed memories and enabling the patient to discharge the pent-up emotions associated with them. It was, indeed, Freud's eventual recognition that 'finally every conflict has to be fought out in the sphere of transference' which transformed psychoanalysis from a quasi-neurological theory about the pathological effects of inhibition into an investigation of the nature and origin of inter-personal relationships.

Rather similarly, the concept of infantile sexuality arose not as the result of direct observations of infants at the breast, or of children at play or being house-trained, but as an attempt to explain themes recurrently encountered in the free associations (spontaneous utterances) of adult patients. The idea that hysterical patients were fixated at the phallic level, that obsessional patients were fixated at the anal level, or melancholic patients at the oral level derives not from studies made in childhood of children who later developed hysterical, obsessional, or melancholic illnesses, but from the fact that adult patients with these illnesses recurrently and obsessively returned to childhood recollections which suggested that they had gone through phases in which they had been preoccupied, both anxiously and pleasurably, with their genitals or their bowel functions; or, in the case of melancholic patients, that they were nostalgic about some unremembered bliss and were curiously preoccupied with their mouths.

This example differs, however, from that of transference in that the concept of infantile sexuality, and its companion, the concept of infantile stages of libidinal development, contains a higher concentration of inference. Whereas transference phenomena can be directly observed, since the analyst has immediate personal experience of his patients treating him as a father- or mother-figure, and may indeed sense paternal and maternal responses being evoked in himself, the concept of infantile sexuality is a construct built up by piecing together fragmentary pieces of evidence, such as obsessive recollections, recurrent dream imagery, and details of symptoms, to form a theoretical pattern. As a result, the theory is in principle capable of criticism, re-evaluation, and revision in two different ways: by discovering whether children do in fact behave in the way which the concept suggests; and by considering whether it is in fact the only or the most satisfactory of accounting for the analytical data on which it is based.

Criticisms, re-evaluations, and revisions of the concepts of infantile sexuality and infantile stages of development have, of course, frequently been made from both these two points of view, but before considering some of them briefly, it is necessary to draw attention to the fact that these developmental ideas are historical concepts which seek to explain phenomena encountered during treatment by reference to presumed events in the patient's past. They attempt to explain the clinical present by the construction of a historical theory which, as it were, unfolds it backwards in time, locating the various aspects of the patient's illness and personality at differing points in his biography, without, as a rule, reference to any documentary or hearsay extra-analytical evidence that may be available. One effect of this procedure is that concepts which have been arrived at by backward extrapolation from adults tend to be formulated in terms of the forward development of a theoretical construct, 'the infant' or 'the child' who looms so large in the analytical literature. The unwary reader who does not realize this may, as a result, be led astray, since it may not occur to him that a chapter entitled, say, 'The Emotional Development of the Child' may be expressing ideas derived from the psycho-analytical treatment of grown-ups and not from direct experience of children; or that an analyst's account of what goes on between infants and their mothers may derive as much from his experience of transference and counter-transference in the psychoanalysis of adults as it does from his direct contact with mothers and babies.

Of recent years, it is true, many analysts have observed children or have treated children psychoanalytically, but none the less it remains important for readers of the psychoanalytical literature to realize that all the basic concepts of classical psychoanalysis derive from the treatment of grown-ups and that, for instance, Mrs Klein's theories about the origins of mental illness in the first year of life derive not from work with infants but from the psychoanalytical treatment of schizoid and depressive adult patients and of children after they have learnt to talk.

This psychoanalytical habit of explaining its data by reference to events which are inferred to have occurred prior to the onset of treatment is, of course, a natural one. Historically speaking, it derives from a straightforward form of medical thinking, that of assuming that illnesses are due either to something that happened to the patient (e.g. trauma and infection) or to some disturbance of growth (e.g. congenital disease and malnutrition). Freud him-self regarded the childhood experiences which in his view caused neurosis as traumata which interfered with psychological growth, a view of the origin of neuroses which enabled them to be fitted neatly into the medical scheme of things. Comparatively recently, however, a number of analysts have begun to question whether the neuroses are in fact illnesses in the sense that physical illnesses are, and have pointed out that whereas physical illnesses are the result of things that have happened to the patient's body, or more usually to specific parts of it, the neuroses seem to be disturbances of the whole personality which arise within the context of his relationships with others; the essential difference between the two being that in the case of physical illness the patient is clearly a victim of circumstances which have impinged on his body with-out his own will being in any way implicated, whereas in the case of the neuroses the patient is suffering the consequences of relationships in which he must have been, to some extent at least, a wilful agent. According to this view, the human ego is not a passive entity, acted upon by environmental and instinctual forces, but an active agent, capable of initiating behaviour, in-cluding those ultimately self-defeating forms of behaviour we know as neuroses. If this proves to be true, it will cease to be possible to maintain that everything that goes on between analyst and patient is a scrambled repetition of the patient's childhood, with the analyst acting as a completely detached, though benevo-lent, observer.

Of the various revisions and elaborations of Freud's develop-mental concepts, only two need to be mentioned here. The first is the shift in emphasis from instinct and erotic pleasure to ego and object relationships. In Freud's original formulations, develop-ment was conceived of as a number of stages during which children were successively preoccupied with their mouth, anus, and geni-tals, these organs (erotogenic zones) being regarded primarily as sources of pleasurable sensations. During the last thirty-five years or so, Freudian analysts of all schools have increasingly tended to regard these organs as vehicles by which the child's relationships to its parents are mediated. As a result, the oral phase is now regarded as not only a period during which infants seek oral gratification, as the jargon puts it, but as one during which their relationship to their mothers forms the centre of their being and in which they have yet to be confronted with the fact that they and she are separate beings. Similarly, the anal phase is now regarded not simply as a period during which small children are preoccupied with their anal functions, but also as one during which they are learning mastery of their body and are being confronted with the problem of rendering their behaviour acceptable to the adults around them; while in the phallic and oedipal phases, children are now conceived to be assimilating their first intimations of the existence of a form of relationship between their parents from which they are totally excluded and which is liable to make them envious and jealous and acutely aware of their own physical and emotional immaturity.

It is noteworthy that although both of the predominant schools of contemporary psychoanalysis – ego psychology and object theory – have modified Freud's instinct theory in this direction, the routes they have taken to do so are quite different. Ego psychology has proceeded by emphasizing the growth of the ego and self-awareness and by relating the stages of libidinal development described by Freud to the emergence of a sense of identity, while object theory has proceeded by emphasizing the developing child's need for and constant involvement with objects. It is as though Freud had provided the verbs for a human psychology, and ego psychology and object theory, both sensing that the sentence was incomplete, have concentrated on providing the subject and object respectively. The remarkable confluence of what are, historically and even geographically, very different streams of thought is exemplified by the similarities that can be discovered in the writings of the Vienna-trained American analyst Erik Erikson and D. W. Winnicott in Britain.

The second elaboration of Freud's theories which requires mention consists in the emergence of depression as a central analytical concept. This elaboration is secondary to the one just mentioned, since it is based on recognition that separation from objects (e.g. loss of parents) in infancy and childhood leads not only to anxiety and deprivation but also to grief and mourning, processes which all analysts since Freud (1917) and Abraham (1912) have agreed are the normal analogues of pathological depression. Here again different schools have come to the same conclusion by different routes, the Kleinians having arrived at it by applying concepts derived from the study of depressive states to normal development, while Bowlby and Spitz reached it by follow-up studies of children known to have suffered losses of maternal care during childhood and by direct observation of children in orphanages and hospital. The reader is, however, warned that two incompatible theories about the origin and importance of depression can be encountered in the psychoanalytical literature: the Kleinian school attributing the predisposition to depression to the infant's fear that its innate destructive drives may destroy the object (i.e. the mother) on which it depends, while analysts of other schools attribute it to the child's and infant's actual experience of separation from her.

A

ABREACTION The DISCHARGE of EMOTION attaching to a previously repressed experience (see REPRESSION). In the early days of psychoanalysis, abreaction was held to be in itself therapeutic, regardless of whether the patient understood the significance of the repressed experience. See Freud (1895). See INSIGHT.

ABSTINENCE One of the rules of psychoanalytical technique is the so-called *rule of abstinence*, though it is not clear what the patient should be made to abstain from. In Freud (1915) the phrase, 'The treatment must be carried out in abstinence', refers specifically to the fact that 'analytical technique requires of the physician that he should deny to the patient who is craving for love the satisfaction she demands'. In Freud (1919), however, an almost identical phrase refers to the need to ensure that the patient's suffering is not relieved too quickly. 'If, owing to the symptoms having been taken apart and having lost their value, his suffering becomes mitigated, we must reinstate it elsewhere in the form of appreciable privation; otherwise we run the danger of never achieving any improvements except quite insignificant and transitory ones.' The idea that sexual abstinence in itself causes ANXIETY and NEUROSIS occurs only in Freud's earliest papers.

ACTING OUT A patient is said to be acting out if he engages in activity which can be interpreted as a substitute for remembering past events. The essence of the concept is the replacement of thought by action and it implies that either (a) the IMPULSE being acted out has never acquired verbal representation, or (b) the impulse is too intense to be dischargeable in words, or (c) that the patient lacks the capacity for INHIBITION. Since psychoanalysis is a 'talking cure' carried out in a state of reflection, acting out is anti-therapeutic. Acting out is characteristic of PSYCHOPATHY and BEHAVIOUR DISORDERS and reduces the accessibility of these conditions to psychoanalysis.

ACCESSIBLE AND INACCESSIBLE A patient is said to be

accessible if the psychiatrist or analyst succeeds in making RAPPORT with him, and inaccessible if he fails. The term is pseudo-objective, since it implies that the capacity for rapport is a constant, identical in every examining physician. In general, NEUROTICS are deemed to be accessible and PSYCHOTICS inaccessible.

ACTIVE AND PASSIVE   Freud made extensive use of the idea that there exists a polarity between activity and passivity; MASCULINITY, AGGRESSION, SADISM and VOYEURISM being active, and FEMININITY, SUBMISSIVENESS, MASOCHISM and EXHIBITIONISM being passive. As a result there is a tendency in CLASSICAL THEORY to equate active and masculine, passive and feminine, and to define masculinity in terms of the ability to adopt an active role and femininity in terms of the ability to accept [*sic*] the passive role; and to regard sadism as a masculine propensity and masochism as a feminine propensity. The situation is, however, complicated by a further assumption that instincts can undergo REVERSAL into their opposite, in particular that active instincts can become passive, sadism and voyeurism being usually cited as examples of instincts capable of this reversal. See Freud (1915).

Freud's equation of passive and feminine has been much criticized, particularly by women analysts – Horney (1926), Klein (1948), and Payne (1935) – and is an example of what Jones called Freud's PHALLOCENTRIC view of women. Only Hermann (1935) has questioned the active–masculine equation. Attempts to describe heterosexual relationships in terms of male activity and female passivity can lead to absurdity, as when Deutsch (1946) describes 'the active pursuit of passive aims' as a feminine characteristic. There also exists a tendency to assume that mothers are active while their infants are passive, this despite the fact that both sucking and suckling involve activity. In both instances formulations in terms of active and passive roles assume that relationships are collisions rather than interactions and confuse activity with initiation of action and passivity with responsiveness and receptiveness.

ACTUAL NEUROSIS   In his early writings Freud distinguished between PSYCHONEUROSES and actual neuroses, the former being due to psychological CONFLICTS and past events, the latter being the physiological consequences of present disturbances in sexual functioning. He further distinguished two forms of actual neurosis: *neurasthenia*, the result of sexual excess, and *anxiety neurosis*, the result of unrelieved sexual stimulation. See Freud (1894). See also under NEURASTHENIA and ANXIETY NEUROSIS.

ADAPTATION   This almost always refers to adaptation to the ENVIRONMENT as a whole, i.e. to the capacity to discriminate between subjective images (PHANTASY) and external percepts (see PERCEPTION) and to the ability to act effectively on the environment. Since CLASSICAL THEORY assumes that the human infant satisfies its wishes by hallucinatory WISH-FULFILMENT (see also HALLUCINATION) and has no EGO or mental structure, adaptation tends to be regarded as a function which is imposed on the developing individual from without as a result of his experience of FRUSTRATION. For the alternative view, that the infant starts life already adapted to the environment it is likely to encounter and that its adaptation increases in complexity as it matures and acquires experience, see Fairbairn (1952), Winnicott (1958), Hartmann (1958). See ENVIRONMENT, AVERAGE EXPECTABLE; MOTHER, ORDINARY DEVOTED; ALLOPLASTIC AND AUTOPLASTIC ADAPTATION.

ADLERIAN   1. A follower of Alfred Adler (1870–1937), early disciple of Freud, who seceded and founded his own movement in 1911. 2. Adj. referring to ideas formulated by him. See IN-FERIORITY COMPLEX; MASCULINE PROTEST.

ADULTOMORPHIC   The adultomorphic fallacy is attributing to infants and young children the thoughts and feelings which an adult would have under analogous conditions. The reference is usually to theories about the psychology of infants which the speaker believes overestimate their level of DEVELOPMENT.

AETIOLOGY AND PATHOLOGY   These are frequently confused. *Aetiology* refers to the causes of disease and *pathology* to the abnormal processes inferred to be responsible for the manifest symptoms. For instance, SEPARATION ANXIETY and ORAL FIXATION may form part of a patient's pathology, while a history of SEPARATION from the MOTHER during the oral phase may be part of the aetiology of his illness.

AFFECT   General term for feelings and EMOTIONS. No generally accepted psychoanalytical theory of affects exists, but a distinction is made between *discharge-affects*, which accompany expression

3

of a drive, and *tension-affects*, which accompany damming-up of a drive. Affects are regarded as being attached to ideas, and not vice versa. The concepts affect and emotion differ in that whereas the former regards them as affixed to ideas, the latter regards them as valid, independent experiences. See Glover E. (1939), Brierley (1951), Rapaport (1953).

AFFECTIVE DISORDER, PSYCHOSIS Psychiatric diagnostic term for those psychoses which are characterized by disturbance of MOOD. See MANIC-DEPRESSIVE PSYCHOSIS; DEPRESSION; MANIA.

AFFERENT Adj., qualifying nerves which conduct IMPULSES, messages, towards the centre, in contrast to EFFERENT nerves which carry them from the centre to the periphery.

AGAPE (Gk.: brotherly love) Sometimes used in conjunction with EROS, to contrast altruistic LOVE (*caritas*) with sensual love.

AGENT Many of the more puzzling aspects of psychoanalytical theory derive from the fact that one of its basic premisses, PSYCHIC DETERMINISM, implicitly denies the possibility that human beings can be agents who make decisions and are responsible for their own actions. As a result we not only have general puzzles about the relationship of causal theories (see CAUSALITY) of human behaviour to moral and legal concepts, but also specific psychoanalytical puzzles such as: (a) What significance can be attached to acts of deciding, choosing, etc., if these acts are already predetermined by UNCONSCIOUS forces? (b) Who or what initiates a DEFENCE? Or (c) If the EGO is built up by INTROJECTION, who or what introjects the initial introjects? For some of the difficulties involved in applied causal theories derived from physics and chemistry to the behaviour of living organisms capable of CONSCIOUSNESS, see Szasz (1961), Home (1966), Rycroft (1966). See also CREATIVITY; MEANING.

AGGRESSION Hypothetical force, INSTINCT, or principle imagined to actuate a range of acts and feelings. It is frequently regarded as antithetical to SEX or LIBIDO, in which case it is being used to refer to destructive drives. Even when being used as a synonym for destructiveness, controversy exists as to whether it is a primary drive, i.e. whether there is an aggressive, destructive instinct, or whether it is a reaction to FRUSTRATION. Opinion also differs as to whether it is an instinct with its own aims or whether it provides the ENERGY to enable the EGO to overcome obstacles in the way of satisfying other drives. The almost universal tendency of analysts to equate aggression with HATE, destructiveness, and SADISM runs counter to both its etymology (*ad-gradior*: I move forwards) and to its traditional meaning of dynamism, self-assertiveness, expansiveness, drive. The psychoanalytical usage derives from Freud's later writings, in which he conceived of aggression as a derivative of the DEATH INSTINCT. EGO PSYCHOLOGY uses *aggressification* and *deaggressification* as homologous with *libidinization* and *delibidinization*. For the biology of aggressive behaviour, see Lorenz (1966).

AGITATED Agitated DEPRESSION and MELANCHOLIA are PSYCHIATRIC diagnostic terms referring to patients who are both deeply depressed and tense, restless, and anxious.

AGORAPHOBIA Form of PHOBIA in which the patient avoids open spaces and becomes anxious (see ANXIETY) when confronted with one.

AIM-INHIBITION A relationship is said to be aim-inhibited if the subject has no conscious EROTIC interest in the OBJECT. Common examples are friendships, platonic love, and domestic affections between relatives. The concept assumes that, in the absence of inhibition, friendships would be overt HOMOSEXUAL relationships, platonic love would be consummated, and INCEST would occur.

ALGOLAGNIA Enjoyment of PAIN.

ALIENATION The state of being, or the process of becoming, estranged from either (a) oneself or parts of oneself or (b) others. Freudian psychoanalysis tends to concern itself with (a), EXISTENTIALISM and Marxism with (b). Since, however, self-alienation limits the capacity to relate to others and alienation from others limits the capacity to discover oneself, (a) and (b) are interdependent.

ALIENIST Obsolescent term for a PSYCHIATRIST.

ALLOPLASTIC AND AUTOPLASTIC ADAPTATION Terms introduced by F. Alexander (1930) to distinguish between

5

adaptive responses which alter the ENVIRONMENT and those which alter the self. DEFENCE mechanisms as used in the PSYCHONEUROSES are the classic examples of autoplastic ADAPTATION.

AMBIVALENCE Term introduced by Eugen Bleuler to describe the co-existence of contradictory IMPULSES and EMOTIONS towards the same object. Usually the term refers to the co-existence of LOVE and HATE. Ambivalence has to be distinguished from having mixed feelings about someone. It refers to an underlying emotional attitude in which the contradictory attitudes derive from a common source and are interdependent, whereas mixed feelings may be based on a realistic assessment of the imperfect nature of the object. The curate of the curate's egg story was not ambivalent about the egg though he probably was about the bishop. Although ambivalence is engendered by all neurotic CONFLICT, it is mostly easily observed in OBSESSIONAL NEUROSIS, in which an attempt is made to balance the two sides of the ambivalence in CONSCIOUSNESS; in the other neuroses, one or other side is usually repressed (see REPRESSION).

AMNESIA Loss of the capacity to remember. *Infantile amnesia* is the loss of childhood and INFANTILE memories. *Hysterical amnesia* is a neurotic symptom in which the patient complains of loss of memory, usually for a circumscribed period of time.

ANACLITIC (lit.: leaning on) Freud (1914) distinguished two types of OBJECT-CHOICE: narcissistic and anaclitic. *Narcissistic object-choice* (see also under NARCISSISM) occurs when a person chooses an object on the basis of some real or imagined similarity with himself, while *anaclitic object-choice* occurs when the choice is based on the pattern of childhood DEPENDENCE on someone unlike himself. According to this formulation, HOMOSEXUALITY is narcissistic, while HETEROSEXUALITY is anaclitic. The implication is that the man rediscovers a mother and the woman rediscovers a father. Alternatively, since Freud considered infantile dependence was a manifestation of the self-preservative instinct (see SELF-PRESERVATION), in anaclitic object-choice the sexual choice follows a path laid down by the self-preservative instinct. See also DEPRESSION, ANACLITIC.

ANAMNESIS Medical term for the history of an illness as given by the patient at consultation, i.e. for his recall of the relevant past.

ANAL CHARACTER   Type of CHARACTER neurosis inferred to be the result of FIXATION at the ANAL STAGE. The term is usually used to refer to REACTION-FORMATIONS against ANAL-EROTISM, in particular to COMPULSIVE obstinacy, orderliness, and parsimony, but can refer to their opposites, viz. compulsive pliancy, untidiness, and generosity. See OBSESSIONAL NEUROSIS.

ANAL-EROTIC, -EROTISM   Refer to sensuous pleasure derived from anal sensations.

ANAL-SADISTIC, -SADISM   Refer to sadistic phantasies (see SADISM) inferred to originate in the ANAL STAGE.

ANAL STAGE, PHASE   Stage of (a) infantile LIBIDINAL DEVELOPMENT postulated by INSTINCT THEORY, in which the anus and defaecation are the major source of sensuous pleasure and form the centre of the infant's SELF-AWARENESS; and (b) of infantile EGO DEVELOPMENT, in which mastery of the body, particularly of its SPHINCTERS, and socialization of impulses are the infant's major preoccupations.

ANALYSAND   A person who is being analysed. The word owes what little currency it has to the fact that it makes it possible to avoid calling students patients.

ANGER   Primary EMOTION, provoked typically by FRUSTRATION. Surprisingly frequently confused with HATE, despite the fact that it is a short-lasting emotion readily experienced towards those we LOVE, whereas hate is a lasting SENTIMENT.

ANHEDONIA   Absence of the capacity to experience pleasure.

ANIMA, ANIMUS   JUNGIAN terms describing the unconscious female image in men and the unconscious male image in women.

ANOREXIA   Absence of appetite. *Anorexia nervosa*: PSYCHO-GENIC absence of appetite of sufficient severity to threaten health or life.

ANXIETY   The usual definition of anxiety as irrational fear applies strictly only to *phobic anxiety* (see PHOBIA), which is evoked by objects and situations such as open spaces (*agoraphobic anxiety*), closed spaces (*claustrophobic anxiety*), heights, spiders, snakes, thunder, travel, crowds, strangers, etc., to an extent which is out of all proportion to their actual danger. It is better defined as the response to some as yet unrecognized factor, either in the ENVIRONMENT or in the SELF, and may be evoked either by changes in the environment or by the stirrings of UNCONSCIOUS, repressed (see REPRESSION) forces in the self. Psychoanalysis is mainly concerned with the latter. Freud had three theories of anxiety. The first was that it was a manifestation of repressed LIBIDO, the second was that it represented a repetition of the experience of birth (Freud, 1915), while the third, which can be regarded as the definitive psychoanalytical theory of anxiety, is that there are two forms: *primary anxiety* and *signal-anxiety*, both of which are responses of the EGO to increases of instinctual or emotional TENSION (see also INSTINCT and EMOTION); SIGNAL-ANXIETY being an alerting mechanism which forewarns the ego of an impending threat to its equilibrium, PRIMARY ANXIETY being the emotion which accompanies dissolution of the ego. The function of signal-anxiety is to ensure that primary anxiety is never experienced by enabling the ego to institute defensive precautions (see DEFENCE) and it can be regarded as an inwardly directed form of VIGILANCE. Primary anxiety represents a failure of defence and occurs in NIGHTMARES. See Freud (1926), Hoch and Zubin (1950), Rycroft (1968), Rosenberg (1949).

Other forms of anxiety described in the literature are: (a) *Castration anxiety*, provoked by real or imagined threats to the sexual function. (b) *Separation anxiety*, provoked by the threat of separation from OBJECTS conceived to be essential for survival. (c) *Depressive anxiety*, provoked by fear of one's own hostility towards 'GOOD objects'. (d) *Paranoid (persecutory) anxiety*, provoked by fear of being attacked by 'BAD objects'. (e) *Objective anxiety*, fear provoked by real, external danger. (f) *Neurotic anxiety*, a term which covers either all forms of the above other than (e), or (a) and (b) in contrast to (c) and (d), which are covered by (g). (g) *Psychotic anxiety*. This last, however, sometimes refers to threats to IDENTITY. See also separate entries under CASTRATION; SEPARATION; DEPRESSIVE; PARANOID-SCHIZOID POSITION; PSYCHOTIC.

ANXIETY HYSTERIA Diagnostic term for what is now generally called PHOBIA, or phobic illness.

ANXIETY NEUROSIS *Either* 1. one of the two ACTUAL NEUROSES, *or* 2. any PSYCHONEUROSIS in which ANXIETY is the predominant symptom.

APATHY   The absence of any EMOTION whatsoever. It is to be distinguished from DESPAIR, which is the loss of hope, and BOREDOM, which is due to blocking of expressive activity, whether for external or neurotic reasons. According to Greenson (1949) apathy can be a life-saving defence in extreme situations; by, as it were, putting the mind into neutral, both despair and the exhaustion following unjustified hopefulness can be avoided. See also Fenichel (1954).

APHANISIS   Term coined by Jones (1948) to describe the ultimate dread of losing all capacity for PLEASURE.

APHONIA   Inability to utter, phonate. When PSYCHOGENIC, a HYSTERICAL CONVERSION symptom.

APPARATUS, PSYCHI(C)AL, MENTAL   See PSYCHIC APPARATUS.

ARCHETYPE   JUNGIAN term for the contents of the *collective unconscious*, i.e. for innate ideas or the tendency to organize experience in innately predetermined patterns.

'AS IF' PERSONALITY   Type of SCHIZOID character who behaves *as though* he had normal emotional responses to situations.

AUTHENTIC AND INAUTHENTIC   Existential terms (see EXISTENTIALISM) used to distinguish between acts which are done in good and bad faith, which are TRUE AND FALSE to the SELF. Psychoanalytical theory has no means of making this distinction, nor the similar one between 'sincere' and 'insincere', even though psychoanalytical practice largely depends on the therapist being able to make it. However, inauthentic behaviour is regularly interpreted as defensive (see DEFENCE), the implication being that the patient's 'real' feelings and motives are other than he himself realizes, or alternatively, that he was insincere to avoid confronting some aspect of the situation or of himself which would have made him anxious (see ANXIETY). The criteria for deciding whether behaviour which is based on IDENTIFICATIONS is authentic are obscure, though that which is based on identification with a loved object is more likely to be authentic than that which is based on identification with a hated or feared object.

AUTISM, AUTISTIC   (lit. self-orientated   *Autistic thinking* is thought which is determined solely by the subject's wishes and

PHANTASIES without reference to the ENVIRONMENT or to realistic (see REAL) considerations of space and time. *Infantile autism* is a childhood PSYCHOSIS in which the patient lacks any capacity to trust or communicate with anyone whatsoever, is either mute or has complex disturbances of speech, and would be diagnosed as mentally defective were it not for his ability to handle inanimate objects. Many, perhaps most, psychiatrists believe it to be an inherited organic disease, but see Bettelheim (1967) for a radical psychoanalytical interpretation.

AUTO-EROTISM, -EROTIC   Refer either to pleasurable activity in which the self is used as an object (e.g. MASTURBATION, thumb-sucking) or to a LIBIDINAL attitude, orientation, or stage of DEVELOPMENT. In the former case, the words are being used objectively to describe observable behaviour, in the latter they are being used inferentially to describe a hypothesis about the patient's or infant's disregard of external objects. According to classical INSTINCT THEORY infants are auto-erotically orientated, i.e. their attitude towards their MOTHER is based solely on self-love and their need for her is based on her capacity to provide them with gratification. When used in this sense, auto-erotic is synonymous with narcissistic (see NARCISSISM). OBJECT-THEORY is opposed to the idea of an auto-erotic phase in infancy and takes the view that the infant is mother-related from the very beginning, that, to quote Fairbairn (1952), the infant is 'object-seeking not pleasure-seeking'. According to this view, auto-erotic behaviour is substitutive, the subject using a part of himself as a symbolic equivalent of someone else.

AUTONOMOUS FUNCTIONS OF THE EGO   These are functions which have ceased to be directly influenced by the INSTINCTS of which they are derivatives and which cannot, therefore, be interfered with by CONFLICTS. In healthy persons, speech, breathing, walking are autonomous functions of the EGO and conflict does not produce stammering, asthma, or paralysis of the legs. Activities which have become functionally autonomous are examples of successful EGO DEVELOPMENT and SUBLIMATION, and they use deaggressified and desexualized ENERGY (see DEAGGRES-SIFICATION and DESEXUALIZATION). In TOPOGRAPHICAL formulations, autonomous functions occupy the CONFLICT-FREE AREA OF THE EGO. See Hartmann (1958).

AUTONOMY AND HETERONOMY Piaget's distinction between the heteronomy of infants and autonomy of adults is made in psychoanalysis by the contrast between INFANTILE dependence and adult independence. Neurotic dependence is a condition in which an autonomous adult imagines himself to be heteronomous. '*Autonomy v. Shame and Doubt*' is Erikson's (1963) term for the second of his eight STAGES OF MAN. It corresponds approximately to the ANAL STAGE of CLASSICAL THEORY, SPHINCTER-control marking the achievement of autonomy.

AUTOPLASTIC ADAPTATION See ALLOPLASTIC.

AVERAGE EXPECTABLE ENVIRONMENT See ENVIRON-MENT, AVERAGE EXPECTABLE.

B

BAD When qualifying OBJECT, BREAST, PENIS, MOTHER, FATHER, this refers to one of the two images or OBJECT-REPRESENTATIONS formed by SPLITTING of the INTERNALIZED object, breast, etc. Bad in this context is an omnibus word embracing 'frustrating', 'hateful', 'feared', 'malevolent', 'persecuting'. It is sometimes printed 'bad' in quotes.

BASIC FAULT Term used by Balint (1952) to describe an aspect of the pathology of a certain type of patient whose whole development has been faulty and false. According to Balint the basic fault can only be overcome if the patient is allowed to REGRESS to a state of oral DEPENDENCE on the analyst (see also ORAL) and experience a NEW BEGINNING. The metaphor is presumably geological not moral.

BASIC RULE The basic or fundamental rule of psychoanalysis governs the patient and not the analyst and is the injunction that he do his best to tell the analyst whatever comes into his mind without reservation. The rule is a counsel of perfection, RESISTANCE and DEFENCE manifesting themselves clinically by failures to carry it out. See FREE ASSOCIATION.

11

BASIC TRUST AND DISTRUST   Terms used by Erikson, Winnicott, and Balint to describe the underlying effects of good and bad experiences of mothering. Basic trust, which is the first of Erikson's eight STAGES OF MAN, corresponds to the ORAL PHASE of CLASSICAL THEORY and to the PRIMARY ONTOLOGICAL SECURITY of the existentialists (see EXISTENTIALISM). Basic distrust corresponds to some usages of PARANOID ANXIETY.

BEHAVIOUR DISORDER   Psychiatric diagnostic term embracing PSYCHOPATHY, the PERVERSIONS, and the addictions, conditions which have in common that their 'SYMPTOMS' consist of behaviour of which society (and sometimes the 'patient' himself when in reflective mood) disapproves. The behaviour disorders raise in acute form problems about the nature of MENTAL ILLNESS, since the 'symptoms' are, on the face of it at least, voluntary acts for which society as a whole, and the law in particular, holds the patient responsible. (Hence the complete failure in communication which so often occurs when psychiatrists are called as expert witnesses in court.) Theoretically they can be regarded as the opposite of the NEUROSES, since they are characterized by deficiency not excess of INHIBITION. They are, in general, amenable to psychoanalytical explanation, but only infrequently to psychoanalytical treatment.

BEHAVIOUR THERAPY   Form of PSYCHOTHERAPY based on LEARNING THEORY. It assumes that symptoms are due to faulty learning and conditioning and aims to remove them by deconditioning and reconditioning procedures. Its theoretical basis differs sharply from psychoanalysis in rejecting the idea that there is any underlying process or illness of which the symptoms are merely a superficial manifestation. It asserts, on the contrary, that the symptom is the illness. Most of the successes claimed for behaviour therapy have been with PHOBIAS and BEHAVIOUR DISORDERS, conditions in which it is possible to isolate one specific symptom as the target of therapeutic intervention. Although theoretically an impersonal technique, papers on the role of TRANSFERENCE in behaviour therapy have recently begun to appear, e.g. Crisp (1966). It differs from psychoanalysis in being applicable to unwilling patients. See Eysenck and Rachman (1965).

BELLE INDIFFERENCE   Psychiatric diagnostic term describing the indifference with which HYSTERICAL patients often seem to view conversion symptoms (see CONVERSION HYSTERIA) which should, on the face of it, be extremely distressing.

BIRTH-TRAUMA. The idea that birth is a traumatic experience (see TRAUMA) was originally propounded by Otto Rank. It enjoyed a certain vogue for some years and was used, e.g. by Freud (1915), to account for the human predisposition to ANXIETY. It is now only of historical interest. The theory that anxiety is a repetition of the traumatic experience of birth seems to have owed its appeal to the fact that it enabled one universal human experience, viz. anxiety, to be explained by reference to another one, birth; and that it made it possible to regard the PSYCHO-NEUROSES as a special form of TRAUMATIC NEUROSIS.

BISEXUAL, BISEXUALITY These refer only occasionally to persons who are bisexual in the sense of engaging in both heterosexual and homosexual relations, but usually to the presence of MASCULINE and FEMININE psychological attributes and attitudes in a single person. Psychoanalytical theory has always assumed that all human beings are constitutionally psychosexually bisexual. Freud (1890) took over this idea from his friend Fliess, and it was originally justified by reference to the biological and anatomical data which suggest that males contain vestigial female organs (and vice versa). Contemporary theory, however, tends to explain psychosexual bisexuality by reference to the fact that children identify (to varying degrees) with both parents (see IDENTIFICATION). The theory of bisexuality assumes that it is possible to attach a sexual connotation to non-sexual functions and to designate as feminine PASSIVE, SUBMISSIVE, MASOCHISTIC, intuitive, and receptive behaviour, and as masculine ACTIVE, assertive, SADISTIC, intellectual, and penetrative behaviour, and that shifts in attitude imply changes in sexual orientation. The problem of bisexuality is bedevilled by social preconceptions about male and female roles. See Margaret Mead (1935, 1949) for evidence as to their variability from one society to another. Any satisfactory analysis of bisexuality would have to take into account (a) biological and constitutional factors, (b) identifications with parents and social STEREOTYPES, (c) confusions between the active–passive and male–female dichotomies, and (d) the relation of intuitive and analytical modes of thinking to (a) and (b).

BODY EGO, BODY IMAGE, BODY SCHEMA *Body ego* is Freud's term for that part of the EGO which derives from the SELF's self-perceptions (i.e. as opposed to perceptions of external objects). 'The ego is first and foremost a body ego, i.e. the ego is ultimately derived from bodily sensations, chiefly from those springing from the surface of the body' – Freud (1927). *Body image* is a psychological term for the self's conception of his own body. *Body schema* is a neurological term for the organic representation of the body in the brain.

BORDERLINE A borderline case is a patient who is on the border between NEUROSIS and PSYCHOSIS, i.e. either one whose PSYCHOPATHOLOGY defies categorization or one whose mechanisms are psychotic but whose behaviour does not warrant his being treated as psychotic. The usage arises from the fact that diagnostic systems (see DIAGNOSIS) assume that neurosis and psychosis are mutually exclusive while clinical observation shows they are not.

BOREDOM The emotion that ensues when an individual fails to find interests and activities which fully engage him. It may arise either as a result of external limitations, e.g. solitary confinement, sensory deprivation, or monotonous work, or as a result of internal inhibition. According to Fenichel (1954), neurotic boredom is a state of instinctual TENSION (see also INSTINCT) in which the instinctual aim is missing. As a result, the bored person seeks an object 'not in order to act upon it with his instinctual impulses, but rather to be helped by it to find an instinctual aim which he lacks'. He knows he wants something, but doesn't know what it is. Hence the irritability and restlessness inseparable from boredom and absent in APATHY.

BREAST This word refers either to the anatomical organ itself or to the idea (OBJECT-REPRESENTATION) of it existing in the subject's mind. 'The breast' is the object of ORAL wishes, IMPULSES, PHANTASIES, and ANXIETIES and is synonymous with 'the MOTHER regarded as a PART OBJECT' or 'the mother regarded as a NEED-SATISFYING OBJECT', i.e. the concept refers not only to the breast as a suckling organ but also to the infant's obliviousness of the mother's person. '*Splitting of the breast*' refers to the psychological process by which the infant divides its image of a complete breast into two, one part becoming 'the GOOD breast', conceived to be perfect, lovable, and all-satisfying, the other part being conceived to be hateful and rejecting ('the BAD breast'). SPLITTING of the breast is a DEFENCE against recognizing that LOVE and HATE are directed against the same object; it purchases freedom from AMBIVALENCE at the price of persecutory anxiety (see PERSECUTION). See PARANOID-SCHIZOID POSITION; DEPRESSIVE POSITION. In the writings of Fairbairn and Klein, both of whom held that all PSYCHOPATHOLOGY originates in the relation to the mother, 'the breast' often means 'the primary object' with only a theoretical implication that this was (is) a part of the mother's body.

C

CASTRATING Word used frequently by analysts in conversation but only rarely in theoretical formulations. It refers to persons who habitually undermine the self-confidence of others. In the first instance, it applies to women who suffer from PENIS-ENVY and therefore disparage or compete with men. In the second instance, it applies to fathers who undermine their sons, but by extension it can even be used to refer to men who habitually make women feel unattractive or incompetent with their children.

CASTRATION, CASTRATION ANXIETY According to CLASSICAL THEORY, all men and male children are liable to castration anxiety, though what the precise nature of this dread is has been subject to both controversy and elaboration. The concept only rarely refers to castration in its anatomical, surgical sense (removal of the testes), but more frequently to either (a) loss of the PENIS – as in *castration threats* used to deter little boys caught masturbating; (b) loss of the capacity for EROTIC pleasure; or (c) demoralization in respect of the MASCULINE role.

Although, for obvious reasons, women cannot suffer from castration anxiety in its primary sense, classical theory asserts that they, too, have a *castration complex*, as a result of which they either feel 'castrated', feel a compulsion to prove that they possess an adequate symbolic substitute (see SYMBOL) for the penis, or experience anxiety in respect of whatever organ or activity has become a penis-equivalent for them. Freud's own writings on the castration complex of women are imbued with his conviction that vaginal sensations (see VAGINA) do not occur until puberty and that, therefore, girls interpret their genital anatomy as evidence that they lack a penis. It was left to the women analysts to assert that girls can be aware of their femininity from the earliest days and to point out that boys can be as envious of their mothers' reproductive powers as girls are of the penis. See FEMININE; PENIS-ENVY; PHALLOCENTRIC. The concept of castration anxiety raises the question of who is the castrator, i.e. whether it tends to be evoked by men or women; and of whether or not it is internalized (see INTERNALIZATION), i.e. whether it is evoked by external or internal OBJECTS. OBJECT THEORY tends to interpret castration anxiety as a variety of PERSECUTORY ANXIETY.

CATATONIA   Form of SCHIZOPHRENIA characterized by periods of excitement and stupor.

CATHARSIS (lit. 'purging')   The reference is usually not to the purging by pity and terror effected by tragedy but to the therapeutic effect of ABREACTION.

CATHEXIS   NEOLOGISM invented by Freud's English translators to translate the German '*Besetzung*' (lit. 'investment') which Freud used to describe the QUANTITY of ENERGY attaching to any OBJECT-REPRESENTATION or mental structure. A cathexis is conceived to be analogous to an electric charge which can shift from one structure except in so far as it becomes bound – or to troops which can be deployed from one position to another. Hence the verbs to *cathect*, *decathect*, and *hypercathect*, the last referring to the defensive manoeuvre (see DEFENCE) of investing in one process in order to facilitate REPRESSION of another. Hence also *withdrawal of cathexis*, for the process of decathexis. *Object- cathexis* refers to energy invested in external objects as opposed to the self. *Ego* and *id cathexes* are ambiguous; they refer either to cathexes by or of the EGO and ID. Hence also *counter-cathexis*, *anti-cathexis:* the energy invested in maintaining repression of a cathected process. Most statements using the word 'cathexis' can be reformulated in terms of 'interest', 'MEANING', or 'REALITY'.

CAUSALITY   The conception that events can be explained as the necessary consequence of prior events, the latter being the causes and the former the effects. Psychoanalysis is generally regarded as a causal theory, since it explains present events, symptoms, etc., in terms of the prior experiences of the subject. Its habit of explaining present CONSCIOUS mental events in terms of present UNCONSCIOUS forces, motives, etc., is also an example of the conception of causality since it is assumed that the unconscious 'cause' was there first and contains the dynamic of the past. Freud's concept of psychic DETERMINISM is based on the assumption that unconscious processes can be the cause of conscious ones, but not vice versa. Some aspects of psychoanalytical theory, notably those centring round the INTERPRETATION of DREAMS and the use of SYMBOLS, are concerned with MEANING and the grammar of unconscious thinking and not with causation. See Rycroft (1966), Home (1966), Szasz (1961).

CENSOR, CENSORSHIP In Freud's first formulations the mental agency responsible for DREAM distortion and REPRESSION was called the censor. The censor is the theoretical ancestor of the SUPER-EGO.

CHARACTER In analytical writings character usually refers *not* to those of a person's attributes which are most characteristic of him as a unique individual, *but* to those which enable him to be categorized into one of a number of character types. This is owing to the fact that certain *character traits* can be interpreted as either (a) derivatives of specific phases of LIBIDINAL and EGO DEVELOPMENT, or (b) analogues of SYMPTOMS, i.e. as defensive procedures. From (a) derive *oral character, anal character, phallic character, genital character.* From (b) derive *hysterical, phobic, schizoid, obsessional character.* Hence *character neurosis, character disorder, character analysis.* See also separate entries under ORAL; ANAL; PHALLIC; GENITAL; HYSTERICAL; PHOBIC; SCHIZOID; OBSESSIONAL.

CHARACTER ASSASSINATION Term used by Leslie Farber (1967) to describe the misuse of psychoanalytical theory to disparage character and impugn motives. This is done by either (a) interpreting behaviour in terms of INFANTILE motives without reference to the modifications of them produced by SUBLIMATION, education, sophistication, etc., or (b) labelling character traits by reference to whatever psychiatric condition displays them in caricature form.

17

The first technique typically consists in interpreting the envied behaviour (see ENVY) as a DEFENCE, without giving the victim the credit for having mastered the primitive IMPULSE by constructing the defence. This makes it possible to interpret kindness, considerateness, and gentleness as REACTION-FORMATIONS against SADISM, and efficiency, tidiness and cleanliness as reaction-formations against anality (see ANAL). The second technique makes it possible to designate all the qualities mentioned in the previous sentence as obsessional (see OBSESSION), to describe animation, vitality as MANIC, the capacity for objectivity and detachment as SCHIZOID, being observant as PARANOID, spontaneity and emotionality as HYSTERICAL. Although the motives underlying this abuse of psychoanalysis are envy, hatred, and malice, it is made possible by the fact that whereas psychoanalysis claims to be a general psychology, capable of explaining all aspects of human nature, its data are derived from pathology. As a result of this contradiction, concepts and classificatory systems which belong to the consulting-room are all too easily applied without modification outside it. The difficulties in avoiding character assassination are shown clearly by psychoanalytical studies of artists and historical personages, e.g. Freud and Bullitt's study of Wilson (1967). See PATHOBIOGRAPHY.

CHILD ANALYSIS The psychoanalysis of children. This differs technically from the analysis of adults in that PLAY replaces FREE ASSOCIATION. It differs theoretically in that parents and parent-substitutes are still actual, external figures in the patient's life and that DEPENDENCE on them is a social and biological fact not a neurotic symptom. It differs morally in that the relationship between analyst and patient is not one between consenting adults; the decision to have treatment is made not by the patient but by his parents. According to Anna Freud, the real dependence of the child on its parents necessitates modifications in technique; according to Melanie Klein it doesn't. See A. Freud (1962), Klein (1932).

CLASSICAL ANALYTICAL TECHNIQUE An analyst is said to practise classical technique if he (a) sees his patients daily, (b) puts them on a couch, (c) eschews all giving of advice, prescribing of drugs, management of their lives, (d) confines his own utterances to INTERPRETATIONS, and (e) instructs his patients to obey the fundamental or BASIC RULE of FREE ASSOCIATION. It is possible to practise classical technique without subscribing to CLASSICAL THEORY, since theory determines what is said by the analyst and not the setting in which he says it. Some practitioners of classical theory would, however, include (f) interpretation of DEFENCE in advance of interpretation of unconscious PHANTASY as an essential component of classical technique. KLEINIAN analysts conform to (a)-(e) but not to (f).

Classical technique was designed for the treatment of adult psychoneurotics. Controversy exists as to whether, and if so how, classical technique should be modified when analysing children, adolescents, and psychotics. Planned deviations from classical technique are sometimes called PARAMETERS. For an exposition of classical technique, see Fenichel (1941).

CLASSICAL (ANALYTICAL) THEORY Although this concept is frequently encountered in the literature, it is hard, unless one is already familiar with the author's theoretical position, to know precisely to what it refers. The concept implies that there exists a theoretical 'norm' and that other theoretical positions can be placed in relation to it, either as deviations from it or as advances on it. As a result, the concept tends to be used tendentiously, meaning either 'theory which is in line with Freud's basic insights' or 'theory as understood by those old-fashioned Viennese analysts way back in the twenties'. However, classical theory certainly bears some relation to CLASSICAL ANALYTICAL TECHNIQUE and includes the following concepts: (a) The STRUCTURAL, TOPOGRAPHICAL, and ECONOMIC formulations of METAPSYCHOLOGY. (b) The concept of stages of EGO and infantile LIBIDINAL DEVELOPMENT, these stages being related to the primacy of specific EROTOGENIC ZONES. And (c) the idea that the NEUROSES are REGRESSIVE phenomena in which the patient regresses to infantile FIXATION-POINTS. Anna Freud in England and Heinz Hartmann in the U.S.A. are either the heirs or the exponents of classical theory.

CLAUSTROPHOBIA Fear of enclosed spaces. A symptom of ANXIETY HYSTERIA or PHOBIA.

COITUS Sexual intercourse. Hence *coitus interruptus*, in which the male withdraws before ejaculation, *coitus prolongatus*, in which male ORGASM is delayed, and *coitus reservatus*, in which male orgasm is avoided.

COLLECTIVE UNCONSCIOUS See ARCHETYPE.

COMMUNICATION As Szasz (1961) has pointed out forcibly, much psychoanalytical theory could, and should, be restated in terms of communication and failures in communication, rather than in terms of functions and disturbances of function of single individuals. This criticism, however, applies more directly to INSTINCT THEORY than to OBJECT THEORY, since the latter's emphasis on OBJECT-RELATIONS contains the idea that the individual seeks communication and that the neuroses constitute failures in doing so. See INSTINCT THEORY AND OBJECT THEORY; MEANING; SEMANTICS; CAUSE; PSYCHIC DETERMINISM; PERSONOLOGY; CONVERSION.

COMPLEX A group of interconnected conscious and unconscious ideas and feelings which exert a dynamic effect on behaviour. The OEDIPUS and CASTRATION COMPLEXES are the only ones so called in Freudian psychoanalysis. The superiority and INFERIORITY COMPLEXES are ADLERIAN.

COMPROMISE FORMATION Any mental phenomenon which is the product of CONFLICT and which partially expresses both parties to the conflict. Typically, a symptom which effects a compromise between the repressed impulse and the repressing agency (see REPRESSION).

COMPULSIVE Adj. referring to CONSCIOUS thoughts and actions which the subject feels compelled to think or carry out and which he cannot prevent (or, at least, the omission of which leads to ANXIETY). Compulsive symptoms are characteristic of OBSESSIONAL NEUROSIS. They are either manifestations of 'the return of the repressed', i.e. they correspond to thoughts and wishes which the patient rejects as incompatible with his self-image, or they are a means of keeping such forbidden thoughts out of mind. Compulsive phenomena can be thought of as either due to failure of REPRESSION or as an indication of ALIENATION, since the element of drive in them betokens some force seeking expression while the element of involuntariness indicates that the subject fails to recognize them as part of himself. The opposites of 'compulsive' are 'free', 'voluntary', 'spontaneous', and 'EGO-SYNTONIC'.

CONCEPT The concepts used in psychoanalytical theory can be classified according to the underlying assumptions or FICTIONS which are being used to organize the facts into theoretical formulations. For example:

1. *'Principle' concepts*, which assume that mental life is actuated by, usually, the CONFLICT between opposing forces or principles, e.g. EROS and THANATOS, LIFE and DEATH INSTINCTS, SEX and AGGRESSION, the REALITY and PLEASURE PRINCIPLES. 2. *Structural concepts:* These assume that mental processes are functions of an organism or apparatus consisting of interrelated parts, e.g. the PSYCHIC APPARATUS and its components, the ID, EGO, and SUPER-EGO. 3. *Topographical concepts:* These assume that mental processes are localizable on a diagram, e.g. id, ego, and super-ego, EGO-BOUNDARY, layers or STRATA of mental content by which MEMORIES, IMPULSES, PHANTASIES, etc., are imagined to be at varying distances from the surface. In this instance hypotheses about the accessibility of UNCONSCIOUS phenomena to CONSCIOUSNESS are formulated in terms of their distance from it, it usually being assumed that the longer ago the further down. 4. *Economic concepts:* These assume the existence of some form of mental ENERGY, QUANTA of which may be attached to STRUCTURES (bound energy), or may move from one structure to another (free energy), or may be discharged in action (see DISCHARGE), e.g. LIBIDO, AGGRESSION, DESTRUDO, CATHEXIS, counter-cathexis. 5. *Dynamic concepts:* Those which describe mental activity in terms of process, drive and development, e.g. INSTINCT, DRIVE, IMPULSE, SUBLIMATION. 6. *Faculty concepts:* These are hangovers from pre-freudian psychology, e.g. MEMORY, INSIGHT, both of which can be, but often are not, restated in dynamic terms, i.e. remembering, forgetting, and (perhaps) INTROSPECTION.

All six types of concept do violence to the facts of human experience in as much they formulate them according to MODELS which do not arise directly out of its PHENOMENOLOGY, i.e. they assume either that the subjective data can be explained as the result of the activity of objectifiable impersonal forces or that non-localizable, temporally organized events can be formulated in terms of a fictitious, space-occupying structure. It is difficult to see, however, how one could formulate theories about the effect of past on present experience and the evolution of adult patterns of behaviour from INFANTILE ones without recourse to structural, dynamic, and economic concepts.

CONCEPTUALIZATION The process of deriving concepts from observations, of formulating general statements. A vogue word, the virtue of which is that it enables its user to avoid choosing between formulation, generalization, abstraction, and thought.

CONDENSATION The process by which two (or more) images combine (or can be combined) to form a composite image which is invested with MEANING and ENERGY derived from both. It is one of the PRIMARY PROCESSES characteristic of UNCONSCIOUS thinking and exemplified in DREAMS and SYMPTOM-FORMATION.

CONFLICT Opposition between apparently or actually incompatible forces. Internal or psychological conflict may be between instinctual IMPULSES (e.g. LIBIDINAL and AGGRESSIVE, see also INSTINCT) or between STRUCTURES (e.g. EGO and ID). The idea that all psychological conflict is NEUROTIC is not part of psychoanalytical theory; conflicts are only neurotic if one party is unconscious and/or if they are resolved by the use of DEFENCES other than SUBLIMATION.

CONFLICT-FREE AREA OF THE EGO TOPOGRAPHICAL formulation by which functions which are not liable to disturbances by neurotic CONFLICT are imagined to occupy an area in the ego. See AUTONOMY; EGO; EGO PSYCHOLOGY.

CONFRONTATION Term occasionally used to describe an analyst's communication in which he draws the patient's attention to some aspect of his behaviour without offering an explanation or INTERPRETATION of it.

CONSCIENCE *Either* a person's system of moral values *or* that part of a person which he experiences as voicing moral values. The word properly refers only to CONSCIOUS values and conscious 'still, small voices' and should not be confused with the SUPER-EGO which differs from it in being partly UNCONSCIOUS and in containing imperatives to which the individual does not consciously subscribe. The two concepts belong, in any case, to different frames of reference.

CONSCIOUS According to psychoanalytical theory mental activity can take place in two modes, one conscious, the other UNCONSCIOUS, those in the former mode being 'immediate data' which 'cannot be more fully explained by any kind of description', those in the latter mode being inferred. Theory also postulates that the two modes function according to different rules, conscious mental activity obeying the 'grammar' of the *secondary processes* and unconscious mental activity obeying that of the *primary processes* (see PROCESSES, PRIMARY AND SECONDARY). *The Conscious*, often abbreviated to 'Cs', is the system, or structure, in which conscious mental activity obeying the secondary processes occurs. Since thoughts belonging to the conscious may at times be unconscious, it is possible for mental activity to be simultaneously *descriptively unconscious* and *dynamically conscious*; such activity is termed *pre-conscious* (see separate entry under PRE-CONSCIOUS). The reverse situation occurs in DREAMS, in which we are conscious of manifestations of the unconscious. Contradictions of this kind contributed to Freud's change of terminology in the 1920s, when the conscious became the EGO and the unconscious became the ID.

CONSCIOUSNESS 1. The state of being aware, in contrast to being asleep, anaesthetized, in coma. 2. The faculty of SELF-AWARENESS possessed by man in contrast to other animals. When used in sense 2 it is not always clear whether it refers to primary (self-)awareness, i.e. knowing what one is doing, or to reflective self-awareness, i.e. paying attention to one's own mental processes.

Freud's paper on consciousness, which should have been included in his papers on METAPSYCHOLOGY (1915), is missing; as a result we have only incomplete knowledge of his views on it. We do know, however, that he (a) usually likened it to a sense-organ capable of perceiving INTERNAL mental events and of discriminating them from external PERCEPTIONS. This function of consciousness he termed REALITY-TESTING. (b) That he held that consciousness differed from UNCONSCIOUSNESS in taking cognizance of the categories of space and TIME, in being intolerant of contradictions, and in using bound ENERGY (i.e. in attributing to images a relatively constant meaning) (see PROCESSES, PRIMARY AND SECONDARY). And (c) that he maintained that 'being brought into connexion with verbal images' was an essential prerequisite for the entry of an unconscious thought into consciousness. It is also possible to deduce from his views on treatment and the therapeutic value of making the unconscious conscious that he held that consciousness had an integrative function (see INTEGRATION). See Freud (1915, 1923). See WORD PRESENTATION.

The tendency of psychoanalysis to regard consciousness of secondary importance and to assume that conscious phenomena are the effect of unconscious ones has led to neglect of problems of consciousness. This neglect forms the basis of much existential (see EXISTENTIALISM) criticism of Freudian psychoanalysis. See PHENOMENOLOGY; ONTOLOGY.

CONSTANCY-PRINCIPLE   Term borrowed by Freud from Fechner to describe the tendency of organisms to maintain a constant level of tension. It corresponds to Cannon's physiological concept of 'HOMEOSTASIS'. Although sometimes used by Freud to imply that organisms seek to abolish all internal TENSION, i.e. have a DEATH INSTINCT, it is best used to refer to a need to maintain an optimal level of tension. See Freud (1920). See PLEASURE PRINCIPLE.

CONSTRUCTIONS IN ANALYSIS   Hypotheses concerning an event in a patient's childhood, reconstructed from data provided by his FREE ASSOCIATIONS but not recollected by him. Freud's belief in the importance of specific events (TRAUMATA) in the causation of NEUROSIS led him to attach great practical and theoretical importance to accurate and convincing constructions, even when they were of events so early in life that eventual remembering was unlikely. Constructions which *are* later confirmed by recollection or by information acquired from other sources were also highly valued by Freud as confirmation of the historical, scientific accuracy of psychoanalysis (see SCIENCE).

CONVERSION   When used as a technical term, this refers to the process by which a psychological complex of ideas, wishes, feelings, etc., is replaced by a physical symptom. According to Freud (1893), it is the AFFECT attaching to the 'ideational complex' which is converted into a physical phenomenon, not the 'ideational complex' itself. Although Freud's discovery that physical 'HYSTERICAL' symptoms are PSYCHOGENIC was the seminal observation from which PSYCHOANALYSIS developed, the 'conversion' hypo-

thesis is unsatisfactory since it leaves unexplained what is sometimes called 'the mysterious leap' from the mental to the physical.
The mystery vanishes if hysterical symptoms are regarded as
gestures. See Home (1966), Szasz (1961).

CONVERSION HYSTERIA   Form of psychoneurosis in which
the symptoms are physical complaints. *Conversion symptoms* differ
from physical symptoms in that (a) the loss of function corresponds to the patient's idea of how his body works and not to the
facts of anatomy and physiology, e.g. a hysterical anaesthesia of,
say, the hand corresponds to the area embraced by the concept
'hand' (covered by a glove), not to the area served by the nerves to
the hand; (b) the symptom can be demonstrated to fulfil a function in the patient's life; and (c) the patient adopts a curious
attitude towards the symptom, typically either a histrionic one or
one of indifference.

COPRO-   Relating to faeces, e.g. *Coprophagia*: eating faeces, a
symptom occurring in disturbed, deprived children and in
SCHIZOPHRENIA. *Coprophilia*: pleasure in touching, looking at, or
eating faeces.

COUNTER-CATHEXIS   See CATHEXIS.

COUNTER-PHOBIC   See under PHOBIC CHARACTER.

COUNTER-TRANSFERENCE   1. The analyst's TRANSFERENCE
on his patient. In this, the correct, sense, counter-transference is a
disturbing, distorting element in treatment. 2. By extension, the
analyst's emotional attitude towards his patient, including his
response to specific items of the patient's behaviour. According to
Heimann (1950), Little (1951), Gitelson (1952), and others, the
analyst can use this latter kind of counter-transference as clinical
evidence, i.e. he can assume that his own emotional response is
based on a correct interpretation of the patient's true intentions or
meaning.

COUNTER-WILL   See WILL and NEGATIVISM.

COVER MEMORY   See SCREEN MEMORY.

CREATIVITY   The capacity to arrive at novel but valid solutions to problems. The capacity to create imaginative products
(see IMAGINATION) which are compelling, convincing, significant,

etc. From its earliest days, psychoanalysis has been tempted to proffer explanations of creative activity, these being invariably based on demonstration of the similarity between creative activity and some neurotic process. The simplest version of this procedure is to demonstrate that the content of novels and paintings can be interpreted as an OEDIPAL phantasy and then deduce from this that creative activity is a form of neurotic daydreaming (Freud, 1908). The difficulty with this hypothesis is that it fails to explain why all daydreams are not creative and it therefore involves secondary hypotheses as to how the formal and technical aspects of creative work enable private neurotic 'creations' to be converted into publicly acceptable and comprehensible works of art. At the end of his life Freud rejected the idea that psychoanalysis had anything to contribute to aesthetics. (But see Ehrenzweig (1967) for a contrary view.) More recently, and usually under the influence of KLEINIAN ideas, there have been attempts to prove that creative activity is either DEPRESSIVE or SCHIZOID, i.e. that it either represents an attempt to make REPARATION for destructive PHANTASIES (Klein, 1948, Sharpe, 1950, Levey, 1939), or is in some way analogous to the delusional system-making of SCHIZOPHRENICS (see also DELUSION). Here again the reason why some people have the capacity to find creative solutions for their depressive or schizoid problems remains unexplained.

Since classical psychoanalysis designates imaginative activity as primitive, INFANTILE, and as a function of the ID, writers such as Hartmann and Kris have been compelled to describe in terms of REGRESSION activities which they clearly in fact regard as creative and progressive. This has led to the use of phrases such as 're-gression at the service of the EGO' to describe the 'negative capability' (Keats) of the creative. Since the results of creative activity are, by definition, novel, unexpected, and therefore unpredictable, creativity is a concept hard to include within a causal-determinist framework (see CAUSALITY and DETERMINISM); hence presumably the AMBIVALENCE of psychoanalysis towards it. The concept also raises problems as to whether it is a general aptitude, in which case everyone could become creative if his INHIBITIONS were removed, or a special gift, in which case psychoanalysis has to admit exceptions to its categories. For the former view, see Kubie's *Neurotic Distortion of the Creative Process* (1958); for the latter, see Phyllis Greenacre's *The Childhood of the Artist* (1957), where she argues that gifted persons are different from the beginning of life, that they actively seek objects who will recognize their difference and their gifts, and that, if analysed, they require a different technique than others. See also MEANING.

D

DEAGGRESSIFICATION The process by which INFANTILE aggressive ENERGY (see also AGGRESSION) loses its primitive, agressive quality when the IMPULSES to which it is attached participate in SUBLIMATION. See NEUTRALIZATION; AUTONOMOUS FUNCTIONS OF THE EGO.

DEATH INSTINCT In his *Beyond the Pleasure Principle* (1922) Freud introduced the concept of a death instinct. 'We . . . have been led to distinguish two kinds of instincts; those which seek to lead what is living to death, and others, the sexual instincts, which are perpetually attempting and achieving a renewal of life.' Despite the fact that, as Jones (1957) points out, 'No biological observation can be found to support the idea of a death instinct, one which contradicts all biological principles', the idea still has a certain currency and forms an essential part of KLEINIAN theory, which conceives of AGGRESSION as a PROJECTION of the individual's own innate self-destructive drive. Attempts to work out the death instinct in detail, postulating a death-instinct form of ENERGY analogous to LIBIDO, have never got further than suggesting a name for such energy, e.g. MORTIDO, DESTRUDO. The concept needs to be carefully differentiated from that of an aggressive or destructive instinct, since the death-instinct concept postulates a wish to dissolve, annihilate *oneself*, while the destructive-instinct concept implies a wish to kill *others*.

DEEP AND SUPERFICIAL Qualifiers of either 'MATERIAL' or INTERPRETATIONS. When referring to the former, 'deep' means that the material brought by the patient (i.e. what he talks about) derives either from early in his life or from repressed areas of his personality (see REPRESSION), while 'superficial' means either 'recent' or 'easily accessible'. When referring to the latter, 'deep' means that the interpretation relates either to early events or to strongly resisted ideas (see RESISTANCE). The usage derives from the use of geological metaphors to describe differences in accessibility and resistance. The metaphor tends to insinuate the assumption that early events are harder of access and of greater importance than recent ones.

DEFENCE 'A general designation for all the techniques which the ego makes use of in conflicts which may lead to neurosis' – Freud (1922). The function of defence is to protect the EGO, and defences may be instigated by (a) ANXIETY due to increases in instinctual TENSION (see also INSTINCT); (b) anxiety due to a bad CONSCIENCE (SUPER-EGO threats); or (c) realistic dangers. The concept of defence is usually stated in terms which imply that the human ego is beset by threats to its survival emanating from the ID, the super-ego, and the outside world, and that it is, therefore, perpetually on the defensive. But the concept is better regarded less negatively and taken to include all techniques used by the ego to master, control, canalize, and use forces 'which may lead to a NEUROSIS'. The concept also implies that neurosis is due to a failure of defence; according to this view the INHIBITIONS resulting from successful REPRESSION are not neurotic symptoms. Anna Freud (1937) lists nine defences: REGRESSION, repression, REACTION-FORMATION, ISOLATION, UNDOING, PROJECTION, INTROJECTION, TURNING AGAINST THE SELF, and REVERSAL – plus a tenth, SUBLIMATION, 'which pertains rather to the study of the normal than to that of neurosis'. SPLITTING and DENIAL are also usually listed as defences.

Since psychoanalysis holds that anxiety is a spur to DEVELOPMENT, some, perhaps all, of the defences play a part in normal development and it is usually assumed that certain defences belong to specific stages of development, e.g. introjection, projection, denial, and splitting to the ORAL phase; reaction-formation, isolation, and undoing to the ANAL phase. See also TECHNIQUE.

DEJA VU The subjective sense that a present novel experience has been gone through previously. See Freud (1914).

DELUSION Term used in psychiatry to refer to a belief voiced by a patient which is both untrue and uninfluenceable by logic or evidence; a fixed idea. A common-sense, clinical concept which turns out to be unexpectedly difficult the moment one asks two questions: (a) How does the psychiatrist know his corresponding belief is true? (b) In what sense does the patient believe his delusion? (a) can be answered only if it is possible to discover the function of the beliefs in the mental economy of the patient and the psychiatrist. (b) leads to the conclusion that the delusion is a manifestation of a thought-disturbance, viz. loss of the capacity to distinguish between categories of thought – in the simplest instance, between metaphorical and factual statements. If the correct mode can be discovered, delusional ideas can often be shown to make sense.

Delusions of grandeur and persecution occur in SCHIZOPHRENIA and PARANOIA. Internally consistent *delusional systems* characterize paranoia. *Delusions of unworthiness*, e.g. the belief in having committed a crime, occur in MELANCHOLIA. See DOUBLE BIND.

DEMENTIA PARANOIDES Obsolete term for paranoid SCHIZOPHRENIA and PARANOIA.

DEMENTIA PRAECOX Obsolete psychiatric term corresponding approximately to what is now called SCHIZOPHRENIA. The term was coined by Kraepelin, the father of modern psychiatry, and implied the illness that was incurable, deteriorating, dementing, and that began in adolescence.

DEMENTIA, SENILE AND PRE-SENILE Organic diseases of the brain characterized by progressive mental deterioration.

DENIAL DEFENCE mechanism by which either (a) some painful experience is denied or (b) some impulse or aspect of the SELF is denied. (a) and (b) are not certainly the same process. According to Freud, denial of painful PERCEPTIONS is a general manifestation of the PLEASURE-PRINCIPLE, the denial being part of hallucinatory WISH-FULFILMENT (see also HALLUCINATION). As a result, all painful perceptions have to overcome the resistance of the pleasure-principle. Denial of aspects of the self is something more complicated, since, according to Klein, it is followed by SPLITTING and PROJECTION, as a result of which the patient denies that he has such and such feelings but goes on to assert that someone else does (see KLEINIAN). *Denial of psychical reality* is a manifestation of MANIC DEFENCE; it consists in denying the inner significance of experience, and in particular of DEPRESSIVE feelings (see also REALITY). Denial has to be distinguished from NEGATION, in which an unpleasant perception is announced by assertion of its negative, e.g. the first sign of a headache is the thought, 'How lucky I am not to have had a headache for so long.'

DEPENDENCE, INFANTILE AND ADULT INFANTILE dependence refers either (a) to the fact that children are helpless and dependent on their parents, or (b) to the fact that NEUROTICS are fixated on their parents and imagine themselves to be dependent on them (see FIXATION). The use of 'dependence' and 'independence' to make the distinction between the helplessness of the immature and the viability of the mature (which Piaget dealt with by using 'heteronomy' and 'AUTONOMY') has led to endless confusion and hair-splitting; since adults need objects to satisfy their adult needs, they can be argued to be dependent on them. Fairbairn defined maturation as a progression from infantile dependence to MATURE dependence. In this sense dependence is the antithesis of NARCISSISM not of self-reliance. *Oral dependence* is the infant's dependence on its MOTHER (see also ORAL).

DEPENDENCY Dependence is almost always intended (see Fowler), though a case could be made out for the idea that dependence is a manifestation of a state of dependency.

DEPERSONALIZATION Psychiatric term for the symptom which leads a patient to complain that he feels unreal.

DEPRESSION This refers either to an EMOTION or a DIAGNOSIS. When referring to an emotion, it means in low spirits, gloomy; when referring to a diagnosis, it refers to a SYNDROME of which the emotion 'depression' constitutes one element. PSYCHIATRY nowadays uses the diagnosis 'depression' to describe what used to be called MELANCHOLIA, the condition in which the patient suffers from low spirits, RETARDATION of thoughts and action, and delusional SELF-REPROACHES (see also DELUSION). This is one of the affective disorders (see AFFECTIVE DISORDER; PSYCHOSIS), so called because the disturbance is one of MOOD; the other is MANIA. Persons who alternate between depression and mania are said to have a MANIC-DEPRESSIVE PSYCHOSIS. Psychiatry distinguishes between *endogenous* and *exogenous depression*, the former being presumed to be the result of some (unspecified) constitutional disturbance, the latter being a comprehensible but none the less excessive response to some distressing event (see also entries under ENDOGENOUS and EXOGENOUS). *Involutional depression* is a depressive illness occurring in the second half of life; its use implies belief in a constitutional origin.

The psychoanalytical literature is unanimous in regarding melancholic depression as a pathological form of MOURNING, the lost object being an 'INTERNAL OBJECT' not an actual person. This internal object was ambivalently invested (see AMBIVALENCE), so that the depressed person felt dependent on an object to which he was none the less hostile. In depression he imagines that he has destroyed this object (hence the self-reproaches), but is incapable of surviving without it (hence the depression). This view of melancholic depression assumes that persons subject to it are, even in health, in a state of precarious balance, since their stability is based on a complex, ambivalent relationship towards an internal object. According to Abraham (1927), depression occurs in persons who use OBSESSIONAL DEFENCES, and the necessary INFANTILE preconditions for depression in adult life are (a) ambivalence towards and FIXATION on the BREAST, INTROJECTION of which creates the 'internal object'; and (b) a severe injury to SELF-ESTEEM occurring later in childhood than weaning, as a result of which the patient fails to achieve self-reliance and reverts to his ambivalent dependence on the breast. See also Freud (1917). Abraham's views on depression formed the basis of Melanie Klein's views (see KLEINIAN) on the DEPRESSIVE POSITION and its role in normal DEVELOPMENT.

Neurotic depression refers to the symptom complained of by many neurotics. Sometimes it is a mild form of the condition discussed above; sometimes it refers to a mixture of ANXIETY, GUILT, and a sense of INHIBITION.

DEPRESSION, ANACLITIC Term coined by Spitz (1946) to describe the state of DEPRESSION, withdrawal, and listlessness into which infants fall when separated from their MOTHERS. The 'anaclitic' refers to the fact that the separation, and the resulting depression, occurs at an age at which the infant is still objectively dependent on its mother. See also ANACLITIC.

DEPRESSIVE When applied to a person or his CHARACTER and/or temperament, the implication is either that he is prone to DEPRESSION or that he has the kind of temperament which leads the speaker to surmise that, if analysed, he would prove to have a PSYCHOPATHOLOGY similar to that discussed under depression (see above). *Depressive anxiety* is anxiety concerning the effect of one's own AGGRESSION on others or on one's INTERNAL OBJECTS.

Depressive illness is a synonym for depression in its diagnostic sense.

DEPRESSIVE POSITION   A KLEINIAN concept. It describes the position reached (in her scheme of things) by the infant (or by the patient in analysis) when he realizes that both his LOVE and HATE are directed towards the same object – the MOTHER – becomes aware of his AMBIVALENCE and concerned to protect her from his hate and to make REPARATION for what damage he imagines his hate has done. Since Klein's system includes the DEATH INSTINCT and innate hostility and ENVY of the mother, this crisis is conceived as playing an essential part in every infant's development, regardless of the quality of its mothering, and its outcome is held to determine all later development. Healthy and neurotic persons are considered to have passed the depressive position, while persons with depressive problems are fixated at it and persons with SCHIZOID and PARANOID problems have failed to reach it. See PARANOID-SCHIZOID POSITION. See Segal (1964).

DEPRIVATION   The experience of receiving an insufficiency of a necessary commodity. Psychoanalysis has concerned itself with two forms of deprivation: *maternal* and *sexual*. Both, but especially in recent years the former, have been adduced as causes of NEUROSIS, particularly in Great Britain by Bowlby (1951). The maternal deprivation theory of neurosis exists in various degrees of sophistication, according to how the insufficient commodity is defined. Statistical theories of maternal deprivation have, of necessity, to define the deprivation in terms of the duration of the physical absence of the MOTHER. Theories such as Winnicott's, which are based on both pediatric observation and analytical CONSTRUCTIONS, can define deprivation in terms of love received or not received and can even break up the concept of mothering into sub-categories, e.g. feeding, handling, cuddling, smiling, warmth, as a result of which a mother may fail to be a 'good enough' or ORDINARY DEVOTED MOTHER in one sub-category while succeeding in the others.

Deprivation theories of neurosis imply that deprivation beyond a certain THRESHOLD produces relatively irreversible effects either by retarding DEVELOPMENT or by initiating DEFENCES. According to one possible schema, the sequence is deprivation→FRUSTRATION →AGGRESSION→ANXIETY→DEFENCE→INHIBITION→return of the repressed→SYMPTON-FORMATION; another is deprivation→FIXA-TION→inhibited development→persistence of the INFANTILE need for mothering and REGRESSIVE behaviour. For the effects of gross maternal deprivation, see SEPARATION, MOTHER–CHILD.

DEPTH PSYCHOLOGY Obsolescent term for PSYCHOANALY-SIS, for the psychology of the UNCONSCIOUS.

DEREALIZATION Psychiatric term for the symptom which leads the patient to complain that the world seems unreal.

DESEXUALIZATION The process by which INFANTILE libidinal ENERGY loses its primitive, EROTIC quality when the PREGENITAL impulses to which it is attached participate in SUBLI-MATION and EGO DEVELOPMENT. See LIBIDINAL DEVELOPMENT, INFANTILE; NEUTRALIZATION; AUTONOMOUS FUNCTIONS OF THE EGO.

DESPAIR The absence of hope. As a pathological phenomenon it occurs in SCHIZOID and schizophrenic disorders (see SCHIZO-PHRENIA), in which it appears to be the result of feelings of un-surmountable ALIENATION and AMBIVALENCE, and in the NEUROSES, in which it is a defensive attitude (see DEFENCE) designed to reduce ANXIETY. 'There is no hope without fear and no fear without hope' – Spinoza.

DESTRUDO Rarely used term for the ENERGY of the DEATH INSTINCT and therefore analogous to the LIBIDO of the LIFE INSTINCT.

DETERMINISM, PSYCHIC The assumption made by Freud that mental phenomena have CAUSES in whatever sense physical ones do. See Jones (1953–7), vol. I, ch. xvii, for Freud's views on causality, determinism and free will, and their relation to the scientific thought of this time. He seems to have held that demon-stration of the existence of UNCONSCIOUS mental processes proved the assumption of determinism, since it made it possible to assert that conscious processes were the effects of unconscious ones. He did not, however, regard consciousness as a mere epipheno-menon, but as a regulator capable of a 'more stable control and

33

guidance of the flow of mental processes' – Jones (op. cit.). The assumption of psychic determinism, at least as usually stated, leaves no place in analytical theory for a SELF or AGENT initiating action or DEFENCE or for the use of explanations other than causal ones.

Most analysts believe that the claims of PSYCHOANALYSIS to be a SCIENCE are based on its use of causal-deterministic assumptions and will have no truck with the idea that it – or at least some parts of its theory – resembles disciplines like linguistics and sociology, which recognize patterns, more than the physical sciences. See Szasz (1961), Home (1966), Rycroft (1966), Gorer (1966). See also MEANING.

DEVELOPMENT Psychoanalysis maintains that human behaviour can be viewed developmentally, i.e. that adult behaviour can be interpreted as an elaboration or evolution of INFANTILE behaviour, and that complex 'higher' forms of behaviour can be interpreted as elaborations of simple, primitive behaviour patterns and drives. The developmental process as a whole can be seen as resulting from two factors, the evolution of innate developmental processes and the impact of experience on these processes. TRAUMATA are experiences which disrupt or pervert development; FIXATION-POINTS are circumscribed INHIBITIONS of development; satisfactory terms do not exist for experiences which accelerate development (i.e. produce precocity) or for negative experiences (STIMULUS-deprivations) which lead to absences of development. Since CLASSICAL ANALYTICAL THEORY is tied to the idea of a division of the PSYCHE into an EGO and an ID, it is forced to conceive of two parallel forms of development, EGO DEVELOPMENT and LIBIDINAL DEVELOPMENT, the former consisting in the acquisition of EGO FUNCTIONS which increase AUTONOMY, the latter consisting in the transformation of PRE-GENITAL sexual and aggressive drives (see SEX and AGGRESSION) into adult sexual and sublimated activities (see SUBLIMATION).

DIAGNOSIS The art of attaching labels to illnesses, of deducing the nature of an illness from the SIGNS and SYMPTOMS presented by the patient. The *differential diagnosis* is the list of labels worthy of serious consideration in any particular instance of making a diagnosis. A *diagnostic formulation* is a more or less complex statement of the PSYCHOPATHOLOGY of a psychiatric patient. The concept diagnosis is a medical one implying that illnesses are specific disease entities, an assumption which is probably invalid when applied to the PSYCHONEUROSES. See MENTAL ILLNESS.

DIRECT ANALYSIS Form of PSYCHOTHERAPY advocated by Rosen (1953) in which the therapist ignores the 'as if' quality of TRANSFERENCE phenomena and asserts that he is the patient's father, mother, etc. Originally advocated for psychotherapy of the PSYCHOSES.

DISCHARGE The concept implies a prior build-up or charge of TENSION, ENERGY, IMPULSE, or EMOTION, the discharge of which lowers tension. The therapeutic effect of ABREACTION was explained by assuming that the damming-up of repressed emotion (see REPRESSION) led to a state of internal tension which was discharged by the abreactive experience. INSTINCT THEORY presupposes that instinctual impulses build up a state of tension which is discharged by instinctual activity. *Discharge of affect* is an impersonal, theoretical formulation of what is conceived to occur in the PSYCHIC APPARATUS when an emotion is expressed. A *discharge-affect* is an emotion which occurs while an impulse is being discharged, in contrast to a *tension-affect*, which accompanies the damming-up of an impulse. See also AFFECT.

DISPLACEMENT The process by which ENERGY (CATHEXIS) is transferred from one mental image to another. Displacement is one of the PRIMARY PROCESSES and is responsible for the fact that, for instance, in DREAMS one image can symbolize another (see SYMBOL). More generally, the process by which the individual shifts interest from one object or an activity to another in such a way that the latter becomes an equivalent or substitute for the other. Symbolization and SUBLIMATION depend on serial displacements.

DISSOCIATION 1. The state of affairs in which two or more mental processes co-exist without becoming connected or integrated (see INTEGRATION). 2. The defensive process (see DEFENCE) leading to 1. No hard and fast distinction can be made between dissociation and SPLITTING, though there is a tendency to use the former when referring to processes and the latter when referring to STRUCTURES, e.g. dissociation of CONSCIOUSNESS when talking about dual personalities or hysterical FUGUES (see also HYSTERIA), but splitting of the EGO.

DOUBLE BIND   According to Bateson, *et al.* (*Towards a Theory of Schizophrenia*, 1956), the childhood of future SCHIZO-PHRENICS is characterized by repeated experiences of being put into a double bind by, typically, their MOTHERS. This experience consists in being made the object of incompatible, contradictory emotional demands in a situation in which there is no avenue of escape and in which no other member of the family rescues the child from the bind by either compensating for or correcting the mother's behaviour or by elucidating it to the child. The schizo-phrenic's response to a double bind is to lose the capacity to dis-tinguish the logical status of thoughts. In other words, his DEFENCE against confusion, and his own and his mother's AMBIVALENCE, is to lose the capacity to understand those nuances which enable one to have INSIGHT into motives and to appreciate discrepancies between overt and concealed meanings. In lay language, a double bind is an 'impossible' position. Strictly speaking, the double bind is not a PSYCHOANALYTICAL concept, since it refers to an INTER-PERSONAL situation and not to an internal CONFLICT or develop-mental process. Although originally formulated as a theory of schizophrenia, it has been adduced as an explanation of neurotic behaviour. The possibility that an analyst may put a patient into a double bind has also been envisaged. See *Family Process* (American journal), Laing (1961), Lidz (1964).

DREAM, DREAMING   Mental activity occurring in SLEEP; a series of pictures or events imagined during sleep. Psychoanaly-sis assumes that dreams have psychological MEANING which can be arrived at by INTERPRETATION. According to Freud's original formulations, dreams have (a) a *manifest content*, which is the dream as experienced, reported, or remembered (see also MANI-FEST), and (b) a *latent content*, which is discovered by interpretation (see also LATENT). He also held that the dreamer performs work (the *dream-work*) in translating the latent into the manifest con-tent, and that, therefore, dream-interpretation is the reverse of dream-work. According to his WISH-FULFILMENT theory of dreams, the latent content is a wish, which is fulfilled in the dream in hallucinatory form (see HALLUCINATION), the translation into the manifest content being necessitated by two factors: (a) the physiological conditions of sleep which determine that dreaming is, in the main, a visual not a verbal process, and (b) that the wish is unacceptable to the waking EGO; it has therefore to be disguised in order to pass the CENSOR. NIGHTMARES and anxiety dreams constitute failures in the dream-work; traumatic dreams (see TRAUMA), in which the dream merely repeats the traumatic experience, are exceptions to the theory.

Freud's interest in dreams derived from the fact that they are normal processes, with which everyone is familiar, but which none the less exemplify the processes at work in the formation of neurotic symptoms. These processes – CONDENSATION, DISPLACEMENT, SYMBOLIZATION, obliviousness to the categories of space and TIME, and toleration of contradictions – Freud called the *primary processes* in contrast to the *secondary processes* of waking thought. Dream interpretation is, therefore, largely a matter of translating primary-process thinking into secondary-process thinking, of expanding the condensed, non-discursive, mainly visual imagery of the dream into the discursive symbolism of language. See PROCESSES, PRIMARY AND SECONDARY.

According to Freud (1900, 1902), the function of dreams is to preserve SLEEP by representing wishes as fulfilled which would otherwise awaken the dreamer. Recent physiological research suggests, however, that sleep is of two kinds, *dreamless* and *dream sleep* (the paradoxical phase of sleep), that phases of the latter occur recurrently in all extended periods of sleep, and that the function of dream sleep is to process the sensory intake of previous periods of wakefulness.

DREAM SCREEN The screen on to which the visual imagery of a dream can be imagined to be projected (see PROJECTION). According to Lewin's original hypothesis, all dreams are projected on to a screen which is only occasionally visible. This screen Lewin interpreted as a SYMBOL of both SLEEP itself and of the BREAST, with which sleep is unconsciously equated, i.e. the screen represented the wish to sleep and the visual imagery represented the wishes disturbing sleep (see DREAM). According to Rycroft and others, the dream screen is not a component of all dreams, but a phenomenon which only occurs in the dreams of persons who are entering a MANIC phase; it symbolizes the manic sense of ecstatic fusion with the breast (MOTHER) and denial of hostility towards it. See Lewin (1946), Rycroft (1951), Boyer (1960).

In his later papers Lewin distinguished between screen dreams and *blank dreams*; the latter is a dream characterized by two convictions on the part of the dreamer: (a) that he has had a dream and (b) that the dreamer had no visual content.

DRIVE   No useful purpose is served by trying to distinguish between an INSTINCT and a drive. Freud used the word '*Trieb*'. See Strachey's general preface to the Standard Edition of Freud for his reasons for preferring 'instinct' to 'drive'.

DUAL INSTINCT THEORY   See under INSTINCT.

DYNAMIC   Psychoanalysis is a *dynamic* psychology since its concepts of PROCESS, INSTINCT, and DEVELOPMENT imply movement; in contrast to static psychologies such as faculty psychology, which merely enumerate and define attributes of the mind.

E

ECONOMIC   When used as a technical term, economic is the adjective corresponding to the noun ENERGY. Economic concepts and formulations refer to the distribution of energy, LIBIDO, and CATHEXES within the PSYCHIC APPARATUS.

EFFERENT   Adj., qualifying nerves which lead impulses away from the centre, in contrast to AFFERENT, which lead them towards it.

EGO   A STRUCTURAL and TOPOGRAPHICAL concept referring to the organized parts of the PSYCHIC APPARATUS, in contrast to the unorganized ID. '. . . The ego is that part of the id which has been modified by the direct influence of the external world. . . . The ego represents what may be called reason and common sense, in contrast to the id, which contains the passions . . . in its relation to the id it is like a man on horseback, who has to hold in check the superior strength of the horse; with this difference, that the rider tries to do so with his own strength while the ego uses borrowed forces' – Freud (1923). For analysts who do not subscribe to the notion of an undifferentiated id out of which the ego develops, the ego is either (a) the whole psyche: 'The pristine personality of the child consists of a unitary dynamic ego' – Fairbairn (1952); (b) that part of the personality which relates to objects and/or is formed by INTROJECTION of objects; or (c) that part of the personality which is experienced as being oneself, which one recognizes as 'I'.

Ego and SELF are often confused; they probably belong to different frames of reference, the ego belonging to an OBJECTIVE frame of reference which views personality as a structure and self belonging to a phenomenological frame of reference (see PHENOMENOLOGY) which views personality as experience.

EGO, BODY   See BODY-EGO.

EGO BOUNDARY   TOPOGRAPHICAL concept by which the distinction between SELF and not-self is imagined to be delineated. A patient is said to lack ego boundaries if he identifies (see IDENTIFICATION) readily with others and does so at the expense of his own sense of IDENTITY. Analysts who hold that the INFANT lives in a state of primary identification with his MOTHER, postulate the gradual development of an ego boundary, i.e. the discovery that objects are not parts of itself.

EGO DEFECT   The absence of an EGO FUNCTION.

EGO DEVELOPMENT   Psychoanalysis's assumption that the psyche is divisible into an ID and an EGO compels it to make a distinction between libidinal and ego development, the former being the progress through various libidinal stages, in which the sources and forms of sexual pleasure change (see LIBIDO), and the latter being the growth and acquisition of functions which enable the individual increasingly to master his IMPULSES, to operate independently of parental figures, and to control his ENVIRONMENT. Attempts have been made to correlate phases of libidinal and ego development and to describe an ORAL ego, which is entirely pleasure-seeking and dependent on the mother, an ANAL ego, which is concerned with control and mastery of impulses, etc. The most ambitious of these is Erikson's STAGES OF MAN, which divides the whole of life from birth to death into eight stages of ego development.

Ego development may also refer to the process by which the ego differentiates out of the id. According to Glover (1939) this occurs by the fusion of a number of originally disparate *ego-nuclei*. On the other hand, according to Fairbairn (1952) the infant starts with a 'unitary, dynamic ego' which reacts to FRUSTRATION by SPLITTING into three parts: the *central ego*, the *libidinal ego* and the *anti-libidinal ego* or INTERNAL SABOTEUR; the first corresponding roughly to Freud's ego, the second to the id, and the third to the SUPER-EGO (see FAIRBAIRN'S REVISED PSYCHO PATHOLOGY). According to Klein, ego development is a process of INTROJECTION of objects (see KLEINIAN).

EGO-DYSTONIC Behaviour and wishes are said to be ego-dystonic if they are incompatible with the subject's ideals or conception of himself; i.e. they refer to a value-judgement made by the subject himself.

EGO FUNCTION Since psychoanalysis ascribes all functions to the EGO, anything which the subject can do is an ego function.

EGO IDEAL The SELF's conception of how he wishes to be. Sometimes used synonymously with the SUPER-EGO, but more often the distinction is made that behaviour which is in conflict with the super-ego evokes GUILT, while that which conflicts with the ego ideal evokes SHAME.

EGO INSTINCT In Freud's formulations prior to 1920 there were two groups of INSTINCTS: the self-preservative or ego instincts (see SELF-PRESERVATION) and the reproductive or sexual instincts (see SEX).

EGO-INTEGRITY The last of Erikson's eight STAGES OF MAN is ego-integrity *v.* DESPAIR. Although Erikson does not use the phrase, 'ego-integrity' seems to mean 'the serenity of old age' and the acceptance of one's own death as natural and as part of the order of things.

EGO LIBIDO LIBIDO which is invested in the EGO. It is not always clear whether this refers to the energy available for EGO FUNCTIONS or to SELF-LOVE.

EGO PSYCHOLOGY Either 'the psychology of the ego', or, and perhaps more frequently, that variety of psychoanalytical theory which has developed from Freud's *The Ego and the Id*

(1923) and Anna Freud's *The Ego and the Mechanisms of Defence* (1936). In this latter sense there is an explicit or implicit contrast with either INSTINCT THEORY, which preceded it, or OBJECT THEORY, which has developed contemporaneously with it. Key concepts of psychoanalytical ego psychology are 'AUTONOMOUS FUNCTIONS OF THE EGO', 'the CONFLICT-FREE AREA OF THE EGO', 'DESEXUALIZATION', 'DEAGGRESSIFICATION'. See Hartmann (1958) for a definitive statement.

EGO-SYNTONIC Behaviour and wishes are said to be ego-syntonic if they are compatible with the subject's ideals and conception of himself.

EGOTIZATION The process by which a mental process or function becomes part of the SELF, structured or deaggressified and desexualized (see STRUCTURAL; DEAGGRESSIFICATION; DESEXUALIZATION).

ELATION The sense of high spirits and triumph occurring typically after a success. As a pathological term, the emotion accompanying MANIA. Pathological elation is usually interpreted as a reversal of the relationship between EGO and SUPER-EGO existing in DEPRESSION. As a result of this reversal, the ego feels as though it had triumphed over (or become fused with) the super-ego; instead of feeling oppressed and alienated it feels liberated and at one with the world. See Lewin (1951) for the psychopathology of elation and its relation to enthusiasm and ecstasy.

ELECTRA COMPLEX Rarely used term for the OEDIPUS COMPLEX of women.

ELUSION Term used by Laing (1961) to describe the process by which a person may avoid confrontation with himself and others by impersonating himself, i.e. by playing at the role that he in fact has. He cites Sartre's waiter and Flaubert's Madame Bovary as examples of elusion. 'It counterfeits truth by a double pretence,' i.e. by pretending that PHANTASY is REAL, and then pretending that reality is a phantasy.

EMBODIED AND UNEMBODIED Terms used by Laing (1960) to describe two states of being, the embodied state being that possessed by persons with primary ontological security (see

41

ONTOLOGY) who 'feel they began when their bodies began and that they will end when their bodies die', the unembodied being that possessed by persons who lack primary ontological security and have a sense of being detached from their bodies.

EMOTION A state of both body and mind consisting of a subjective feeling which is either pleasurable or unpleasant but never neutral, which is accompanied by expressive behaviour or posture and by physiological changes. Psychoanalytical theory tends to assume that emotions are AFFECTS, i.e. that they are QUANTA of ENERGY attached to ideas, that their presence indicates a disturbance in psychic equilibrium, and that they interfere with ADAPTATION. 'From the point of view of the psychology of the neuroses, affective action – in contrast to the theoretical ideal of rational action – often appears as a deplorable residue of primitive mental conditions and as a deviation from the normal. . . . Yet we do know the crucial role of affectivity in organizing and facilitating many ego functions. Freud [1937] implied this when he said that analysis is not expected to free man of all passions' – Hartmann (1958). For some of the complications and paradoxes produced by the 'theoretical ideal of rational action' and the assumption that emotions are primitive and irrational, see Rycroft (1962). Psycho-analysis has made little use of McDougall's (1908) distinction between primary emotions, e.g. fear, anger, tenderness; complex emotions, e.g. admiration, envy; and sentiments, e.g. love, hate, and respect, and tends as a result to interpret simple emotions as manifestations of complex ones, e.g. ANGER as a manifestation of HATE, or to assume that complex emotions can be present at the beginning of life, e.g. to attribute ENVY to the new-born infant. But for a partial exception, see Brierley (1951).

EMPATHY (*Einfühlung*) 'The power of projecting one's personality into (and so fully comprehending) the object of con-templation' – *C.O.D.* The capacity to put oneself into the other's shoes. The concept implies that one is both feeling oneself into the object and remaining aware of one's own identity as another person. The word is necessary since sympathy is only used to refer to the sharing of unpleasant experiences and does not imply that the sympathizer necessarily retains his objectivity. The capacity to *empathize* is an essential pre-condition of doing psychoanalytical therapy. It can be, but rarely is, cited as an example of projective IDENTIFICATION.

ENDOGAMY   Custom or law requiring that marriage be with someone within the tribe or TOTEM group. See also EXOGAMY.

ENDOGENOUS   Arising from within. See DEPRESSION.

END-PLEASURE   See FORE-PLEASURE AND END-PLEASURE.

ENERGY   'Energy is the only life and is from the body; and reason is the bound and outward circumference of energy' – William Blake. 'We assume, as the other natural sciences have taught us to expect, that in mental life some kind of energy is at work; but we have no data which enable us to come nearer to a knowledge of it by an analogy with other forms of energy. We seem to recognize that nervous or psychical energy exists in two forms, one freely mobile and the other, by contrast, bound' – Freud (1940). Mobile energy is characteristic of the ID and bound energy characteristic of the EGO.

Freud's concept of psychical energy is *not* designed to explain phenomena such as mental fatigue, differences in vitality, etc., but to elucidate problems of shifts in attention, interest and attachment from one object or activity to another. These are explained by postulating that QUANTA of energy are invested in the mental REPRESENTATIONS of OBJECTS and that these quanta vary in their mobility. *Bound energy* is relatively immobile and is characteristic of structured parts of the PSYCHIC APPARATUS, i.e. of the ego and the SECONDARY PROCESSES, while investment with free or *mobile energy* characterizes unstructured parts of the psychic apparatus, i.e. the id and the PRIMARY PROCESSES. In other words, in primary-process thinking, e.g. DREAMING, ideas and images are relatively interchangeable, so that one idea or image readily symbolizes another (see SYMBOL), while in the secondary-process thinking of conscious rational thought, images, ideas, and words have relatively constant value and meaning. It is hard to avoid the conclusion that Freud's theory of bound and mobile energy has little to do with the concept of energy as used by the 'other natural sciences', but that it is really a theory of MEANING in disguise. Freud's reasons for trying to explain thinking in terms of movements of energy derive from his *Project for a Scientific Psychology* (1895), where he attempted to explain psychic processes in terms of quanta of energy moving from one NEURONE (brain cell) to another.

The adjective corresponding to 'energy' is 'ECONOMIC'. Quanta of energy invested in particular mental representations are 'CATHEXES'; as a result, representations to which energy is attached are described as being 'cathected', and those from which energy has been withdrawn are described as being 'decathected'.

A problem which has exercised psychoanalysis is the question as to whether different INSTINCTS or STRUCTURES use different forms of energy. When Freud held that there were two groups of instincts, the sexual (see SEX) and the EGO INSTINCTS, he held that the energy of the sexual instincts was LIBIDO, but never came to a clear opinion as to whether the ego-instincts also used libido or some other kind of energy. Similarly, when he believed that the two groups of instincts were the LIFE and DEATH INSTINCTS, he held that libido was the energy of the life instincts but never coined a term for the energy of the death instinct. According to the EGO PSYCHOLOGISTS, the id is invested with sexual and aggressive energy, whereas the ego uses energy borrowed from the id which has been DESEXUALIZED and DEAGGRESSIFIED.

ENGULFMENT   Term used by Laing (1960) to describe a form of ANXIETY suffered by persons who lack primary ontological security (see under ONTOLOGY), in which relationships with others are experienced as overwhelming threats to their IDENTITY.

ENURESIS   Incontinence of urine. Bed-wetting is, strictly, *nocturnal enuresis*.

ENVIRONMENT   That which is outside the organism, person, under consideration. A distinction needs to be made, especially when considering the psychology of animals and infants, between the total environment as perceptible by the observer and the *Merkwelt* (perceptual environment) of the subject being observed. The latter consists solely of those aspects of the total environment which are perceptible and relevant to the subject. Failure to appreciate this distinction leads to anthropomorphic and ADULTO-MORPHIC fallacies. In the psychoanalytical literature 'external REALITY' and 'outer WORLD' are often used as synonyms of environment. Psychoanalysis tends to concern itself solely with human aspects of the environment. But see Searles (1960).

ENVIRONMENT, AVERAGE EXPECTABLE   Term used by Hartmann (1958) to describe the kind of environment for which the infant has built-in expectations and to which maturational processes are geared. In some respects it corresponds to Winnicott's less abstract ORDINARY DEVOTED MOTHER. The concept makes a break with Freud's view that the infant starts life totally maladapted and assumes, on the contrary, that he is born with a number of built-in patterns of response and behaviour and that development 'can count on average expectable stimulations (environmental releasers)'.

ENVY   'Grudging contemplation of more fortunate persons' – *C.O.D.* According to McDougall (1931), 'it is a binary compound of negative self-feeling and of anger'. According to Freud *penis envy* occupies a central position in the psychology of women (see under PENIS ENVY), while according to Melanie Klein innate ENVY of the MOTHER'S BREAST and its CREATIVITY is a primary cause of all mental illness (see KLEINIAN). Both propositions create more problems than they solve. The former raises the question of how feelings of bodily incompleteness can arise in an intact body, i.e. it raises problems about the BODY-IMAGE of girls, while the latter raises questions as to how an EMOTION, and a complex one at that, can be innate and present from birth. Freud's views on penis envy are an example of his PHALLOCENTRIC view of women and are linked with his conviction that vaginal sensations (see VAGINA) never occur in females until puberty. See CASTRATION.

EPINOSIC   Occurs only in the phrase 'epinosic gain', which is synonymous with 'secondary gain'. See GAIN, PRIMARY AND SECONDARY.

EPISTEMOPHILIA   Pleasure in gaining knowledge. There is a tendency to regard the thirst for knowledge as either a derivative of SCOPOPHILIA, i.e. as an extension of sexual curiosity, or as a SUBLIMATION of ORAL drives.

EROS   Greek God of Sexual Love used by Freud to personify the LIFE-force and the sexual instincts. In his later writings, Eros was contrasted with THANATOS, the God of Death, the personification of the DEATH INSTINCT. Freud's use of Eros is poetic metaphor rather than science. The appropriateness of the metaphor derives from (a) the fact that Eros was the secret lover of PSYCHE and (b) the fact that 'his role was to co-ordinate the elements which constitute the universe. It is he who 'brings harmony to chaos' and permits life to develop. This primitive deity, a semi-abstract personification of cosmic force. . . .' – *Larousse Encyclopedia of Mythology*.

EROTIC   Sexual, libidinal, pleasurable (see SEX and LIBIDO). According to psychoanalysis all bodily functions accessible to consciousness may be sources of erotic pleasure, while those which involve the *erotogenic zones* habitually are (see also EROTOGENIC ZONE). Hence ORAL, ANAL, URETHRAL, PHALLIC, GENITAL, etc., erotism. Bodily functions which are not normally sources of erotic pleasure may by displacement become *eroticized*; if this happens, the eroticized organ may become the site of a NEUROTIC or PSYCHOSOMATIC symptom, since it is, as it were, serving two masters. Psychoanalysis's use of 'erotic' as a bridge concept between 'sexual' and 'pleasurable' can lead to confusion; only according to context can one tell whether 'erotic' refers to pleasure which is experienced as having a sexual quality or to pleasure which is inferred to have some connexion with sex.

EROTOGENIC ZONE   Any area of the body from which EROTIC sensations may arise. Typically, the sexual organs and the mucous membrane surrounding bodily openings.

ESSENTIALISM   The opposite of EXISTENTIALISM. Freudian psychoanalysis is an essentialist theory since it explains phenomena in terms of essences, i.e. in terms of forces underlying the phenomena.

ETHOLOGY   Nowadays *not*, as some dictionaries have it, the science of character-formation, *but* the study of animal behaviour under natural conditions. The relevance of ethology to psycho-analysis derives from (a) the possibility that it will provide it with a theory of INSTINCTS based on observation of non-human species and (b) the possibility that some of its techniques will prove applicable to the study of infants and children, thereby enabling psychoanalytical hypotheses about infantile DEVELOPMENT to be tested by direct observation. Psychoanalytical writers such as Spitz (1959), who base their work on direct observation of infants rather than on therapeutic work, are arguably human ethologists rather than psychoanalysts. See Lorenz's *On Aggression* (1966) for some points of convergence between psychoanalysis and ethology.

EXHIBITIONISM   1. Sexual PERVERSION consisting in the exposure, by the male, of his GENITALS to a female. 2. Similar behaviour by male children. 3. By extension, all behaviour which is motivated by pleasure in being looked at, in self-display, in showing off, etc. Although Freud lists exhibitionism as a component-instinct and as a normal component of INFANTILE SEXUALITY, exhibitionism in senses 1 and 3 is regularly interpreted as NEUROTIC and defensive (see DEFENCE); its function being to prove that one has got something by compelling some object to react to it. The generalized exhibitionism of women, which society tends within limits to accept as normal, is often interpreted as a derivative of PENIS ENVY; as being based on the need to prove that one has something despite not having a penis. Latter-day analysts are, however, more likely to regard it as a MANIC DEFENCE against DEPRESSION, FRIGIDITY, or fear of loss of IDENTITY ('I must be real because I'm being looked at'). True exhibitionism of the genitals is almost unknown in women.

For sociological and FORENSIC data about exhibitionism, see Mohr, *et al* (1965).

EXISTENTIALISM   Philosophical theory which gives priority to PHENOMENOLOGY and ONTOLOGY over CAUSATION, which rejects explanations in terms of essences imagined to actuate behaviour from within in favour of study of the phenomena themselves. For general discussions of the relationship between existential and Freudian psychoanalysis, see Hartmann (1964), Lomas (1967), May (1967), and the writings of R. D. Laing. See also ESSENTIALISM.

EXOGAMY   Custom or law requiring that marriage be with someone outside the tribe or TOTEM group. See also ENDOGAMY.

EXOGENOUS   Arising from outside. See DEPRESSION.

EXTERNALIZATION   The process by which a mental image is imagined to be outside the SELF, by which an 'internal OBJECT' (see also INTERNAL) is *projected* on to some figure in the external world. In this sense, synonymous with PROJECTION and the opposite of INTROJECTION not INTERNALIZATION. Fairbairn, however, uses externalization and internalization in a somewhat individual sense to describe the location of objects outside and inside the self during his transitional stage of development. See FAIRBAIRN'S REVISED PSYCHOPATHOLOGY; TECHNIQUE; QUASI-INDEPENDENCE.

EXTRAVERSION AND INTROVERSION   Either **1.** as used by Jung, personality types differing in the importance attached to external perceptions and internal ideas. Or **2.** as used by Eysenck, a dimension of personality, according to which all individuals can be placed at some point along an extraversion–introversion axis. According to Eysenck (1965) extraversion corresponds to the choleric and sanguine, and introversion to the melancholic and phlegmatic temperaments of Galen. He also endorses the popular equation of extravert with 'outgoing' and 'introvert' with 'introspective'. Neither term is used much by either analysts or psychiatrists, though there is a tendency to equate 'introverted' with 'withdrawn' or 'SCHIZOID'. According to Eysenck's findings *psychopaths* and *hysterics* tend to score highly for extraversion and *phobic* and *obsessional patients* tend to score highly for introversion.

F

FAIRBAIRN'S REVISED PSYCHOPATHOLOGY   Fairbairn (1941) in his *Revised Psychopathology of the Psychoses and Psychoneuroses* describes mental DEVELOPMENT in terms of OBJECT-RELATIONSHIPS and asserts that the various PSYCHOSES and NEUROSES differ not, as CLASSICAL PSYCHOANALYTICAL THEORY maintains, in REGRESSIONS to different stages of LIBIDINAL DEVELOPMENT, but in the use of different TECHNIQUES during his second stage of development, the Stage of Transition or QUASI-INDEPENDENCE. During his first stage, the Stage of INFANTILE DEPENDENCE, the infant is objectively totally dependent on the MOTHER (BREAST), towards whom he has initially a non-ambivalent relationship (see AMBIVALENCE). The unavoidable experiences of FRUSTRATION and rejection at her hands lead, however, to the

SCHIZOID POSITION, during which the infant's EGO splits into three, two parts of which, the *libidinal ego* and *anti-libidinal ego* (IN-TERNAL SABOTEUR), become attached to two antithetical conceptions of the breast, the accepted (exciting) object and the rejected (rejecting) object respectively. The third part of the infant's ego becomes the *central ego*, which corresponds to the ego of classical analysis. The libidinal ego corresponds to the ID and the anti-libidinal ego, less precisely, to the SUPER-EGO. SCHIZOPHRENIA and DEPRESSION are in Fairbairn's view aetiologically (see AETIOLOGY) related to disturbances of development during the Stage of Infantile Dependence, but the other neuroses reflect the operation of different techniques during the next stage, the Stage of Transition or Quasi-independence, during which the child achieves partial independence of the mother by manipulations of the accepted and rejected objects created during the schizoid position. In the OBSESSIONAL TECHNIQUE, he conceives both to be inside himself, thereby achieving a measure of independence at the cost of having to control a 'bad' INTERNAL OBJECT (the rejected object); in the hysterical defence (see HYSTERIA), he conceives the accepted object to be outside himself, and the rejected object to be inside himself; in the phobic (see PHOBIA), he conceives both rejected and accepted object to be outside himself; and in the PARANOID, the accepted to be inside, and the rejected outside. Fairbairn's third and last stage is the Stage of Mature Dependence. See also FUTILITY, SENSE OF.

FAECES   Excrement, shit. Since the ANAL is the second of the PRE-GENITAL phases of LIBIDINAL DEVELOPMENT, and the acquisition of SPHINCTER (bowel) control is the achievement of the corresponding phase of EGO DEVELOPMENT, the words 'faeces' and 'defaecation' feature prominently in all psychoanalytical case histories. Anyone inclined to be sceptical as to whether faeces and defaecation really play such an important part in our mental life as the literature implies, should reflect on the extent to which obscene language calls on faecal terms to express abuse, contempt, and disparagement.

FAMILY   The family in psychoanalysis is always what anthropologists call the *nuclear family*, consisting of mother, father, and children who regard themselves, and are regarded by society, as a basic unit; and not the *extended family* of clan or tribe. As a result, phenomena such as the OEDIPUS COMPLEX and sibling-rivalry (see under SIB) are always defined in terms that would make no sense if applied to cultures in which uncles and grandparents are no less significant than fathers or cousins and sibs are not clearly differentiated. As a result, too, phenomena such as adolescent IDENTITY crises, which apparently only occur in nuclear families, are defined as though they were inherent in human nature. *Family therapy* is PSYCHOTHERAPY which regards the family, not the individual 'presenting' patient, as the therapeutic object. *Family Process* is the American journal in which research based on the assumption that the neuroses are intra-familial disturbances is published. The *family romance* is the childhood phantasy that one's apparent parents are not one's real ones, and that one is really of noble or royal birth.

FANTASY AND PHANTASY   According to the *O.E.D.*, 'In modern use *fantasy* and *phantasy*, in spite of their identity in sound and in ultimate etymology, tend to be apprehended as separate words, the predominant sense of the former being "caprice, whim, fanciful invention", while that of the latter is "imagination, visionary notion".' Since the psychoanalytical concept is more akin to IMAGINATION than to whimsy, English psychoanalytical writers invariably use *phantasy* not *fantasy*, but few, if any, American writers have followed them in doing so.

FATHER   Although Freud's own writings attach central importance to the father and the OEDIPUS COMPLEX, almost all contemporary analytical literature centres round the MOTHER and PRE-OEDIPAL phases of development. Whether this is a reflection of social change or a real advance in knowledge remains uncertain. 'The father' means either the patient's father or his internal image of his father, the latter being 'the INTERNAL father', which may by SPLITTING exist in two forms: 'the GOOD father' and 'the BAD father'. The 'PRIMAL FATHER' is the leader of the 'PRIMAL HORDE', whose murder by his sons evoked the primal inherited sense of GUILT; see TOTEM and TABOO. Hence: *father-figure, father-complex.*

FEAR   Primary EMOTION evoked by impending danger and accompanied by the wish to flee. Despite the fact that fear is one of the elemental human experiences and that flight is undoubtedly one of the basic biological responses, psychoanalysis has little to say about fear. There are two reasons for this. Firstly, its primary concern has been with pathology; as a result fear has been over-shadowed by ANXIETY, though this is sometimes defined as irrational fear; alternatively fear is sometimes defined as 'objective anxiety'. Secondly, Freud's insistence of dual instinct theories (see under INSTINCT) left no place for a third primary instinct; as a result psychoanalysis has much to say about how LOVE and HATE can CONFLICT with one another, INHIBIT one another, and even at times reinforce one another (SADISM), but little to say about how fear can interact with love and hate. In view of Freud's passion for antitheses and opposites, it is worth noting that a case could be made for regarding fear as the opposite of both love and hate.

FEMININE, FEMININITY Referring to patterns of be-haviour, attitudes, etc., presumed to be psychological secondary sexual characteristics of the female. CLASSICAL THEORY tends to assume that femininity has an essential connexion with PASSIVITY and MASOCHISM and that feminine psychology centres round the difficulties involved in taking up a helpless position. Whereas, as the jargon has it, men 'adopt the masculine role', women 'accept the feminine role' reluctantly and only after 'renouncing the PENIS'. As Jones pointed out, this view of femininity is an example of Freud's 'PHALLOCENTRIC' bias and it has been criti-cized by many but not all the women analysts. See Payne (1935) for a concept of femininity based on the idea of receptivity. See MASCULINE for some of the obstacles to discovering what mental characteristics are innately masculine or feminine. See also ACTIVE AND PASSIVE; BISEXUAL; CASTRATION.

FETISH 1. Inanimate object worshipped by savages for its magical powers or as being inhabited by a spirit. Hence 2. an object which a *fetishist* endows with sexual significance and in the absence of which he is incapable of sexual excitement. A sexual fetish is either an inanimate object or a non-sexual part of a person, the inanimate ones usually being clothes, footwear, or articles of adornment, the animate ones being typically feet or hair. Fetishists can be said to regard their fetish as being 'in-habited by a spirit', since the fetish is clearly associated with a person without being one, and as having 'magical powers', since its presence gives them the potency they otherwise lack. Fetishism is a classical example of primary-process thinking influencing behaviour since (a) the fetish has multiple meanings derived by CONDENSATION, DISPLACEMENT, and SYMBOLIZATION from other objects, and (b) the fetishist behaves as though it actually were these other objects and is no more disturbed by incongruity or absurdity than a dreamer is while dreaming (see DREAM). See PROCESSES, PRIMARY AND SECONDARY; SPLITTING.

FICTION   Some but not all psychoanalytical CONCEPTS are fictions, i.e. they formulate mental phenomena *as if* they were phenomena of some other kind. The central fiction of CLASSICAL THEORY is the PSYCHIC APPARATUS, which enables mental processes to be conceived as functions of a hypothetical thing or STRUCTURE. The tendency to use fictions seems to derive from the assumption that formulations which sound OBJECTIVE are more scientific (see SCIENCE) than those which admit openly that mental phenomena are subjective. See MODEL; REIFICATION.

FIXATION   The process by which a person becomes or remains ambivalently attached (see AMBIVALENCE) to an OBJECT, this object being one which was appropriate to an earlier stage of DEVELOPMENT. Fixation is therefore evidence of failure to progress satisfactorily through the stages of LIBIDINAL DEVELOPMENT. The concept assumes that the fixated person (a) has a tendency to engage in INFANTILE, outmoded patterns of behaviour or to regress (see REGRESSION) to such patterns under stress; (b) to choose compulsively (see COMPULSIVE) objects on the basis of their resemblance to the one on which he is fixated; and (c) suffers impoverishment of available ENERGY as a result of his investment in the past object. Excessive FRUSTRATION and SATISFACTION, excessive LOVE and HATE have all been adduced as causes of fixation. Hence *oral fixation, mother fixation, anal fixation, father fixation* (all of which q.v.).

FIXATION POINT   That phase, period, or point of infantile DEVELOPMENT at which a person has become fixated (see FIXATION above), through which he has not completely passed, and to which he remains liable to regress (see REGRESSION).

FLIGHT   The instinct or innate behaviour-pattern of flight does

not feature in psychoanalytical theory. See FEAR; ANXIETY; IN-
STINCT.

FLIGHT INTO HEALTH   Phrase used to describe the rapid
symptomatic recovery sometimes displayed by patients who wish
to avoid psychoanalytical investigation. Probably a MANIC DEFENCE.

FLIGHT INTO ILLNESS   Phrase used to describe the escape
from conflict achieved by developing symptoms.

FOCAL THERAPY   Modification of psychoanalytical therapy
in which one specific problem presented by the patient is chosen
as the focus of INTERPRETATION. See Malan (1963).

FORENSIC   Used in courts of law. Hence *forensic medicine,
forensic psychiatry*.

FORE-PLEASURE AND END-PLEASURE   These terms
enable the PLEASURE associated with EROTIC activity to be divided
into (a) that associated with mounting TENSION, *fore-pleasure*, and
(b) that associated with reduction of tension, *end-pleasure*, the
former being a TENSION-AFFECT, the latter a DISCHARGE-AFFECT.
According to Freud (1905), the fore-pleasure of heterosexual
intercourse, i.e. the kissing and cuddling, represents the survival
into adult life of those forms of INFANTILE SEXUALITY which are
aesthetically acceptable. He also argued that fore-pleasure from
the infantile EROTOGENIC ZONES (see also INFANTILE) fulfilled the
'new function' of creating sufficient tension to enable genital
SATISFACTION to be achieved. 'This pleasure then leads to an
increase in tension which in its turn is responsible for producing
the necessary motor energy for the conclusion of the sexual act.'
Fore-pleasure refers strictly only to those activities which enhance
the desire for end-pleasure and not to those which distract from
it. Fore-pleasure is a striking example of a phenomenon which is
extremely difficult to reconcile with Freud's PLEASURE PRINCIPLE,
since (a) the tension produced by it is pleasurable not painful and
(b) it shows that desire can be dependent on external stimulation
and not solely on internal pressure. For an ethological discussion
of the inter-relation of innate behaviour (INSTINCT) and external
stimulation and the dependence of instinctual activity on releasing
mechanisms and reaction chains, see Tinbergen (1951). See also
ETHOLOGY.

FORGETTING Usually discussed under the headings of AMNESIA and PARAPRAXES. There is a tendency to assume that *all* forgetting is due to REPRESSION, though the idea that in perfect health we would remember every experience throughout our lives, however trivial, seems improbable on *a priori* grounds. If, as biological theory maintains, the function of remembering is to make available past experiences while making present decisions, forgetting is only pathological if it occurs in respect of facts which are relevant to the present.

FREE ASSOCIATION Brill's mistranslation of Freud's *'freier Einfall'*, which has, however, become the accepted term in English. *Einfall* means 'irruption', 'sudden idea', not 'association', and the concept refers to ideas which occur to one spontaneously, without straining. When used as a technical term, free association describes the mode of thinking encouraged in the patient by the analyst's injunction that he should obey the 'BASIC RULE', i.e. that he should report his thoughts without reservation and that he should make no attempt to concentrate while doing so. Free association technique relies on three assumptions: (a) that all lines of thought tend to lead to what is significant; (b) that the patient's therapeutic needs and knowledge that he is in treatment will lead his associations towards what is significant except in so far as RESISTANCE operates; and (c) that resistance is minimized by relaxation and maximized by concentration. It was Freud's adoption of free association technique which enabled him to abandon HYPNOSIS. Resistance manifests itself during sessions by failures in the patient's capacity to associate freely. Some accounts of analytical technique make it depend entirely on free association and the resultant emergence of the relevant pathogenic 'MATERIAL', but this is an over-simplification since (a) the analyst makes INTERPRETATIONS, and the following utterances of the patient are associations *to* his intervention and not free; and (b) the analyst's interventions compel the patient to scan his free associations in IDENTIFICATION with the analyst, i.e. the patient does two things at once, or in rapid oscillation: free association and reflection. An alternative formulation is that the patient oscillates between being the SUBJECT and OBJECT of his experience, at one moment letting thoughts come, the next moment inspecting them. See also SPLITTING.

FRIGIDITY   Although some writers use the word 'frigidity' to describe all sexual inhibitions in women, including the inability to have vaginal ORGASMS (see also VAGINA), it is best restricted to the inability to be in any way sexually aroused. Since many women enjoy sexual intercourse without coming to a climax, the wider definition leads to the absurdity of designating as frigid women who are sexually responsive. See 'Medica' (1955), Gorer (1966). Frigidity can only be regarded as a neurotic symptom (a) if it is persistent or (b) if it occurs even under the most favourable circumstances; otherwise it is a sign of either inexperience or insincerity (on the part of either the woman or her partner).

FRUSTRATION   The state of being or having been balked, baffled, or disappointed. Frustration and DEPRIVATION are often confused, but, strictly speaking, frustration refers to the effect of non-satisfaction of a drive or failure to achieve a goal, while deprivation refers to the lack of the commodity or opportunity necessary for satisfaction. Frustration and deprivation theories of neurosis tend none the less to be identical on the assumption that deprivation leads to frustration, frustration leads to AGGRESSION, aggression leads to ANXIETY, anxiety leads to DEFENCES. . . .

Although psychoanalysis is popularly supposed to maintain that frustration is harmful, this is not the whole story since it also maintains that EGO DEVELOPMENT is initiated by frustration. In fact, frustration theories of neurosis assume that both frustration and deprivation *beyond a certain threshold of intensity* are pathogenic (see THRESHOLD).

FUGUE   Psychiatric term for the process by which a person wanders off, not knowing who or where he is. Fugues are generally categorized as HYSTERICAL and cited as examples of DISSOCIATION of consciousness. A rare condition, most of the cases cited in psychiatric textbooks have occurred in persons such as boys in boarding schools and conscript soldiers who feel trapped in situations in which they are no longer free agents.

FUNDAMENTAL RULE   See BASIC RULE.

FUROR THERAPEUTICUS   Disparaging term for therapeutic enthusiasm. According to Freud, *furor therapeuticus* is against the long-term interests of patients being analysed. But see Malan (1963) for its value in short-term therapy.

FUSION AND DEFUSION   According to Freud's later speculative writings, INSTINCTS are not only in CONFLICT but are also capable of fusing and defusing. 'We never have to deal with pure LIFE INSTINCTS and DEATH INSTINCTS at all, but only with combinations of them in different degrees. Corresponding with the fusion of instincts there may under certain conditions occur a defusion of them' – Freud (1924). Analysts who accept this point of view assume that in health the life and death instincts are fused with the life-instincts preponderating, that in sadistic (see SADISM) and masochistic (see MASOCHISM) perversions they are fused with the death instinct preponderating, and that in OBSESSIONAL NEUROSIS defusion occurs, the patient's life instinct becoming the object of his death instinct.

FUTILITY, SENSE OF   Phrase used especially by Fairbairn to describe the predominant effect in SCHIZOID disorders.

G

GAIN, PRIMARY AND SECONDARY (PARANOSIC AND EPINOSIC)   The primary (paranosic) gain of a SYMPTOM is the freedom from ANXIETY and CONFLICT achieved by its formation. The secondary (epinosic) gain consists of the practical advantages which can be achieved by using the symptom to influence or manipulate others. For instance, the primary gain of AGORAPHOBIA is the freedom from anxiety and conflict about AMBIVALENCE towards parental figures achieved by not being able to leave home; the secondary gain is the possibility of using the symptom to avoid unpleasant commitments or to compel others to act as one's companion. Relatives of patients tend to be acutely aware of the secondary gains of neurosis but to be oblivious to its primary gains.

GENERATIVITY *v.* STAGNATION   Erikson's term for the seventh of his eight STAGES OF MAN. It corresponds to middle age.

'Generativity is primarily the interest in establishing and guiding the next generation or whatever in a given case may become the absorbing object of a parental kind of responsibility. When this enrichment fails, a regression from generativity to an obsessive need for pseudo-intimacy, punctuated by moments of mutual repulsion, takes place, often with a pervading sense (and objective evidence) of individual stagnation and interpersonal impoverishment' – Erikson (1963).

GENETIC   In the psychoanalytical literature this almost always means 'ONTOGENETIC', related to the development of the individual, and not 'phylogenetic', relating to the development of the species. Hence the word's associations with 'genetics' and 'genes' should be ignored and it should be regarded as synonymous with 'developmental' (see DEVELOPMENT).

GENITAL CHARACTER   Hypothetical or ideal character displayed by a person who has been fully analysed, who has fully resolved his OEDIPUS COMPLEX, who has 'worked through' (see WORKING THROUGH) his *pre-genital* ambivalence and achieved the post-ambivalent GENITAL LEVEL of PSYCHOSEXUAL development (see also AMBIVALENCE). A genital character would, if such a person existed, be totally free of INFANTILE DEPENDENCE and would be distinguishable from a PHALLIC CHARACTER by the fact that he attached equal importance to his own and his object's satisfaction – to attach more to his object's than his own would reveal him as a masochist (see MASOCHISM). Although there is something absurd about the concept, which illustrates vividly the difficulties inherent in describing healthy phenomena in terms of a language rooted in pathology, it is a logical necessity for anyone who thinks that maturity should be definable in terms of INSTINCT THEORY. Evans (1949) has pointed out the close similarity between the analytical ideal of the genital character and the English ideal of a gentleman. See also GENITALITY.

GENITALITY   'While psychoanalysis has on occasion gone too far in its emphasis on genitality as a universal cure for society and has thus provided a new addiction and a new commodity for many who wished to so [*sic*] interpret its teachings, it has not always indicated all the goals that genitality actually should and must imply. In order to be of lasting social significance, the utopia of genitality should include:

'1. mutuality of orgasm
'2. with a loved partner
'3. of the other sex
'4. with whom one is able and willing to share a mutual trust
'5. and with whom one is able and willing to regulate the cycles of
    'a. work
    'b. procreation
    'c. recreation
'6. so as to secure to the offspring, too, all the stages of a satisfactory development' – Erikson (1963).

GENITAL LEVEL   According to CLASSICAL THEORY, the last phase of LIBIDINAL DEVELOPMENT; after progressing through or up the PRE-GENITAL stages of development and passing through the latency period, the individual reaches or achieves the genital level – presumably a plateau from which no further ascent is possible. Erikson (1963), however, discusses GENITALITY in connexion with the sixth of his eight STAGES OF MAN, INTIMACY *v.* ISOLATION (Young Adulthood), and reserves MATURITY for his eighth, which is only reached in old age. See GENITAL CHARACTER; EGO INTEGRITY.

GLOBUS HYSTERICUS   The subjective sense of a lump in the throat occurring in absence of any palpable lump.

GOOD   When used technically 'good' refers to a particular class of INTERNAL OBJECTS, viz. those which are conceived to be benevolent towards the subject, in contrast to 'BAD' objects, which are imagined to be malevolently disposed towards him. The two types of object good and bad, arise as a result of SPLITTING of the primary or original introjected object (see INTROJECTION), i.e. the subject divides his conception of the BREAST, MOTHER, FATHER, PENIS, etc., into two, the good and bad breast, etc., thereby defending himself against the AMBIVALENCE which would ensue if he recognized that he experienced SATISFACTION and FRUSTRATION from and LOVE and HATE towards the same object. Although this usage derives its wide currency from the writings of Klein and Fairbairn, its origins are to be found in the work of Freud, Abraham, and Rado on melancholia. See also IDEALIZATION; DEPRESSIVE POSITION;

PARANOID-SCHIZOID POSITION; KLEINIAN; FAIRBAIRN'S REVISED PSYCHOPATHOLOGY.

GRIEF   SORROW; the EMOTION accompanying MOURNING.

GROUP   A number of persons united for some purpose or possessing common interests, aspirations, functions, or fears which enable them to be differentiated as a social entity both by themselves and by others.

Group psychology: That branch of psychology concerned with the behaviour of groups and with the psychology of membership of groups. Probably not distinguishable from social psychology or *Massenpsychologie.* Psychoanalytical formulations stress IDENTIFI-CATION between members, identification of members with a leader, and the relationship with the common enemy, all three factors playing an important role in diminishing the disruptive effects of rivalry between members.

Group psychotherapy: Any form of PSYCHOTHERAPY in which more than two patients are present. In most forms of group psychotherapy the group is initially an artefact created by the therapist selecting the members, but it is assumed that the common relationship to the therapist will lead to the formation of a genuine group situation. Group psychotherapy of 'natural' groups, e.g. of whole FAMILIES, seems to be a rarity.

Group analysis: Group psychotherapy in which the therapist restricts his activities to INTERPRETATION of the dynamics of the group. See Foulkes and Anthony (1957).

GUILT   Psychoanalysis is concerned not with the fact of guilt but with the sense of guilt, i.e. with the EMOTION which follows infringement of a moral injunction. More specifically, it is con-cerned with the NEUROTIC sense of guilt, i.e. with those experiences of feeling guilty which are not explicable in terms of infringements of the patient's conscious values. According to CLASSICAL THEORY the neurotic sense of guilt arises as a result of conflict between the SUPER-EGO and INFANTILE sexual and aggressive wishes (see SEX and AGGRESSION), this conflict being an internalized REPRESENTA-TION and perpetuation of conflicts between the child and his parents (see also INTERNALIZATION); the situation is, however, complicated by the fact that the super-ego is conceived to derive its energy from the child's own AGGRESSION; as a result the sense of guilt is influenced directly by the extent to which the individual expresses his aggressive feelings by taking them out on himself in moral condemnation.

Guilt differs from ANXIETY in that (a) anxiety is experienced in relation to a feared future occurrence, while guilt is experienced in relation to an act already committed, and (b) the capacity to experience guilt is contingent on the capacity to internalize objects whereas the capacity to experience anxiety is not; animals and infants may feel anxious, but only human beings with some awareness of time and of others can feel guilty. Neurotic guilt and anxiety may, however, be indistinguishable owing to the fact that the neurotic sense of guilt is associated with dread of punishment and retribution.

Analysts who believe in an innate destructive instinct also believe inevitably in an inherent sense of guilt derived from awareness of the wish to destroy what is also loved, to defy what is also submitted to.

All DEFENCES used to reduce anxiety can also be used to reduce the sense of guilt, but one defence, REPARATION, the making good of damage imagined to have already been done, is used specifically to reduce the sense of guilt.

H

HALLUCINATION 'Apparent PERCEPTION of an external object not actually present' – *O.E.D.* A subjective image which the patient experiences as an external phenomenon. Owing to the failure in 'REALITY-TESTING' involved in hallucinating it tends to be regarded as PSYCHOTIC, though this is not always so. Hallucinations can occur as a result of fever, brain disease, drugs, and sensory deprivation as well as for psychotic reasons. Hallucinations of all senses can occur, those of touch being known as 'HAPTIC'. DREAMS are the hallucinations of the normal.

'HANS, LITTLE' The child patient described in Freud's *Analysis of a Phobia in a Five-Year-Old Boy* (1909).

HAPTIC Relating to touch.

HATE 1. A principle or inner force conceived to actuate behaviour. 2. An AFFECT characterized by an enduring wish to injure or destroy the hated object. Hate is often confused by analysts with ANGER, despite the fact that the latter is a passing not an enduring emotion which can be felt in relation to someone one loves. According to McDougall (1908), hate is a SENTIMENT and anger a simple, primary EMOTION. According to Freud (1915), hate is the response to threats to the EGO, but in his later speculative writings he viewed it as a manifestation of the DEATH-INSTINCT. Analysts influenced by these later ideas tend to regard LOVE and hate as opposites and to see the psyche as a battleground between these two opposed principles.

HEALTH Health and normality (see NORM) are often confused, but, strictly speaking, health refers to states of wholeness and INTEGRATION while normality refers to states corresponding to whatever norm the writer is taking as his standard of comparison. When, however, the writer takes as his norm the ideal of mental health, the two terms become synonymous. In phrases such as 'the mental health movement', health means freedom from ascertainable MENTAL ILLNESS. Health is both a medical and a religious term, *vide* the Book of Common Prayer's, 'We have left undone those things which we ought to have done; and we have done those things which we ought not to have done; and there is no health in us.'

HEBEPHRENIA Form of SCHIZOPHRENIA characterized by withdrawal, bizarre mannerisms, and neglect of the person.

HETERONOMY See AUTONOMY AND HETERONOMY.

HETEROSEXUAL, HETEROSEXUALITY Refer to sexual behaviour, impulses, desires, etc., in which the object is a person of the opposite sex.

HOMEOSTASIS The tendency of organisms to maintain themselves in a constant state. According to Cannon (1932), who coined the term: 'Organisms, composed of material which is characterized by the utmost inconstancy and unsteadiness, have somehow learned the methods of maintaining constancy and keeping steady in the presence of conditions which might reasonably be expected to prove profoundly disturbing.' Freud's PLEASURE-PAIN PRINCIPLE, and his use of Fechner's CONSTANCY

61

PRINCIPLE, are usually regarded as psychological concepts analogous to the physiological concept of homeostasis, i.e. they imply an in-built tendency to keep psychological TENSION at a constant optimal level, similar to that which makes the body keep its blood-chemistry, temperature, etc., constant.

HOMOSEXUAL 1. Adj., referring to sexual behaviour in which the subject's object is a person of the same sex. According to Freud (1914), homosexual love differs from heterosexual love in being narcissistic (see NARCISSISM), since the object is loved on account of its similarity to what the subject is, once was, or hopes some time to become, as opposed to heterosexual love, which is ANACLITIC, being dependent on the object providing what the subject cannot himself be. 2. By extension, adj. referring to all attitudes, feelings, etc., directed towards persons of the same sex. Hence *homosexuality*, which may be male, female (lesbianism), ACTIVE (in which the subject behaves as a man and treats his object as though he were female), PASSIVE (in which the subject behaves as a woman and treats his object as a man), MANIFEST, LATENT, AIM-INHIBITED, and SUBLIMATED. The latter three terms are used to refer to phenomena which the laity would not regard as homosexual. *Latent homosexuality* is the odd one out since it refers not to repressed homosexual feelings (see REPRESSION) which become manifest during psychoanalytical treatment, but to defensive submissive attitudes (see DEFENCE and SUBMISSION) adopted towards more powerful males. The justification for the concept derives from the theoretical assumption that the defence is regressive (see REGRESSION), that it consists in reactivation of passive, FEMININE wishes towards the FATHER during the negative oedipal phase (see NEGATIVE OEDIPAL COMPLEX). Latent homosexuality can, however, be regarded as a defence against PARANOID ANXIETY and as analogous to the intimidated, appeasing, submissive attitude adopted by animals when attacked by a member of their own species. See Tinbergen (1951), Lorenz (1966).

The 'homo' in homosexual derives from the Greek '*homos*', meaning 'same', and not from the Latin '*homo*', a 'man'; hence 'homosexual' can be applied to women as well as men.

HYPNAGOGIC Adj. referring to the drowsy state occurring while falling asleep (see SLEEP) and to experiences such as HALLUCINATIONS occurring during this state.

HYPNOANALYSIS Form of PSYCHOTHERAPY in which the patient is made drowsy by sedation prior to his therapeutic session. The rationale of such treatment is based on the idea that the patient's sleepiness will reduce RESISTANCE and make him more receptive of the therapist's INTERPRETATIONS and suggestions.

HYPNOID Sleep-like. According to Breuer, Freud's collaborator in *Studies in Hysteria* (1895), hypnoid states occur frequently in women who engage in activities such as housework which do not engage their full attention and predispose to HYSTERIA.

HYPNOPOMPIC Adj. referring to the drowsy state occurring while awakening from SLEEP and to experiences such as HALLUCINATIONS occurring during this state.

HYPNOSIS Artificially induced SLEEP. The TRANCE-like state induced by HYPNOTISM.

HYPNOTISM The process of putting a person into a state of TRANCE, in which he is awake but suffers an impoverishment of his critical faculty and is amenable to *hypnotic suggestion*. According to Ferenczi (1909), the hypnotic state is a TRANSFERENCE phenomenon, in which the hypnotist temporarily acquires the authority of a parent, some techniques being paternal (the authoritative, imposing voice *à la* Svengali), others maternal (stroking the forehead, the soothing voice). Hypnotism played an important part in the history of PSYCHOANALYSIS, since it was Freud's dissatisfaction with it which led him to discover the technique of FREE ASSOCIATION. For an account of hypnotic techniques, including some which can be used on unwilling and unwitting subjects, see Hartland (1966).

HYPOCHONDRIACAL Adj. referring either to a person who imagines he is suffering from a physical illness or to the DELUSIONS or PHANTASIES of such a person. Hence *hypochondriasis*, a PSYCHOSIS of which the main symptom is the patient's belief that he has an incurable physical illness.

HYPOMANIA Psychiatric term for the condition of persons who display in mild form the ELATION and PSYCHOMOTOR ACCELERATION of MANIA. Differentiation of hypomania from exuberant and indefatigable vitality depends on demonstrating that the patient uses MANIC DEFENCES against DEPRESSION.

HYSTERIA 1. Medical diagnostic term for (a) illnesses characterized by the presence of physical SYMPTOMS, (b) the absence of physical SIGNS, or any evidence of physical pathology, and (c) behaviour suggesting that the symptoms fulfil some psychological function. The notion of hysteria derives from the ancient Greeks, who applied the term solely to diseases of women, which were explained as being due to malfunctioning of the UTERUS (*hysteron*). According to one theory, the uterus is a mobile organ capable of moving about the body and pressing on other organs; according to another, sexual abstinence leads to 'starvation of the womb' or to retention of unused animal spirits which passed out of the uterus leading to disturbance in other organs. One of the effects of psychoanalysis has been to demolish uterine theories of the causation of hysteria while retaining the idea that it is in some way connected with SEXUALITY. For the history of the medical concept, see Veith (1965). 2. CLASSICAL THEORY distinguishes between two forms of hysteria: *conversion-hysteria* (q.v.), which corresponds to the traditional medical concept, and *anxiety-hysteria* (q.v.), which is now more commonly known as PHOBIA. Hysteria occupies an important place in the history of PSYCHOANALYSIS, which began with the publication of Freud and Breuer's *Studies on Hysteria* (1895), in which hysterical symptoms were explained as the result of repressed memories (see REPRESSION) and the CONVERSION of ideas into physical symptoms.

Although both these concepts survive in psychoanalytical theory, no contemporary analyst would maintain that they provide an adequate explanation of hysteria. A curious fact, to which Wisdom (1961) has drawn attention, is that Freud never wrote a definitive formulation of his views on hysteria and that it is extremely difficult to discover what the classical theory of hysteria is. There is, however, a tendency to assume that it asserts that the hysterical FIXATION POINT is during the oedipal phase (see OEDIPUS COMPLEX) and that its characteristic DEFENCE mechanisms are REPRESSION and DISSOCIATION. Melanie Klein was also silent on the subject of hysteria and the only object-theorist to concern himself with it has been Fairbairn (1953), who labelled one of his defensive TECHNIQUES 'the hysterical' and held that the origins of hysteria lay in the SCHIZOID position (see PARANOID-SCHIZOID POSITION). According to Veith (1965), hysteria is an almost extinct disease which only occurs among 'the uneducated of the lower social strata' who have not been influenced by the dissemination of psychoanalytical ideas. (Psychoanalysts who work in private practice are none the less quite familiar with hysterical phenomena.)

HYSTERICAL   **1.** When applied to a symptom, see HYSTERIA above. **2.** When applied to a personality, the reference is either to a predisposition to produce CONVERSION-SYMPTOMS or to a histrionic quality in the patient's behaviour. In both cases the implication is that the observed phenomena should not be taken at their face value and that they are intended either to draw or distract attention. **3.** When applied to DEFENCES, the reference is either to the tendency to produce conversion-symptoms, or to the use of DISSOCIATION (SPLITTING), or to simultaneous use of IDEALIZATION and REPRESSION. According to Fairbairn (1952) the *hysterical technique* consists in EXTERNALIZATION of the GOOD OBJECT and INTERNALIZATION of the BAD OBJECT, as a result of which the hysterical person regards some external object as ideally good and his own impulses as bad.

I

I   When used simply as the nominative of the first person singular, 'I' creates no difficulties, but when used substantively to refer to a STRUCTURE, viz. 'the I', its relations to 'the SELF' and 'the EGO' are not always clear. In German, indeed, 'the I' and 'the ego' are identical: '*das Ich*'. However, given the fact that the English language permits a choice between 'the I' and 'the ego', it seems logical to use 'the I' for the self when it is the SUBJECT of experience, i.e. for that part of the self which can assert 'I am', and the 'ego' for the self or person when it is the OBJECT of scrutiny.

I-THOU RELATION   Term used by Martin Buber to describe mutual experiences of reciprocity, of shared relations in which the self discovers itself in relation to the other. The 'I-Thou' relation is contrasted by existentialist writers (see EXISTENTIALISM) with CLASSICAL THEORY's conception of OBJECT-RELATIONS between genital CHARACTERS (see also GENITAL) whose EGOS are distinct entities. 'Buber's emphasis upon the relation between selves, rather than upon the individual self in its relations to the world, constitutes an obvious difference from Freudian psychology.' See 'Martin Buber and Psychoanalysis', in Farber (1966).

ID The Latin word for 'it', used by Freud's translators to translate his *'das Es'*, the term he borrowed from Groddeck and used to designate unorganized parts of the PSYCHIC APPARATUS. (Groddeck's translators prefer 'the IT'.) Historically the id is the descendant of the UNCONSCIOUS in the same way as the EGO is the descendant of the CONSCIOUS. According to CLASSICAL THEORY the id is developmentally anterior to the ego, i.e. the PSYCHIC APPARATUS begins as an undifferentiated id, part of which develops into a structured ego. The id 'contains everything that is present at birth, that is fixed in the constitution – above all, therefore, the instincts, which originate from the somatic organization and which find a first psychical expression here [in the id] in forms unknown to us' – Freud (1940). 'It is the dark, inaccessible part of our personality; what little we know of it we have learnt from our study of the dream-work and of the construction of neurotic symptoms, and most of that is of a negative character and can be described only as a contrast to the ego. We approach the id with analogies: we call it a chaos, a cauldron full of seething excitations . . . it is filled with energy reaching it from the instincts, but it has no organization, produces no collective will, but only a striving to bring about the satisfaction of instinctual needs subject to the observance of the pleasure-principle' – Freud (1933). The concept is one of many examples of Freud's passion for explaining mental phenomena in terms of the opposition of antithetical forces. The id is primitive, the ego civilized; the id is unorganized, the ego organized; the id observes the PLEASURE-PRINCIPLE, the ego the REALITY-PRINCIPLE; the id is emotional, the ego rational; the id conforms to the PRIMARY PROCESSES which ignore differences and are oblivious of contradictions and of space and time, the ego conforms to the SECONDARY PROCESSES which are analytical and respect the principles of contradiction and the categories of space and time. For a summary of the arguments *against* conceiving of mental life in terms of such antitheses and in favour of the view that the psyche has structure from the very beginning, see Rycroft (1962).

IDEALIZATION   Defensive process (see DEFENCE) by which an ambivalently regarded (see AMBIVALENCE) (INTERNAL) OBJECT is split into two (see SPLITTING), one resulting object being conceived of as ideally GOOD, the other as wholly BAD. The concept includes two notions: the construction of an ideal, perfect object and the REIFICATION of an idea. Idealization in its wider and non-technical sense of regarding some person as perfect and wonderful involves PROJECTION as well as idealization. Idealization differs from admiration in that (a) the idealizing person needs a perfect person to exist and ignores (denies, see DENIAL) the existence of those attributes of the idealized person which do not fit the picture, and (b) it leads to DEPENDENCE on and subservience to the idealized person and not to emulation and imitation. Idealization is a defence against the consequences of recognizing ambivalence and purchases freedom from GUILT and DEPRESSION at the cost of loss of SELF-ESTEEM. Failure of the defence leads to disillusion and depression. See Rycroft (1955).

IDEAS OF REFERENCE   See REFERENCE, IDEAS OF.

IDENTIFICATION   The process by which a person either (a) extends his IDENTITY *into* someone else, (b) borrows his identity *from* someone else, or (c) fuses or confuses his identity *with* someone else. In analytical writings it never means establishing the identity of oneself or someone else.

Four types of identification are distinguished: primary, secondary, projective, and introjective. *Primary identification* is the state of affairs presumed to exist in infancy when the individual has yet to distinguish his identity from that of his objects, when the distinction between 'I' and 'you' is meaningless. *Secondary identification* is the process of identifying with an object the separate identity of which has been discovered. Unlike primary identification, secondary identification is a defence since it reduces hostility between the self and the object and enables experiences of SEPARATION from it to be denied. None the less, secondary identification with parental figures is held to be part of the normal developmental process (see DEVELOPMENT). *Projective identification* is the process by which a person imagines himself to be inside some object external to himself. This again is a defence since it creates the ILLUSION of control over the object and enables the subject to deny his powerlessness over it and to gain vicarious

67

satisfaction from its activities. *Introjective identification* is either the process of identifying with an INTROJECT or the process by which a person imagines another to be inside and part of him. In some usages this is indistinguishable from secondary identification and introjection.

Identification is often confused with INTROJECTION, INTERNALIZATION, and INCORPORATION. See Koff (1961), and Fuchs (1937) for attempts to define the term accurately. See also EGO; EGO DEVELOPMENT; EGO BOUNDARY.

IDENTITY   The sense of one's continuous being as an entity distinguishable from all others. According to Erikson (1953), many aspects of EGO DEVELOPMENT can be formulated in terms of the growth of the sense of identity, an *identity-crisis* of greater or lesser severity being characteristic of late adolescence and early adulthood. The sense of identity is lost in FUGUES and perverted in schizophrenic DELUSIONS of identity (see also SCHIZOPHRENIA) in which, typically, an underlying sense of nonentity is compensated for by delusions of grandeur. Many of the problems about identity centre round the part played by IDENTIFICATIONS in enhancing or diminishing identity. Failure to identify with parents, particularly the parent of one's own sex, during childhood is held to diminish the sense of identity, but failure to disidentify with them in adolescence has a similar effect. The sense of identity is probably synonymous with SELF-AWARENESS and can be regarded as the subjective equivalent of the EGO, which psychoanalytical theory tends to use only objectively. It is not clear whether the *search for identity* which preoccupies many American writers is a search for a role or for enhanced self-awareness. See Erikson (1953), Wheelis (1958), Lynd (1958). See also SELF; I; IDENTITY *v.* ROLE DIFFUSION.

IDENTITY *v.* ROLE DIFFUSION   The fifth of Erikson's eight STAGES OF MAN. It corresponds to adolescence and early manhood, during which, according to Erikson, the individual has to redefine his identity, particularly in relation to the parents he is growing away from and the society he is growing into. 'Role diffusion' refers to the adolescent tendency to 'over-identify, to the point of apparent complete loss of identity, with the heroes of cliques and crowds' – Erikson (1953).

ILLUSION   'A subjective perversion of the objective content' of a perception. It differs from a HALLUCINATION in that it is due to misinterpretation of an actual experience, and from a DELUSION in that the question of belief does not arise. Illusions are not pathological phenomena and are of more interest to psychologists, particularly to students of perception, than they are to psychiatrists and psychoanalysts. The word is, however, used by Winnicott in a somewhat special sense to describe the infant's experience on those happy occasions when the MOTHER succeeds in realizing his expectations, i.e. when the infant's wish-fulfilling hallucinations (see WISH-FULFILMENT) are met by actual mothering. According to Winnicott, healthy development is dependent on such experiences of illusion. See Winnicott (1958). Patients who use the defence of IDEALIZATION can also be said to be in a state of illusion. See Rycroft (1955).

IMAGINATION The process, or faculty, of conceiving REPRESENTATIONS of objects, events, etc., not actually present. The process produces results which are either (a) *imaginary*, in the sense of being fictitious, unreal, etc., or (b) *imaginative*, in the sense of providing solutions to problems which have never previously been so solved or, in the arts, creating artefacts which none the less reflect or enhance experience. The psychoanalytical literature tends to subsume imagination under the heading of PHANTASY and has the same difficulty as do the arts in deciding whether and when phantasy (imagination) is escapist or creative, defensive, or adaptive (see CREATIVITY, DEFENCE and ADAPTATION). It is generally accepted, however, that creative imaginative activity involves the participation of unconscious non-verbal phantasy. See Rycroft (1956), Beres (1955).

IMAGO Word used by Freud to describe (unconscious) OBJECT-REPRESENTATIONS. Not to be confused with an insect after its final metamorphosis.

IMPLOSION Term used by Laing (1960) to describe the fear of being annihilated by reality which is experienced by persons who lack primary ontological security (see ONTOLOGY). Such persons feel like vacuums, long to be filled, but fear that whatever could fill them would destroy their IDENTITY.

IMPOTENCE When describing a symptom, sexual incapacity of the male is always intended. Sexual impotence may be due to either physical or psychological factors. Psychoanalysis is only concerned with the latter. Psychogenic impotence can only be regarded as a neurotic symptom if it is persistent, if it defeats the patient's conscious intentions and occurs even under the most favourable conditions. Otherwise it is the result of either inexperience or insincerity.

IMPULSE The psychoanalytical usage of this word derives from NEUROLOGY, where it refers to the wave of electrical charge passing along a nerve fibre. In CLASSICAL THEORY instinctual impulses are similarly conceived to pass from some point in the ID along channels leading into the EGO, where they are either (a) discharged in action (see DISCHARGE), (b) inhibited (see INHIBITION), (c) diverted by the operation of DEFENCE mechanisms, or (d) sublimated (see SUBLIMATION) into non-instinctual channels. When used correctly the concept is an ECONOMIC one, used to describe the movements of psychic ENERGY within the PSYCHIC APPARATUS, but in fact it is often used as a synonym for wish, desire, or drive, all of which refer to subjective experiences.

INACCESSIBLE See ACCESSIBLE AND INACCESSIBLE.

INCEST Sexual relations between blood relatives; the prohibited degree of relationship being determined by canon or secular law. For Freud's views on the origins of the INCEST TABOO, see his *Totem and Taboo* (1913). The OEDIPUS COMPLEX implies that all individuals have *incestuous phantasies*. In conversation, analysts and persons who have been in close contact with psychoanalytical circles habitually use 'incestuous' for 'in-bred', to refer, for instance, to the social atmosphere created by the fact that everyone and his wife has been in analysis with everyone else.

INCORPORATION Although sometimes used synonymously with INTERNALIZATION or INTROJECTION, incorporation properly refers only to a PHANTASY, viz. to the phantasy that the subject has ingested an EXTERNAL OBJECT. Incorporation-phantasies are typically ORAL, i.e. that the subject has swallowed the object, but they may also occur in relation to other openings of the body, including such organs as the eye and ear which can be imagined as openings. The confusion with introjection arises from the fact that the structural process of introjection may be accompanied by the phantasy of incorporation. When used as a technical term, incorporation never refers to the process of assimilating something into a previously existing structure or to the combining of units to form a larger body or structure. Incorporation-phantasies were first described as occurring in melancholic (DEPRESSIVE) patients (see MELANCHOLIA), whose introjections (IDENTIFICATIONS) are made during the oral stage of LIBIDINAL DEVELOPMENT and are accompanied by cannibalistic phantasies. See Freud (1917), Abraham (1927).

INDIVIDUATION   The process of becoming an individual, or of becoming aware that one is one. As used by Jung, the term seems to include not only the idea of becoming aware that one is separate and different from others, but also the idea that one is oneself a whole, indivisible person. According to Jung, individuation is one of the tasks of middle age. See Bennet (1966).

INDUSTRY *v.* INFERIORITY   The fourth of Erikson's eight STAGES OF MAN. It corresponds to the LATENCY PERIOD of CLASSICAL THEORY. The 'industry' refers to the preoccupation with acquiring physical skills characteristic of the phase (ages 8–13) and the 'inferiority' to the danger of being discouraged by a sense of inferiority in comparison with grown-ups. See Erikson (1953).

INFANTILE   When applied to behaviour, emotions, phantasies, etc., infantile means PRE-GENITAL and not childish or immature. *Infantile sexuality* embraces sexual phenomena assumed to be normal, ubiquitous, and inevitable during the infantile phases of LIBIDINAL DEVELOPMENT and which persist into adult life only in so far as (a) the OEDIPUS COMPLEX has not been resolved, (b) SUBLIMATIONS have not occurred, and (c) the activities have not been integrated into the FORE-PLEASURE of adult sexuality. The psychoanalytical usage of 'infantile' to mean pre-genital, PRE-OEDIPAL, unsublimated is accompanied by an analogous use of 'infant' to mean any child under, say, 4 or 5. In medical and statistical literature, 'infant' means 'a child under 1 year of age'; in legal usage any person under 21.

INFERIORITY COMPLEX   Originally an Adlerian term describing the cluster of ideas and feelings which arise in reaction to the sense of *organ inferiority*. Now a popular term for the sense of inadequacy.

INHIBITION   A process or function is said to be in a state of inhibition if it is being rendered quiescent by the operation of some other process or function. In NEUROLOGY, a reflex response is said to inhibit another if its operation precludes the possibility of the other occurring. Fear can also be said to inhibit appetite, sexual desire, etc. The essence of the notion is that of holding in check. In psychoanalysis the term is usually used to refer to instances in which the state of inhibition can be regarded as a symptom, the inhibiting agency usually being the EGO or SUPER-EGO and the inhibited process being an INSTINCTUAL IMPULSE or a sublimated derivative thereof (see SUBLIMATION). In some contexts, however, inhibition is contrasted with SYMPTOM, the former referring to a loss of function, the latter to disturbance of function. See Freud's *Symptoms, Inhibitions and Anxiety* (1926). Inhibition and repression differ in that the former implies that something is switched off, the latter that something is being held back.

INITIATIVE *v.* GUILT   The third of Erikson's eight STAGES OF MAN. It corresponds to the oedipal phase (see OEDIPUS COMPLEX) of CLASSICAL THEORY, the 'initiative' manifesting itself *inter alia* in 'anticipatory rivalry with those who have been there first', leading 'to a climax in a final contest for a favoured position with the mother; the inevitable failure leads to resignation, guilt, and anxiety' – Erikson (1953).

INSANITY   See SANITY AND INSANITY.

INSIGHT   1. In PSYCHIATRY: the capacity to appreciate that one's disturbances of thought and feeling are subjective and invalid. Loss of insight characterizes PSYCHOSIS, retention characterizes NEUROSIS. 2. In PSYCHOANALYSIS: the capacity to understand one's own MOTIVES, to be aware of one's own PSYCHODYNAMICS, to appreciate the MEANING of symbolic behaviour (see SYMBOL). Analysts distinguish between *intellectual insight*, the capacity to formulate correctly one's own PSYCHO-PATHOLOGY and dynamics, and *emotional insight*, the capacity to feel and apprehend fully the significance of 'UNCONSCIOUS' and symbolic manifestations. Intellectual insight is usually classified as an OBSESSIONAL DEFENCE since it enables the subject to understand and control aspects of himself from which he remains alienated (see ALIENATION). Emotional insight, on the other hand, is evidence of freedom from alienation and of 'being in touch with the unconscious'. It is possible to have insight in sense **1** and to lack it in sense **2**, i.e. to be sane and yet clueless. Although insight refers in the first instance to SELF-AWARENESS and self-knowledge, it is also used to refer to the capacity to understand others. Insight is a faculty necessary for the practice of psychoanalysis.

The aim of psychoanalytical treatment is sometimes defined in terms of the acquisition of insight, though Freud himself never used this formulation, preferring the idea that its aim is to make CONSCIOUS the UNCONSCIOUS. Both definitions imply that consciousness has an integrating function (see INTEGRATION).

INSTINCT   An innate biologically determined drive to action. According to CLASSICAL THEORY, an instinct has (a) a biological source, (b) a supply of ENERGY derived therefrom, (c) an aim, viz. carrying out the behaviour specific to the instinct, leading to *instinctual satisfaction* (see also SATISFACTION) and DISCHARGE of the energy invested in it, and (d) an OBJECT, in relation to which the aim can be achieved. Failure to find an object and to achieve the *instinctual aim* leads to *instinctual frustration* (see also FRUSTRATION) and increase in instinctual TENSION, the heightened tension being experienced as PAIN. In accordance with the PLEASURE PRINCIPLE, this pain leads either to increased activity in pursuit of relief or to the introduction of DEFENCE-mechanisms to reduce the tension. The EGO reacts to the threat of instinctual tension over and above its THRESHOLD of tolerance by ANXIETY (SIGNAL-ANXIETY), which is the ego's STIMULUS to institute defensive measures. According to Freud (1915), an instinct may undergo four vicissitudes, viz. (a) REVERSAL into its opposite, typically the replacement of an active role by a passive one; (b) TURNING AGAINST THE SELF, i.e. use of the self as the instinctual object; (c) REPRESSION, a term which in 1915 included all the defence-mechanisms, later described; and (d) SUBLIMATION, as a result of which the instinctual energy is eventually discharged in activities bearing only a symbolic connexion (see SYMBOL) with the primary instinctual aim. This conception of instinct is clearly only applicable with any degree of plausibility to the sexual and aggressive drives (see SEX and AGGRESSION), and attempts to apply it to other innate behaviour patterns, such as sleep or nutrition, would lead to immediate and obvious absurdities. In fact it was constructed with the sexual disorders of hysterics in mind (see HYSTERIA and HYSTERICAL), though the relation of instinctual tension to signal-anxiety derives from study of the defences against aggression occurring in OBSESSIONAL NEUROSIS.

Freud was consistently a proponent of a *dual instinct theory*, holding that instincts could be categorized into two groups, which tended to be antagonistic towards one another, and that the conflicts between the two groups were responsible for neurosis. He was not, however, consistent in his view as to what the two (groups of) instincts were. Until the early 1920s they were the *ego-instincts* (see EGO-INSTINCT) and the *sexual instinct*, corresponding to the self-preservative and reproductive instincts of biology (see SELF-PRESERVATION), but in his later speculative writings they were the LIFE and DEATH INSTINCTS. The scheme outlined above was never intended to apply to ego-instincts, and it is not clear whether it was meant to apply to the death instinct – though there certainly exists a tendency among analysts to assume that there is an instinct and a form of energy both called 'aggression' to which it does. Many analysts have pointed out that, although the notion of CONFLICT implies the existence of at least two drives, there is no particular reason for preferring a dual to a triple or even a multiple instinct theory. Contemporary animal psychology (ETHOLOGY) postulates at least seven instincts or innate behaviour patterns: nutrition, SEX, fighting, parental, SLEEP, TERRITORIALITY, and grooming. The last two are unrepresented in psychoanalytical theory.

INSTINCT, COMPONENT According to CLASSICAL THEORY, the adult sexual instinct 'gradually develops out of successive contributions from a number of component instincts which represent particular EROTOGENIC ZONES' – Freud (1940).

INSTINCT THEORY AND OBJECT THEORY These terms are used to distinguish between formulations which concern themselves with INSTINCTS and their vicissitudes and those concerned with the individual's relations with his OBJECTS. Formally the distinction is a false one, since instincts are directed towards objects and objects can only be of significance if the individual has some drive to relate to them. In practice, however, it is a real one, viz. between theories which assume that the individual acquires the capacity to relate to objects at some stage of DEVELOP-

MENT and those which assume that he is born related to an object (the MOTHER); between those which assume that ADAPTATION is a reluctantly learned process and those which assume that the infant is born adapted; between those which assume that the value of objects lies in their capacity to give instinctual pleasure and those which assume that the value of pleasure lies in its capacity to enrich relationships. *Instinct theory* provides psychoanalysis with a link with biology; *object theory* gives it one with the social sciences. Classical psychoanalysis is an instinct theory; the KLEINIAN and Fairbairnian (see FAIRBAIRN'S REVISED PSYCHOPATHOLOGY) systems are object theories. Hartmann's EGO-PSYCHOLOGY has some aspects of both. See Klein (1948), Fairbairn (1952), Hartmann (1958).

INTEGRATION   The process by which parts are combined into a whole. According to CLASSICAL THEORY the human psyche starts as an unintegrated, unorganized ID and becomes integrated as a result of EGO-DEVELOPMENT. According to OBJECT THEORY the infant begins life in a state of primary integration. 'The pristine personality of the child consists of a unitary, dynamic ego' – Fairbairn (1952). All DEFENCES, other than SUBLIMATION, operate at the expense of integration, purchasing freedom from ANXIETY at the price of SPLITTING off or REPRESSION of parts of the potential integrated SELF. Psychoanalytical treatment aims to restore lost parts to the self and to increase integration. See Fairbairn (1952), Rycroft (1962), Storr (1960).

INTERNAL   This is frequently used as a synonym for 'psychical', 'mental', on the assumption that mental processes are located in an inner space. Hence *internal reality, internal conflict, internal object* (see also REALITY, CONFLICT, OBJECT), all of which are conceived and defined in contrast to their 'external' equivalents.

INTERNALIZATION   Although sometimes used synonymously with INTROJECTION, it is best used only to describe that process by which objects in the external world acquire permanent mental REPRESENTATION, i.e. by which PERCEPTS are converted into images forming part of our mental furniture and structure.

INTERNAL SABOTEUR   Term used by Fairbairn (1952) to describe one of the three parts into which the original 'unitary, dynamic EGO' becomes split. The internal saboteur is anti-libidinal, is attached to the INTERNAL 'rejecting OBJECT', and is the precursor of Freud's SUPER-EGO.

INTERPERSONAL   1. *Interpersonal theories* and concepts are concerned with how persons interact on one another, in contrast to the intrapersonal theories of CLASSICAL THEORY, which are concerned with how single individuals develop and behave. 2. *Interpersonal relationships* are relationships between persons; the 'inter' is redundant unless a contrast is being made with relationships between parts of a person. A man's relation to (with) his boss is interpersonal, to his SUPER-EGO is intrapersonal.

INTERPRETATION   The process of elucidating and expounding the MEANING of something abstruse, obscure, etc. Psychoanalytical interpretations are statements made by the analyst to the patient in which he attributes to a DREAM, a SYMPTOM, or a chain of FREE ASSOCIATIONS some meaning over and above (under and below) that given to it by the patient. The paradigm of interpretation is *dream-interpretation*, the activity of discovering the LATENT content of meaning of a dream by analysis of its MANIFEST content. The assumptions underlying this activity are (a) that the dream has meaning; (b) that this can be elucidated by a person familiar with symbolism (see SYMBOL) and the PRIMARY PROCESSES (the rules governing UNCONSCIOUS mental activity), with the circumstances of the dreamer and with his associations to the dream; and (c) that the dreamer can confirm the accuracy of the interpretation by his response to it – in the most simple instance by recollecting some event corresponding to one surmised by the interpreter. It is assumption (c) which prevents dream-interpretation from becoming an arbitrary and dogmatic procedure.

Transference-interpretations relate the patient's behaviour and associations to his relationship to the analyst. *Content interpretations* refer to unconscious IMPULSES and PHANTASIES without reference to the defensive processes which have been keeping them unconscious. *Direct interpretations* are based solely on the analyst's knowledge of symbolism without reference to the patient's associations. *Correct interpretations* are those which both (a) explain adequately the 'MATERIAL' being interpreted and (b) are formulated in such a way and communicated at such a time that they have actuality for (make sense to) the patient. *Premature interpretations* are 'true' interpretations communicated to the patient before they can make sense to him. *Mutative interpretations* alter the patient. (See Strachey (1934) for an explanation as to why interpretations have a therapeutic effect and for the preconditions necessary for an interpretation being effective.) The function of interpretation is to increase SELF-AWARENESS and therefore facilitate INTEGRATION by making the patient CONSCIOUS of processes within himself of which he was previously unconscious.

Analysts habitually talk as though *all* their utterances were interpretations, but this is not, strictly speaking, the case. Some are CONFRONTATIONS, i.e. remarks which draw the patient's attention to something without explaining it, while others reflect what the patient is saying and show that the analyst is still 'with' him.

See Freud (1900, 1902), for the original account of psycho-analytical dream-interpretation. See Sharpe (1937, 1950), for vivid pictures of an analyst at work. See Rycroft (1958), for a discussion of the emotional significance of interpretations.

INTIMACY *v.* ISOLATION The sixth of Erikson's eight STAGES OF MAN. It is during this stage that the healthy individual reaches the GENITAL LEVEL of classical psychoanalysis (see CLASSICAL THEORY) and becomes capable of intimate love and creative work. It apparently lasts from the early twenties to early middle age. The hazard of this phase is 'the fear of EGO loss in situations which call for self-abandon' and a resulting sense of isolation. See GENITALITY for an extended quotation from Erikson's description of this phase. See Erikson (1953).

INTRAPSYCHIC Adj. referring to processes occurring within the mind. *Intrapsychic conflict* refers to CONFLICT occurring between two parts of the same mind, in contrast to conflict between persons.

INTROJECTION The process by which the functions of an EXTERNAL OBJECT are taken over by its mental REPRESENTATION, by which the relationship with an object 'out there' is replaced by one with an imagined object 'inside'. The resulting mental structure is variously called an *introject*, an *introjected object*, or an *internal object*. Introjection is preceded by INTERNALIZATION, may or may not be accompanied by the PHANTASY of INCORPORATION, and may be succeeded by SECONDARY IDENTIFICATION. The SUPER-EGO is formed by introjection of parental figures and it may be analysed into a number of component introjects (the GOOD (BAD) INTERNAL FATHER (MOTHER)). Introjection is both a DEFENCE and a normal developmental process; a defence because it diminishes SEPARATION ANXIETY, a developmental process because it renders the subject increasingly AUTONOMOUS.

INTROSPECTION Looking inwards, examining one's thoughts and feelings. It is sometimes distinguished from SELF-OBSERVATION by using the former to describe worried or narcissistic self-preoccupation (see NARCISSISM), the latter objective self-scrutiny. According to this distinction, one of the aims of psychoanalytical treatment is to decrease introspection and to increase the capacity for self-observation.

INTROVERSION, INTROVERT See EXTRAVERSION AND INTROVERSION.

INVERT, INVERSION *Sexual inversion* is an obsolescent term for male HOMOSEXUALITY; hence *invert* for male homosexual.

ISAKOWER PHENOMENON HYPNAGOGIC experience first described by Isakower (1938) in which the subject imagines soft, doughy masses to be moving towards his face. Isakower interpreted this phenomenon as a revival of the infant's experience of being at the BREAST. See Lewin (1946) for an account of its relevance to his DREAM SCREEN concept and the psychology of SLEEP.

ISOLATION DEFENCE-mechanism by which the subject isolates an occurrence, preventing it from becoming part of the continuum of his significant experience. 'When something unpleasant has happened to the subject or when he has done something which has a significance for his neurosis, he interpolates an interval during which nothing further must happen – during which he must perceive nothing and do nothing . . . the experience is not forgotten, but, instead, it is deprived of its AFFECT, and its associative connexions are suppressed or interrupted so that it remains as though isolated and is not reproduced in the ordinary processes of thought' – Freud (1926). Isolation is used typically by obsessional neurotics (see OBSESSIONAL NEUROSIS) in whom it plays the same role as does REPRESSION in hysteria. It has connexions with SPLITTING and DISSOCIATION.

'IT, THE' The English translators of Groddeck (1866–1934), from whom Freud borrowed the concept of the ID (*'das Es'*), use 'the It' to refer to Groddeck's original concept, which Freud modified considerably. Although 'the Id' and 'the It' have in common the idea of an impersonal force within, with which the EGO has to come to terms, they differ in that 'the id' is a *psychological* concept, that part of the PSYCHIC APPARATUS within which the instinctual and innate are mentally represented and out of which the ego arises, while 'the *Es*' is a *psychosomatic* concept: 'the body and mind are a joint thing which harbours an It, a power by which we are lived, while we think we live. . . . The It, which is mysteriously connected with sexuality, Eros, or whatever you choose to call it, shapes the nose as well as the hand of the human, just as it shapes his thoughts and emotions. . . . And just as the symptomatic activity of the It in hysteria and neurosis calls for psychoanalytical treatment, so does heart trouble and cancer.' See Grossman (1965).

J

JEALOUSY Differs from ENVY in that it involves three parties: the SUBJECT, an OBJECT whom the subject loves, and a third party who arouses ANXIETY in the subject about his security of tenure of the second party's affections; whereas envy involves only two parties: the subject and an object whose good fortune or possessions the subject envies. *Jealousy* is related to possessiveness of the other, *envy* to comparison of the self with the other. According to McDougall, jealousy is a complex emotion implying the existence of the sentiment of LOVE. It is typically evoked by the oedipal triangle and forms part of the OEDIPUS COMPLEX. *Pathological jealousy*, i.e. persistent, unfounded, delusional jealousy (see also DELUSION), appears to have some intrinsic connexion with HOMOSEXUALITY and PARANOIA. According to Freud (1911), the jealousy and the paranoia are defences against the homosexuality, but the contemporary tendency is to regard the paranoia as the primary member of the triad.

JUNGIAN 1. N. a follower of C. G. Jung (1875–1961), Swiss psychiatrist who was a disciple of Freud's from 1907 to 1913 but later founded his own school and system of PSYCHOPATHOLOGY. Jungian therapists are correctly called *analytical psychologists* and not psychoanalysts, though this is far from being general usage. 2. Adj. referring to ideas propounded by Jung. See Bennet (1966) for a comprehensible summary of Jung's ideas.

K

KATATONIA   See CATATONIA.

KLEINIAN 1. N. a follower of Melanie Klein (1882–1960), pioneer of CHILD ANALYSIS and of research into DEPRESSIVE and SCHIZOID states. 2. Adj. referring to ideas and theories formulated by Melanie Klein. Although the *Kleinian school* of psychoanalysis remains within the Freudian fold, its theories differ in several fundamental respects from CLASSICAL THEORY. The main differences are: (a) The DEATH INSTINCT is taken seriously as a clinical concept; innate AMBIVALENCE is assumed, the destructive component of the ambivalence being interpreted as a defensive PROJECTION (see also DEFENCE) outwards of the innate self-destructive instinct. (b) EGO-DEVELOPMENT is regarded as a process of continual INTROJECTION and PROJECTION of objects and not as progress of the self through a number of stages in which a variety of defences are used. (c) The origins of NEUROSIS are held to lie in the first year of life and not in the first few years and to consist in failures to pass through the *depressive position*, and not to FIXATION at a variety of stages (FIXATION POINTS) through childhood. As a result, the depressive position plays the same part in Kleinian theory as the OEDIPUS COMPLEX does in classical theory. (d) Kleinian theory is an OBJECT THEORY not an INSTINCT THEORY inasmuch as it attaches central importance to resolution of ambivalence towards the MOTHER, the BREAST, and regards ego-development as being based primarily on introjection of the mother and/or breast. It differs, however, from the object theories of Fairbairn (see FAIRBAIRN'S REVISED PSYCHOPATHOLOGY) and

Winnicott in attaching little importance to the infant's actual experience of mothering, this being overshadowed in the Kleinian view by the infant's difficulties in overcoming its innate ambivalence towards the breast. Being endowed with both innate ENVY of it and the need to use it as the recipient of its own projected death-instinct, the infant has first to work through its fear and suspicion of the breast (the PARANOID-SCHIZOID POSITION) and then work through its discovery that the breast it hates and the breast it loves are the same breast (the DEPRESSIVE POSITION). (e) It assumes that the infant has a much more vivid, violent PHANTASY life than does classical theory and that the main task of analysis is to interpret unconscious phantasies rather than to interpret DEFENCES against unconscious impulses. Phantasies are, however, regarded as the psychic representatives of libidinal and destructive instincts and to be the processes against which defences are erected. In summary, Kleinian analysis resembles classical analysis in subscribing to a dual INSTINCT theory and indeed in being more Freudian than the Freudians in its use of the death instinct but differs from it in rejecting the concepts of stages of development and fixation-points in favour of a theory of positions and in attributing greater importance to the first year of life than to childhood as a whole. See Segal (1964) for an exposition of Kleinian theory and Glover (1945) for sharp criticism of it from a classical point of view.

L

LAMARCKIANISM Evolutionary theory, first stated by Lamarck (1744–1829), which asserts that characteristics acquired by the individual can be inherited by his descendants. This theory of the 'inheritance of acquired characteristics' is generally held to be incompatible with the Darwinian theory that evolution occurs by natural selection, i.e. by the survival and transmission of chance variations. Much to the embarrassment of most of his followers Freud was a Lamarckian. 'In spite of innumerable similar strictures Freud remained from the beginning to the end of his life what one must call an obstinate adherent of this discredited Lamarckism,' wrote Jones (1957). This adherence explains his anthropological theory that the sense of guilt of contemporary man derives from PARRICIDE committed in prehistoric times; and his historical theory that the consciousness of GUILT which pervades Jewish history is an inherited, unconscious memory of the guilt felt by Moses' murderers. Jones (1957), vol. III, ch. 10, is at a loss to explain this aberration of Freud's. See Freud (1913, 1939). See ONTOGENY AND PHYLOGENY; TOTEM; TABOO; PRIMAL.

LATENCY PERIOD Developmental phase postulated by psychoanalysis in which psychosexual maturation marks time. It occurs after the OEDIPAL phase and ends at puberty and is a period of emotional quiescence between the dramas and turmoils of childhood and adolescence. It is unclear whether the latency period is an innate, universal phenomenon related to the prolonging of biological immaturity which characterizes human development or whether it is confined to repressive cultures (see REPRESSION) in which INFANTILE and immature sexual behaviour is subject to restriction. The latency period corresponds to the fourth of Erikson's eight STAGES OF MAN, INDUSTRY *v.* INFERIORITY, a formulation which emphasizes the preoccupation of this stage with acquiring skills.

LATENT See MANIFEST AND LATENT.

LAY ANALYST A PSYCHOANALYST who is not medically qualified. Although in most countries other than England the practice of psychoanalysis is confined to members of the medical profession, it was Freud's opinion that psychoanalysis should become a profession independent of medicine, 'a profession of lay curers of souls who need not be doctors and should not be priests'. This quotation is exceptional in that 'lay' here means 'non-clerical' and not 'non-medical'.

LEARNING THEORY 1. Any theory which attempts to explain learning. 2. (And more usually) that body of psychological theory which seeks to explain behaviour in terms of learned responses to environmental stimuli – in contrast to DYNAMIC theories such as psychoanalysis which explain it in terms of innate or instinctual developmental processes. In sense 2 learning theory is the heir of Pavlov's work on conditioned reflexes and of Watson's behaviourism, which it resembles in rejecting introspective data and in regarding PSYCHOLOGY as a 'purely OBJECTIVE experimental branch of natural SCIENCE'. Learning theory provides the theoretical basis for BEHAVIOUR THERAPY, which proceeds from the assumption that neurotic behaviour is the end-result of faulty, maladaptive learning and can, therefore, be modified by deconditioning and relearning techniques. Learning theorists claim that its reliance on experiment and sophisticated statistical techniques gives it a scientific respectability which psychoanalysis, with its clinical origins, sadly lacks. See Eysenck (1965).

LIBIDINAL INFANTILE DEVELOPMENT CLASSICAL THEORY postulates a series of phases of libidinal development through which the individual passes from infancy until he reaches the LATENCY PERIOD, these phases being synchronous with a parallel series of phases of EGO-DEVELOPMENT. In most formulations the phases are the ORAL, ANAL, PHALLIC, and OEDIPAL, the first three being conjointly 'PRE-OEDIPAL'. The oral, anal, and phallic phases are so named because during them the mouth, anus, and penis are respectively the main source of libidinal pleasure; according to some formulations they are narcissistic (see under NARCISSISM), on the ground that only in the oedipal phase does the capacity for OBJECT-LOVE emerge. In some formulations the oral phase is subdivided into *oral-sucking* and *oral-biting* substages, and the anal phase divided into *anal-expressive* and *anal-retentive*. OBJECT THEORY continues to use the terms 'oral' and 'anal' to describe phases or aspects of the MOTHER-child relationship, despite its abandonment of the classical notion that the infant is narcissistic and pleasure-seeking – and despite its rejection of the distinction between an ID in which libidinal development occurs and an EGO in which EGO DEVELOPMENT takes place. See also INSTINCT THEORY AND OBJECT THEORY; LIBIDO.

LIBIDINAL AND LIBIDINOUS The former is the correct form for the adjective corresponding to the technical term LIBIDO.

LIBIDO Hypothetical form of mental ENERGY, with which processes, STRUCTURES and OBJECT-REPRESENTATIONS are invested. Libido is conceived as having a source, the body or the ID, as existing in various forms related to specific EROTOGENIC ZONES (i.e. ORAL, ANAL, GENITAL libido), as being distributed between various structures or processes, which are *libidinized* (or, alternatively, carry a *libidinal cathexis* (see CATHEXIS)). In Freud's first formulations, libido was the energy attached specifically to the sexual instincts (see SEX), but later the EGO was assumed to possess libido, this *ego-libido* being derived from libido attached to object-representations (object-libido). This rather curious formulation derives from two others: viz. (a) that the ego differentiates out of the id; hence ego-energy must be a differentiated form of id-energy; (b) that the development of the ego is the result of FRUSTRATION by parental objects, and is accompanied by IDENTIFICATION with and INTROJECTION of them; hence the libido originally attached to them becomes attached to the ego, SELF-LOVE and SELF-AWARENESS increasing as the attachment to the parents decreases. This formulation implies that the ego is its own object; hence the distinction made by Federn (1952) between *subject-libido*, the energy available to the self qua subject, and *object-libido*, the energy available for investment in objects. Object-libido invested in the ego is *narcissistic libido*. Believers in the LIFE INSTINCT and DEATH INSTINCT are logically compelled to contrast libido, the energy of the life instincts, with another form of energy specific to the death instinct. Although attempts have been made to introduce 'MORTIDO' and 'DESTRUDO' to fill this gap, neither has caught on.

LIBIDO THEORY   See LIBIDO; INSTINCT THEORY.

LIFE INSTINCT   In his later speculative writings Freud abandoned his earlier idea that the two groups of INSTINCTS were the sexual (see SEX) and the EGO-INSTINCTS, corresponding to the reproductive and self-preservative instincts of biology (see SELF-PRESERVATION), in favour of the LIFE INSTINCT and DEATH INSTINCT, the life instinct including both the sexual and the self-preservative instincts, the death instinct being the drive to return to the inanimate state.

LIMEN, LIMINAL   Subliminal, supraliminal. See THRESHOLD.

LOVE   Psychoanalysts have as much difficulty defining such a protean concept as do others. It appears in the literature as (a) EROS, a personified force or principle; (b) an INSTINCT or group of instincts liable to come into CONFLICT with either self-preservative (see SELF-PRESERVATION) or destructive instincts; (c) an AFFECT more often contrasted with HATE than with FEAR; and (d) a capacity or function liable to INHIBITION, PERVERSION, and SUBLIMATION. INSTINCT THEORY assumes that all forms of loving are, in the last resort, derivatives of instinct and that their function is to provide instinctual SATISFACTION; OBJECT THEORY assumes that they are all manifestations of the need to relate to objects. The distinction between love which recognizes the needs and reality of the other and that which fails to is usually made by contrasting OBJECT-LOVE and INFANTILE or dependent love (see DEPENDENCE). A *love-object* is an object whom the subject loves in contrast to either (a) an object whom he hates or to whom he is indifferent, or (b) a need-satisfying object. *Oedipal love* is love for a parent or for a parent-substitute. *Genital love* is not a synonym for sexual desire but the form of love of which a person who has reached the GENITAL LEVEL is capable.

M

MAGIC   Primitive, superstitious practices based on the assumption that natural processes can be affected by actions which influence or propitiate supernatural agencies, or, as in the case of *sympathetic magic*, by actions which resemble those which the magician wishes to induce. See OMNIPOTENCE; OBSESSIONAL NEUROSIS; RITUAL.

MALIGNANT   In medicine, cancerous growths are *malignant*, in contrast to non-cancerous ones, which are *benign*. Severe hysteria is sometimes termed *malignant hysteria*, possibly partly because of the unconcious malice so often present.

MANIA   PSYCHOSIS characterized by ELATION, PSYCHOMOTOR ACCELERATION, i.e. gross acceleration of both physical and mental activity leading to excitement, severe insomnia and eventual exhaustion, and flight of ideas, i.e. rapid thought in which the connexions between one idea and the next are based on superficial associations and which is undisciplined by self-criticism. Acute and chronic forms are described and the illness is regarded as being a phase of MANIC-DEPRESSIVE PSYCHOSIS. The few psycho-analytical studies made of mania suggest that its PSYCHOPATHOLOGY is the reverse of that of DEPRESSION and that the elation is due to a sense of triumph at having overcome the SUPER-EGO (INTERNAL OBJECTS), whose imagined hostility is responsible for the depression of the DEPRESSIVE phase of the psychosis. See Abraham (1927), Lewin (1951).

MANIC DEFENCE Form of defensive behaviour (see also DEFENCE) exhibited by persons who defend themselves against ANXIETY, GUILT, and DEPRESSION by (a) DENIAL of the guilt anxiety and depression; (b) the operation of a PHANTASY of OMNIPOTENT control, by means of which they imagine themselves to be in control of all situations which might provoke anxiety or feelings of helplessness; (c) IDENTIFICATION with objects from whom a sense of power can be borrowed; and (d) PROJECTION of 'BAD' aspects of the self on to others. Manic defences purchase freedom from guilt and anxiety at the expense of depth of character and appreciation of the motives and feelings of others.

Use of the manic defence is not confined to persons liable to develop MANIA or a MANIC-DEPRESSIVE PSYCHOSIS. The concept belongs to OBJECT THEORY. According to Fairbairn it is an emergency defence brought into operation when the non-specific TECHNIQUES (PARANOID, OBSESSIONAL, HYSTERICAL, and PHOBIC) have failed to protect the EGO against the onset of a depressive state (see FAIRBAIRN'S REVISED PSYCHOPATHOLOGY).

MANIC-DEPRESSIVE PSYCHOSIS PSYCHOSIS in which periods of MANIA and DEPRESSION alternate. According to Kraepelin, the major mental illnesses could be divided into two groups, DEMENTIA PRAECOX and manic-depressive psychosis, the latter being a cyclical illness in which the patient suffers a series of attacks of ELATION and depression with intervening normal intervals. The concept is descriptive and prognostic (see PROGNOSIS) and has no psychopathological implications (see PSYCHOPATHOLOGY). Contemporary psychiatry tends to prefer AFFECTIVE PSYCHOSIS or affective disorder, terms which exclude the implication of an in-built cycle of moods.

MANIFEST AND LATENT The *manifest content* of a DREAM

is the dream as reported by the dreamer; the *latent content* is its meaning as revealed by interpretation. Freud seems to have believed that dreams have, as it were, an original text, the publication of which encounters CENSORSHIP so that the dream has to be redrafted in a form that the censor cannot understand. The original draft is the latent content, the redrafting is the DREAM-WORK, and the final, published draft is the manifest content. The distinction between manifest and latent can also be applied to a SYMPTOM and its unconscious MEANING. The distinction between manifest and latent homosexuality is, however, anomalous; *manifest homosexuality* refers to overt HOMOSEXUAL behaviour, *latent homosexuality* refers to submissive attitudes adopted by neurotic men towards men imagined to be more powerful than themselves (see SUBMISSION). Since manifest homosexual behaviour is regarded as defensive (see DEFENCE), its latent equivalent is not homosexuality but fear of either men or women. Since latent homosexuality describes a form of behaviour it cannot be latent. What has happened is that a hypothesis about the cause of submissiveness, viz. that it is a manifestation of latent (i.e. unconscious) homosexuality, has been introduced into its description.

MASCULINE, MASCULINITY Referring to patterns of behaviour, attitudes, etc., presumed to be psychological secondary sexual characteristics (see SEX) of the male. CLASSICAL THEORY tends to assume that masculinity has an inherent connexion with activity, aggressiveness (see AGGRESSION), SADISM, and competitiveness; and further that all these propensities are related to sex; e.g. aggressiveness and competitiveness are related to the OEDIPUS COMPLEX rather than to a non-sexual instinct such as TERRITORIALITY. The question as to what forms of behaviour and what mental characteristics are innately masculine is bedevilled by (a) the assumption that all characteristics must be either masculine or feminine; (b) the absence of human societies in which any individual comes to MATURITY without being influenced by social STEREOTYPES; and (c) the absence of any neutral neuters to view the issue without bias. See ACTIVE AND PASSIVE; FEMININE; BISEXUAL.

MASCULINE PROTEST ADLERIAN term for reactive behaviour in women who feel they are members of an inferior sex. See ENVY; PENIS ENVY.

MASOCHISM **1.** Sexual PERVERSION in which the subject claims to get erotic pleasure from having pain inflicted upon himself. **2.** Character-trait presented by persons who bring ill-treatment, humiliation, and suffering upon themselves. **3.** *Moral masochism*: term used by Freud to describe the tendency to submit to one's own sadistic SUPER-EGO (see SADISM). The concept hinges on the idea that the super-ego derives its moral force from instinctual aggressive ENERGY (see also INSTINCT and AGGRESSION) which is discharged by 'taking it out on' the EGO. Masochism is either a real or an apparent exception to the PLEASURE-PRINCIPLE. It tends to be explained in terms of either (a) REVERSAL of sadism; (b) IDENTIFICATION with the sadistic partner; (c) alleviation of GUILT by experiencing punishment and pain simultaneously with pleasure; (d) eroticization of a submissive role (see EROTIC and SUBMISSION) originally adopted to appease authority figures; and (e) the DEATH INSTINCT.

CLASSICAL THEORY assumes an intrinsic connexion between masochism, passivity (see PASSIVE), and FEMININITY. In doing so it confuses abandoning oneself to the WILL of another with experiencing pain.

MASTURBATION Although the word literally means genital excitement, it is only used to refer to self-induced genital excitement. Hence:

Masturbation phantasy The imaginative activity accompanying masturbation.

Infantile masturbation Masturbation occurring in childhood.

Masturbation equivalent or substitute Activity inferred to be an equivalent or substitute for masturbation.

MATERIAL Analysts often refer to material brought by patients. This means their utterances. The usage derives from the fact that what the patient says is used by the analyst as evidence on which to base INTERPRETATIONS. As a result a patient can be thought of as producing material for the analyst to interpret, ORAL material being evidence making possible interpretations at the oral level, etc. Although this elision of the notions of utterance and evidence is convenient and natural, it also encourages the tendency of analysts to think of their work as inspection of some*thing* rather than as COMMUNICATION with some*one*.

MATURE AND IMMATURE Although these tend to be words of praise or abuse, they have in biology precise meanings. A mature individual (organism) is one in whom DEVELOPMENT is complete; an immature individual is one in whom it is incomplete: a child is immature and a grown-up is mature. When applied to psychological processes and behaviour, their use seems always to imply comparison with NORMS, the origins of which are unclear; to label someone immature implies that one knows what sort of behaviour is appropriate to his age and that he is in fact behaving in a way appropriate to someone younger.

MEANING Although psychoanalysis is usually presented as a CAUSAL theory which explains psychological phenomena as the consequences of prior events, a number of analysts, notably Szasz (1961), Home (1966), Rycroft (1966), have recently argued that it (or some aspects of it) is really a theory of meaning, and that Freud's crucial observation that HYSTERICAL symptoms were psychogenic was really the discovery that they have meaning, i.e. that they could be interpreted as gestures and COMMUNICATIONS. Advocates of this view argue that theories of causality are only applicable to the world of inanimate objects and that Freud's attempt to apply deterministic principles derived from the physical sciences to human behaviour fails to take account of the fact that man is a living AGENT capable of making decisions and choices and of being creative (see CREATIVITY). They also hold (a) that Freud was misguided in supposing that his discovery of UNCONSCIOUS mental processes and of the 'PRIMARY PROCESSESS' governing them proved that mental life demonstrated the principle of psychic DETERMINISM; and (b) that in so supposing he involved psychoanalysis in a contradiction, viz. that of maintaining both that CONSCIOUS processes are determined by unconscious ones and that making unconscious processes conscious increased the individual's freedom of choice and action. In some aspects of his work Freud clearly realized that he was concerned with meanings and not causes. He entitled his most famous book *The Interpretation of Dreams*, not the 'Cause of Dreams', and his chapter on symptoms in his *Introductory Lectures* is 'The Sense of Symptoms'.

MELANCHOLIA Obsolescent term for what is now called DEPRESSION (particularly ENDOGENOUS depression), DEPRESSIVE illness, or the depressive phase of MANIC-DEPRESSIVE PSYCHOSIS. When *melancholic* qualifies depression, the implication is that the patient is not simply in low spirits but is also retarded, suicidal, and self-reproachful (self-accusatory); (see RETARDATION; SUICIDE; SELF-REPROACHES).

MEMORY Memory fulfils the biological function of enabling organisms to respond to present circumstances in the light of past experience and thereby to replace simple, automatic, 'instinctual' reactions by complex, selective, learned responses. Freud's theory of memory is in reality a theory of FORGETTING. It assumes that all experiences, or at least all significant experiences, are recorded, but that some cease to be available to CONSCIOUSNESS as a result of REPRESSION, this mechanism being activated by the need to diminish ANXIETY. Although this theory explains those instances of forgetting that can be demonstrated to be related to neurotic CONFLICT, other factors presumably contribute to the fact that AMNESIA for infancy and very early childhood is universal and is not decreased by even the 'deepest' analysis.

MENARCHE The onset of menstruation in puberty.

MENTAL ILLNESS This term embraces the PSYCHOSES, the PSYCHONEUROSES, and the BEHAVIOUR DISORDERS, three clinical entities which differ in kind. Some at least of the psychoses are illnesses similar in kind to physical illnesses; they have demonstrable physical CAUSES which explain the SYMPTOMS without reference to either the patient's personality or to any motives which he might have for wishing to be ill. The neuroses resemble physical illnesses in that they have symptoms of which the patient complains, but they are inexplicable without reference to the patient's personality and motives, i.e. they are creations of the patient himself and not simply the effects of causes operating on him. The behaviour disorders are conditions in which there are no symptoms in the sense of phenomena of which the 'patient' himself complains; it is society not the patient who objects to the disordered behaviour. The idea that the neuroses – and, *a fortiori*, the behaviour disorders – are illnesses is a useful social fiction since it enables neurotic phenomena to be dealt with therapeutically, but it is based on a confusion of thought, viz. the equation of unconscious motives with causes. See Szasz (1961), Home (1966), Rycroft (1966).

METAPSYCHOLOGY   Term invented by Freud to describe what other sciences call 'general theory', i.e. statements at the highest level of abstraction. Metapsychological formulations describe mental phenomena in terms of the fictive PSYCHIC APPARATUS (see FICTION) and ideally contain references to the TOPOGRAPHICAL, DYNAMIC, and ECONOMIC aspects of the phenomenon in question; the topographical referring to its location within the psychic apparatus, i.e. whether in the ID, EGO, or SUPER-EGO, the dynamic to the INSTINCTS involved, and the economic to the distribution of ENERGY within the apparatus. Metapsychology is part of CLASSICAL THEORY and is not used by OBJECT-THEORISTS.

MIGRAINE   Correctly, severe one-sided headache with *photophobia* (painful sensitivity to light) and *castellations* (visual images resembling the battlements of a castle).

MIND   In Strachey's translation of Freud, 'mind' translates '*Seele*' and 'psyche' translates '*Psyche*'. The two terms are, however, synonymous, as are also 'psychical' and 'mental'. As Brierley has pointed out, psychoanalysis regards mind as a process and not a thing, despite Freud's habit of relating mental phenomena to a PSYCHICAL APPARATUS. 'The general theory of psycho-analysis, in its most abstract definition, is a psychology of mental processes and their organization. For such a psychology, mind has ceased to be a static structure or a substantial thing and has become a dynamic entity, a nexus of activities and a sequence of adaptive responses' – Brierley (1951). Psychoanalysis also regards mind (mental processes) as being in some way intrinsically connected with body (bodily processes). Despite conforming to the linguistic conventions which compel one to talk of a body and a mind which are different and yet interact, it contains a number of concepts which tie its psychology to physiology and biology. Among these are INSTINCT, ID, UNCONSCIOUS, AFFECT, sexuality (see SEX), EROTOGENIC ZONES, and SYMBOLISM.

MNEME   MEMORY. Hence *mnemic image*, the psychological equivalent of a memory-trace.

MODEL   When analysts talk of constructing models, they are

referring to the formulation of a system of concepts which can be expressed diagrammatically. The classic example of a psycho-analytical model is Freud's PSYCHIC APPARATUS, in which the relations between the ID, EGO, SUPER-EGO, and the ENVIRONMENT are represented topographically (see TOPOGRAPHICAL). The danger of models is that they may be taken too seriously; the fact that mental activity and conflict *can* be conceived of in terms of a visible diagram, parts of which are labelled id, ego, and super-ego, leads all too readily to the conviction that there really are things called the id, ego, and super-ego. See REIFICATION.

MOOD   Psychiatry only recognizes two moods – ELATION and DEPRESSION. Disturbances of mood characterize the AFFECTIVE DISORDERS. See MANIA; MANIC-DEPRESSIVE PSYCHOSIS.

MORTIDO   Term coined by Federn (1936) to describe a form of ENERGY belonging to the DEATH INSTINCT and analogous to LIBIDO. Although such a concept is logically necessary for analysts who believe in the LIFE and death instincts, no one, not even Federn himself, has had the nerve to work out the implications of conceiving of a PSYCHIC APPARATUS in which two opposed instincts are simultaneously at work, and two different forms of energy circulate.

MOTHER   Since psychoanalytical theory is formulated in terms of what anthropologists call the *nuclear family*, consisting of father, mother, and children, it assumes that the person who mothers a child and the person who gave it birth are identical. Hence formulations about mothering are stated in terms of 'the relationship to the mother', the real-life complications arising from the contributions of grandmothers, aunts, nurses, elder sisters, and *au pair* girls being dealt with, if at all, by calling them 'mother-figures'. Even fathers may on occasion be mother-figures.

According to most formulations, the mother is the central person in the child's life throughout the PRE-OEDIPAL phases of DEVELOPMENT, though Melanie Klein (see under KLEINIAN) dates the onset of the OEDIPUS COMPLEX in the first year of life, i.e. during what CLASSICAL THEORY holds to be the ORAL PHASE. Again accord-ing to most, but not all, formulations, the mother is a NEED-SATIS-FYING or PART OBJECT during the first few months of life, i.e. she is 'loved' solely for her capacity to provide SATISFACTION and only later does she become a WHOLE OBJECT, whose own personality and needs are in any way recognized by the infant. The phrases '*the good mother*' (see also GOOD), '*the bad mother*' (see also BAD), '*the ideal mother*', and '*the persecuting mother*' all refer to conceptions of the mother existing in the infant's mind formed by SPLITTING of the mother image. The *phallic mother* (see PHALLIC WOMAN) is also, strictly speaking, a conception in the infant's mind, though the term is sometimes also applied to women whose personality encourages such a conception. '*The rejecting mother*' and '*over-protective*' and *schizophrenogenic mothers* are actual mothers, so described by psychiatrists and analysts who attribute to them pathogenic effects on their offspring (see entries under OVER- and SCHIZOPHRENOGENIC). The *ordinary devoted mother* is Winnicott's (1958) term for the mother who provides her child with mothering adequate for his development and who is capable of *primary maternal preoccupation*. For the effects of maternal deprivation and of separation from the mother, see DEPRIVATION; SEPARATION, MOTHER–CHILD.

MOTIVE That which drives a person towards an end or goal. The concept does not distinguish between 'internal' factors, such as instincts, and 'external' ones, such as incentives. See WILL.

MOURNING 'The psychological processes that are set in train by the loss of a loved object and that commonly lead to relinquishing of the object' – Bowlby (1942). It follows bereavement, is accompanied by GRIEF, and may or may not be followed by attachment to a new object; it is typically accompanied by (a degree of) IDENTIFICATION with the lost object. Although terminologies differ, mourning seems to be divisible into three stages: (a) That of protest or DENIAL, in which the subject attempts to reject the idea that the loss has occurred, feels incredulous, and experiences anger, reproaching himself, the dead person, or his medical attendants for having allowed the loss to occur. Darwin called this stage 'frantic grief'. (b) That of resignation, acceptance, or despair, in which the reality of the loss is admitted and SORROW supervenes. (c) That of detachment in which the subject relinquishes the object, weans himself from it, and adapts himself to life without it. If mourning occurs 'normally', the subject 'gets over' the loss and becomes capable of reattaching himself to a new object.

All schools of psychoanalysis regard mourning as the normal analogue of DEPRESSION, the loss in depression being not that of an actual person but of an ambivalently invested 'INTERNAL OBJECT' (see also AMBIVALENCE). See Freud (1917), Abraham (1927). According to Bowlby (1951, 1961), infants and children react to separation from their mothers by mourning processes which predispose to psychiatric illness in later life.

MUSCLE EROTISM   Pleasure in bodily activity.

N

NARCISSISM   1. Sexual PERVERSION in which the subject's preferred object is his own body (first used in this sense by Havelock Ellis and Näcke). 2. By extension, any form of self-love.

CLASSICAL THEORY distinguishes between *primary narcissism*, the love of self which precedes loving others, and *secondary narcissism*, love of self which results from introjecting and identifying with an OBJECT (see also INTROJECTION and IDENTIFICATION). The latter is either a defensive activity or attitude (see DEFENCE), since it enables the subject to deny (see DENIAL) that he has lost the introjected object, or part of the developmental process (see DEVELOPMENT). A major difficulty of the concept is that, on the one hand, the word 'narcissism' has inescapable disparaging overtones, while, on the other hand, it is used as a technical term to categorize all forms of investment of ENERGY (LIBIDO) in the SELF. Hence the not infrequent references to 'healthy narcissism' to distinguish proper self-respect from 'over-valuation of the ego'.

Narcissistic object-choice is based on the object's similarity to the subject. A *narcissistic wound* is an injury to self-esteem. A *narcissistic neurosis* is one in which the patient is incapable of forming a TRANSFERENCE. *Narcissistic supplies* are indications of affection, flattery, praise, etc., which enhance self-esteem. Narcissism also on occasion means egocentrism or SOLIPSISM, i.e. it can refer to the tendency to use oneself as the point of reference round which experience is organized. In this sense the discovery that one is not the only pebble on the beach and that the world was not constructed solely for one's own benefit involves a loss of narcissism.

See AUTO-EROTIC.

NARCO-ANALYSIS   Form of PSYCHOTHERAPY in which the patient receives INTERPRETATION while under the influence of a hypnotic drug (see HYPNOTISM).

NEED-SATISFYING OBJECT   OBJECT which is 'loved' solely for its capacity to satisfy instinctual needs without cognizance being taken of *its* needs or personality.

NEGATION   Process by which a PERCEPTION or thought is admitted to CONSCIOUSNESS in negative form, e.g. the onset of a headache is registered by the thought, 'How lucky I am to have been free from headaches for so long'; the fact that a figure in a dream stands for the mother is admitted by the statement, 'It wasn't my mother anyhow.' (The point here is that none the less the idea that it might be the mother must have occurred for it to be denied.) Not to be confused with DENIAL; NEGATIVISM.

NEGATIVE   Often used as synonym for 'hostile', but see below.

NEGATIVE OEDIPUS COMPLEX   Form of OEDIPUS COMPLEX in which the subject wishes to possess the parent of its own sex and regards that of the opposite sex as its rival.

NEGATIVE THERAPEUTIC REACTION   Technical term for a fortunately rare hazard of psychoanalytical treatment, viz. exacerbation of the patient's symptoms in response to precisely those INTERPRETATIONS which are expected to alleviate them. Although the phenomenon has been used as evidence in favour of the existence of primary MASOCHISM, it is more usually explained in terms of GUILT provoked by the prospect of health achieved at the expense of someone else.

NEGATIVISM   Counter-suggestibility; cussedness; rejection of overtures of help. Attitude displayed by patients who have a compulsion to oppose their WILL to that of others, even to the extent of 'cutting off their nose to spite their face', and who react to the prospect of therapeutic change as though it would be a defeat. It is not synonymous with NEGATIVE THERAPEUTIC REACTION.

NEO-FREUDIAN   Term used to describe a number of American writers who attempted to restate Freudian theory in sociological terms and to eliminate its connexions with biology. Karen Horney, Erich Fromm, and Harry Stack Sullivan are the best-known neo-Freudians. Horney and Fromm were and are concerned with the relations of personality and individual development to social structure. Sullivan was concerned with the role of INTERPERSONAL relations in determining behaviour and personality and could be classified as an object theorist (see OBJECT THEORY). See Brown (1961).

NEURALGIA   Pain due, usually, to inflammation in a nerve.

NEURASTHENIA   1. Obsolescent medical and psychiatric term for a state of excessive fatiguability and lack of vigour once supposed to be due to exhaustion or malnutrition of the nerves. 2. In Freud's writings, one of the ACTUAL NEUROSES.

NEURITIS   Inflammation of a nerve.

NEUROLOGY   That branch of medicine concerned with disorders of the nervous system. Freud was a neurologist before he became a psychoanalyst and many psychoanalytical concepts derive from neurology, notably IMPULSE, INHIBITION, DISCHARGE, and CATHEXIS – the last being a transposition of the idea that neural activity consists in the movement of QUANTA of ENERGY from one NEURONE (nerve-cell) to another into the field of psychology, so that 'ideas', 'mental REPRESENTATIONS', 'images' are treated as the unit structures (neurones) of a PSYCHIC APPARATUS analogous to the nervous system. See Freud's *Project for a Scientific Psychology* (1895) for his attempt to base a psychology directly on the movement of energy from neurone to neurone. The *Project* was never published in Freud's lifetime and is now only of interest in showing to what extent psychoanalysis developed out of neurology.

NEURONE   A nerve-cell, the basic structural unit of the central nervous system, consisting of a cell-body and processes along which IMPULSES pass.

NEUROPSYCHIATRY   That branch of medicine concerned

with the treatment of nervous and psychological disorders. A *neuropsychiatrist* is at home both in NEUROLOGY and PSYCHIATRY and is primarily interested in the interrelations of the two disciplines.

NEUROSIS This term, which dates from the second half of the eighteenth century, originally meant a disease of the nerves. Then later, in the nineteenth century, it was used to describe 'functional disorders', i.e. diseases believed to be due to functional disturbances of the nervous system which were unaccompanied by structural changes. Since Freud's discovery that one of the neuroses, HYSTERIA, was a disorder of the personality and not of the nerves, it has been used to describe precisely those mental disorders which are *not* diseases of the nervous system. CLASSICAL THEORY distinguishes the following types of neurosis:

Psychoneurosis Due to past causes and explicable only in terms of the patient's personality and life history. There are three types of PSYCHONEUROSIS: CONVERSION-HYSTERIA, ANXIETY-HYSTERIA (PHOBIA), and OBSESSIONAL NEUROSIS.

Actual neurosis Due to present causes and explicable in terms of the patient's sexual habits (see also entry under ACTUAL NEUROSIS).

Traumatic neurosis Due to shock (see also entry under TRAUMATIC NEUROSIS).

Narcissistic neurosis Neurosis in which the patient is incapable of forming a TRANSFERENCE (see also entry under NARCISSISM).

Character neurosis In which the 'SYMPTOMS' are CHARACTER traits.

Organ neurosis A rarely used term for a PSYCHOSOMATIC illness (see also entry under ORGAN NEUROSIS).

Infantile neurosis Neurosis in childhood (see also INFANTILE). Classical theory assumes that all neuroses in adult life have been preceded by one in childhood.

A *transference-neurosis* is either a neurosis in which the patient is capable of TRANSFERENCE, or the obsessive interest in the analyst which develops during the course of psychoanalytical treatment.

An *anxiety neurosis* is either any neurosis in which ANXIETY is the major symptom or one of the actual neuroses (see also entry under ANXIETY NEUROSIS).

NEUROTIC **1.** Adj. from NEUROSIS. According to context, it is used to assert that the phenomenon so qualified is not HEALTHY (NORMAL), not ORGANIC (physical), not PSYCHOTIC, and is capable of psychological explanation. **2.** Popularly: 'nervy', 'anxious', 'tense', 'highly-strung', with the implication that the state referred to has a psychological explanation.

NEUTRALIZATION The process by which infantile sexual and aggressive IMPULSES (see SEX and AGGRESSION, ENERGIES, are desexualized and deaggressified (see DESEXUALIZATION and DE-AGGRESSIFICATION) and lose their INFANTILE quality. Sublimated activities (see SUBLIMATION) and AUTONOMOUS FUNCTIONS OF THE EGO use *neutralized energy*. The concept belongs to EGO-PSYCHOLOGY. See Hartmann (1958).

NEW BEGINNING Term used by M. Balint to describe the start of the process of recovery occurring in patients whose cure necessitates a REGRESSION to extreme DEPENDENCE on the analyst. It corresponds to what Winnicott (1958) calls emergence of the true self (see TRUE AND FALSE). See BASIC FAULT.

NIGHTMARE **1.** A DREAM of being sat upon and in danger of being suffocated by a female monster. **2.** The female monster herself; an incubus. **3.** Loosely: any terrifying dream. Nightmares are an example of gross failure of DEFENCE against internal forces, and as a result of this failure, the dreamer experiences terror rather than ANXIETY. Nightmares are commoner in childhood than in adult life. The suffocating monster is a good example of a BAD internal OBJECT (see also OBJECT, BAD; OBJECT, INTERNAL), since it is a mental REPRESENTATION, a phantom (a PHANTASY image), which the dreamer's EGO responds to as though it were a person. See Jones (1931), Rycroft (1968).

NORM, NORMAL, AND ABNORMAL A norm is that member of a class by comparison with which other members are described. In medicine, psychoanalysis, psychology, and sociology there is a tendency to use as the norm some ideal member of the class and to designate as abnormal any member who deviates appreciably from this norm. In medicine, the norm is 'health' and signs and symptoms are abnormal (hence the medical abbreviation 'N.A.D.' – nothing abnormal detected). Behaviour is designated abnormal by psychologists, sociologists, and psychoanalysts if it deviates from the behaviour considered normal by either the society in which the subject lives, or by the theory to which the scientist subscribes. For instance, HOMOSEXUAL behaviour may be described as abnormal either because society considers HETERO-SEXUALITY the norm or because theory regards it as a PERVERSION of DEVELOPMENT. In the former case, 'abnormal' means 'socially deviant', in the latter 'unhealthy'. Workers who accept society's values are tempted to confuse these two conceptions of normality and to regard as 'unhealthy' all behaviour which is deviant and to equate 'health' with conformity and adjustment. The links between psychoanalysis and biology compel psychoanalysts to define normality in terms of HEALTH (i.e. in terms of INTEGRATION and freedom from CONFLICT), and not in terms of successful adjustment to any particular society. See NEO-FREUDIAN.

NUCLEUS 'Central part or thing around which others are collected'; 'beginning meant to receive additions' – both *C.O.D.* According to Glover (1939), the EGO begins as a number of discrete nuclei which fuse during DEVELOPMENT, i.e. subjectively: experience of the SELF is at first fragmentary and discontinuous, islands of self-awareness only gradually becoming fused to form a continuous sense of IDENTITY; and objectively: integrated behaviour patterns are at first partial and only gradually fuse to form an integrated person. This idea belongs to CLASSICAL THEORY and EGO PSYCHOLOGY and is, apparently at least, in striking contrast to OBJECT-THEORY's assumption of an original unitary ego liable to fragmentation. See also FAIRBAIRN'S REVISED PSYCHO-PATHOLOGY.

The rarely encountered *nuclear complex* refers to the constellation of ideas and feelings relating to the parents and originating in childhood, which form the kernel of the subject's PSYCHO-PATHOLOGY. See OEDIPUS COMPLEX.

O

OBJECT   N. That towards which action or desire is directed; that which the SUBJECT requires in order to achieve instinctual SATISFACTION; that to which the subject relates himself. In psycho-analytical writings, objects are nearly always persons, parts of persons, or SYMBOLS of one or the other. This terminology confuses readers who are more familiar with 'object' in the sense of a 'thing', i.e. that which is not a person. Hence:

Object, bad   An object whom the subject hates or fears, who is experienced as malevolent. A BAD object may be either an internal or an external object (see below).

Object-cathexis   Investment of ENERGY in an external object, in contrast to its investment in the self (narcissistic CATHEXIS, see also NARCISSISM).

Object-choice   Narcissistic object-choice is based on IDENTIFICATION with an object similar to the subject. *Anaclitic object-choice* is based on the object's difference from the subject (see also ANACLITIC).

Object-constancy   The ability to maintain a lasting relationship with a specific, single object; or, inversely, the tendency to reject substitutes for a familiar object, e.g. an infant who displays object-constancy rejects mothering from anyone other than his MOTHER and misses her specifically when she is absent.

Object, external   An object recognized by the subject as being external to himself; in contrast to an internal object (see above).

Object, good   An object whom the subject loves, who is experienced as benevolent. A good object may be either INTERNAL or EXTERNAL.

Object, internal   OBJECT-REPRESENTATION which has acquired the significance of an external object (see above). Internal objects are phantoms, i.e. they are images occurring in PHANTASIES which are reacted to as 'REAL'. They are derived from external objects by

INTROJECTION and are conceived to be located in internal (psychical) reality.

Object-libido   LIBIDO which is invested in objects, as opposed to *narcissistic libido* which is invested in the self.

Object-loss   The loss of, usually, a good external object. The event which precedes introjection and/or MOURNING.

Object-love   Love of an object which is recognized as a person other than oneself, in contrast to SELF-LOVE and IDENTIFICATION. And *love-object*: an object who is loved, who is the object of object-love.

Object, need-satisfying   An object whom the subject 'loves' solely on account of its capacity to satisfy needs and whom the subject fails to recognize as a person. The term is only used when discussing the nature of an infant's attachment to its *mother*.

Object, part   An object which is part of a person, e.g. a PENIS or a BREAST. The distinction between whole and part object is sometimes used to make what would at first sight appear to be a very different distinction, that between recognizing an object as a person whose feelings and needs are as important as one's own and treating an object as existing solely to satisfy one's own needs. See whole object (below) and need-satisfying object (above).

Object-relations(hip)   The relation of the subject to his object, *not* the relation between the subject and the object which is an *interpersonal* relationship. This is because psychoanalysis is a psychology of the individual and therefore discusses objects and relationships only from the point of view of a single subject. An object-relationship may be either an external or an internal object (see above).

Object (relations) theory   Psychoanalytical theory in which the subject's need to relate to objects occupies the central position; in contrast to INSTINCT THEORY, which centres round the subject's need to reduce instinctual TENSION.

Object-representation   The mental *representation* of an object. Strictly speaking, all ECONOMIC concepts, e.g. object-CATHEXIS, object-LIBIDO, refer to the mental representations of objects and not to objects themselves; otherwise one would have to envisage the possibility of mental *energy* being attached to STRUCTURES outside the PSYCHIC APPARATUS and even perhaps the possibility of energy passing from one apparatus to another. See INTERNALIZA-TION.

Object, transitional Object which the subject treats as being half-way between himself and another person, typically a doll or piece of cloth which a child treasures and uses as a comforter but which does not have to be treated with the consideration appropriate to a person. The concept is Winnicott's (1958), who regards such objects as helping children to make the transition from INFANTILE narcissism to object-love and from DEPENDENCE to self-reliance.

Object, whole An object whom the subject recognizes as being a person with similar rights, feelings, needs, etc., as himself.

OBJECTIVE AND SUBJECTIVE 'Are terms of philosophy and physiology distinguishing concepts and sensations that have an external cause from those which arise only in the mind' – Fowler (1965). Hence physical pain is an objective phenomenon, dreams and hallucinations are subjective. Psychoanalysis is largely concerned with the interconnexion between objective and subjective phenomena and is sometimes described as a mixed psychology on the grounds that it takes cognizance of both types of phenomenon and uses concepts derived both from observation of behaviour and from introspection (either by the observer, i.e. the analyst, or by the subject, i.e. the patient). In this it differs sharply from behaviourism, which attempts to construct a psychology without reference to CONSCIOUSNESS, and less sharply from PHENOMENOLOGY which is concerned solely with how the subject experiences himself and his relation to the external world. The fact that psychoanalysis uses subjective data is used as the starting-point of criticisms of it on the grounds that it is unscientific. This criticism only holds if one defines SCIENCE in a way that only applies to the natural sciences and excludes the moral sciences such as linguistics, SEMANTICS, sociology, and anthropology. See Eysenck (1965), Szasz (1961), Rycroft (1966). See also CAUSALITY; MEANING; BEHAVIOUR THERAPY; SUBJECT AND OBJECT.

OBSESSION When used as a technical term: an idea or group of ideas which persistently obtrudes itself on the patient's CON-SCIOUSNESS despite his WILL and despite the fact that he himself recognizes its abnormality. Obsessions (syn. obsessive or COM-

PULSIVE ideas) are the major symptom of OBSESSIONAL NEUROSIS.

OBSESSIONAL CHARACTER   A person whose personality contains traits which can be interpreted as equivalent to an OBSESSIONAL NEUROSIS; who uses OBSESSIONAL DEFENCES but does not have obsessional symptoms. Conscientiousness, tidiness, meanness, pedantry, rationality combined with cluelessness about human emotions, respect for the letter rather than the spirit of the law and for red tape rather than creative achievement are all liable to be called obsessional character-traits. The common feature of these is that control is valued more highly than expressiveness. The justification for calling them obsessional derives from the theoretical inference that ANXIETY about losing control lies at the back of them. See ANAL CHARACTER.

OBSESSIONAL DEFENCES   This term embraces REACTION-FORMATION, ISOLATION, and UNDOING, defences which have in common their tendency to keep the EGO uncontaminated by instinctual forces (see INSTINCT). See DEFENCE.

OBSESSIONAL NEUROSIS   Form of PSYCHONEUROSIS of which the predominant symptoms are *obsessive thoughts* and *compulsive behaviour* (*obsessional rituals*, see also RITUAL). Obsessional thoughts differ from 'normal' thoughts in that they are experienced by the patient himself as unspontaneous, distracting, repetitive, ruminative, and as coming from elsewhere than himself; their subject-matter is typically absurd, bizarre, irrelevant, and obscene. Compulsive behaviour is repetitive, stereotyped, ritualistic, and superstitious.

According to CLASSICAL THEORY, the PSYCHOPATHOLOGY of obsessional neurosis centres round REGRESSION to the ANAL-SADISTIC stage and AMBIVALENCE towards parental figures and their INTROJECTS. More recent formulations centre round the high degree of INTERNALIZATION and the need to control all IMPULSES, the symptoms constituting failures to achieve control, i.e. they are examples of 'return of the repressed' (see under REPRESSION). It can also be regarded as a disorder occurring in persons whose personality development has been based on ALIENATION from INSTINCT and EMOTION, the obsessional EGO being anti-libidinal, anti-impulsive, anti-emotional, etc., and the symptoms being either breakthroughs from the alienated aspects of the self (obsessional thoughts) or DEFENCES against such breakthroughs (obsessional rituals).

Obsessional neurosis has occupied an important place in the history of psychoanalysis since Freud's *The Ego and the Id* (1923), in which he first described the personality as a tripartite structure consisting of an ID, EGO, and SUPER-EGO, and his *Inhibitions, Symptoms and Anxiety* (1926), in which he first described SIGNAL ANXIETY, were both written with obsessional neurosis in mind. 'Obsessional neurosis is unquestionably the most interesting and repaying subject of analytic research,' he wrote in the latter.

OBSESSIONAL TECHNIQUE   One of the four TECHNIQUES described by Fairbairn in his *A Revised Psychopathology of the Psychoses and Psychoneuroses* (see FAIRBAIRN'S REVISED PSYCHO-PATHOLOGY). These techniques are used by the subject to effect the transition from INFANTILE to mature DEPENDENCE. According to Fairbairn, the infant constructs two images of the MOTHER (BREAST) on whom he is originally dependent, one being that of her as a GOOD, satisfying OBJECT, the other that of her as a BAD, frustrating object, and the four techniques differ in *where* the subject locates these two objects. In the obsessional technique, he locates both inside himself – in Fairbairn's terminology he *internalizes* both the accepted and the rejected object (see INTERNALIZATION) – identifying with the good object (see IDENTIFICATION) but regarding the other as an alien 'content' within him which he must control. As a result, the subject achieves 'QUASI-INDEPENDENCE' from the mother based on identification with her, but only reaches the stage of 'mature dependence' if identification with her is replaced by a relationship to her – or rather some adult, 'genital' equivalent. Since this technique, like the other three, can be regarded as a DEFENCE against SEPARATION-ANXIETY, it tends to be called *the obsessional defence*, though it is clear from Fairbairn's own text that he regarded it as a normal developmental process. See Fairbairn (1952).

See GENITALITY; INSTINCT THEORY AND OBJECT THEORY.

OBSESSIONAL THINKING   This term refers *not* to obsessional thoughts (see above) but to a form of thinking displayed typically by OBSESSIONAL CHARACTERS and accepted by them as a valid form of mental activity. Its function is to reconcile ambivalent attitudes (see AMBIVALENCE), and it tends therefore to consist of highly abstract formulations designed to reconcile contradictions or of statements, typically linked by 'buts', which tend to cancel one another out. Alternatively, all assertions may be so qualified by references to exceptions, conditions, or hints as to the possibility of another and better formulation that the subject in fact avoids committing himself to them.

OCEANIC FEELING   Phrase used by Romain Rolland in a letter to Freud to describe the mystical, cosmic emotion which (according to Rolland) is the true source of religious sentiments (see RELIGION). Freud could not discover this feeling in himself. See Freud (1930), where he offers an interpretation of it, viz. that it is a regression 'to an early phase of EGO-feeling', and revives the experience of the infant at the BREAST before he has learnt to distinguish his ego from the external world.

OEDIPAL   See OEDIPUS COMPLEX.

OEDIPUS COMPLEX   Group of largely UNCONSCIOUS ideas and feelings centring round the wish to possess the parent of the opposite sex and eliminate that of the same sex. The complex emerges, according to CLASSICAL THEORY, during the *oedipal phase* of LIBIDINAL and EGO DEVELOPMENT, i.e. between the ages of three and five, though Oedipal manifestations may be present earlier – even, according to Melanie Klein (see KLEINIAN), during the first year of life. The complex is named after the mythical Oedipus, who killed his father and married his mother without knowing that they were his parents. According to Freud, the Oedipus complex is a universal phenomenon, built in phylogenetically (see PHYLOGENETIC), and is responsible for much unconscious GUILT. *Resolution of the Oedipus complex* is achieved typically by IDENTIFICATION with the parent of the same sex and (partial) temporary renunciation of the parent of the opposite sex, who is 'rediscovered' in his (her) adult sexual object. Persons who are fixated at the *Oedipal level* are *mother-fixated* or *father-fixated*, and reveal this by choosing sexual partners with obvious resemblances to their parent(s). Oedipal rivalry with the father is a cause of CASTRATION ANXIETY.

Freud first mentioned the Oedipus complex in a letter to his friend Fliess in 1897, and the idea arose out of the self-analysis which he conducted after the death of his father. Its first published appearance was in the *Interpretation of Dreams* (1900). It remained a cornerstone of psychoanalytical theory up to, say, 1930, but since then psychoanalysis has become increasingly mother-orientated and concerned with the *pre-oedipal relationship to the mother*, and the modern tendency is to regard the Oedipus complex as a psychic structure itself requiring interpretation in terms of earlier conflicts rather than as a primary source of neurosis itself. However, even the most enthusiastic supporters of psychopathological systems (see PSYCHOPATHOLOGY) centring round the MOTHER have to take account of the fact that children have two parents, that in our society at least they grow up in close proximity to both and are confronted with intimations of their sexual life together and their own exclusion from it.

OMNIPOTENCE   *Omnipotent phantasies* are PHANTASIES that the subject is omnipotent. *Omnipotence of thought* refers to the belief that thoughts can of themselves alter the external world. According to some accounts, all infants believe in the omnipotence of thought and learn by their experience of FRUSTRATION to accept the REALITY PRINCIPLE. According to others, it is a symptom of ALIENATION and the DISSOCIATION of phantasy from any contact with the external world. According to Freud (1912), belief in the omnipotence of thought underlies animism, MAGIC, religious practices (see RELIGION), and OBSESSIONAL NEUROSIS, the RITUALS of the latter two being attempts to *control* the omnipotence of, in the one case, God, in the other, the subject himself (i.e. of the alienated part of himself, see ALIENATION). Omnipotence of thought is also invoked as an explanation of the fact that wishes can arouse as much guilt as actions.

ONEIROMANCY   Divination by means of DREAMS; not to be confused with dream INTERPRETATION, which makes no claim to be predictive and uses the dream solely as evidence of the dreamer's state of mind. *Oneirology* is a rarely used word for the scientific study of dreams.

ONTOGENY AND PHYLOGENY   The former refers to the development of the individual, the latter to the development of the race or species. In biology the formulation 'ontogeny recapitulates phylogeny' is used to describe the fact that the general pattern of embryological development in the individual is only explicable in terms of the evolution of the species. The idea that this formula might also be applicable to human psychological development was responsible for Freud's incursions into anthropology and for his drawing parallels between infantile PHANTASIES (see also INFANTILE) and modes of thinking with those of primitive man. As Jones (1930) put it: '. . . when psycho-analytic methods are applied to data obtained from savage races and from mythology and archaeology, it becomes difficult to resist the conclusion that there is an extensive resemblance between the phantasies and mental peculiarities of our young children and what one must infer to have been characteristic of the race as a whole in primitive times; the ideas of cannibalism, of incest, and of father-murder are prominent among the many I am referring to. Freud himself views these conclusions, perhaps rather uncritically, in the Lamarckian manner.' The reference to LAMARCKIANISM is to Freud's belief that acquired characteristics could be inherited and that, therefore, modern man's neurotic sense of GUILT could be attributed to ancestral crimes committed in prehistoric times. See OMNIPO-TENCE; PARRICIDE; INCEST; TOTEM; PRIMAL HORDE.

ONTOLOGY The science or study of being. According to Rollo May (1967), the American existential analyst (see EXISTEN-TIALISM), man has four ontological characteristics: (a) 'he seeks to preserve some center'; (b) 'the human being's centeredness depends on his courage to affirm it', i.e. it is not automatically maintained as in plants and animals; (c) 'he has the need and possibility of going out from his centeredness to participate in other beings'; and (d) SELF-CONSCIOUSNESS, that development of the awareness possessed by animals which enables man to be aware that he is the being who has a centre, who affirms and who participates in other beings – and which enables him to use abstractions and SYMBOLS to transcend the immediate situation. Existentialist philosophers and analysts criticize Freudian psycho-analysis on the ground that it neglects ontology and that its pre-occupation with the past and with the UNCONSCIOUS has led to neglect of problems of CONSCIOUSNESS and self-consciousness. These criticisms are characteristically levelled at INSTINCT-THEORY and EGO-PSYCHOLOGY and not at OBJECT-THEORY. See May (1967), Sartre (1956), Laing (1967). See INSTINCT-THEORY AND OBJECT-THEORY; IDENTITY.

Hence: *Primary ontological security*, term used by Laing (1960) to describe the existential position of a person with a 'centrally firm sense of his own and other people's reality and identity'. According to Laing it is this that the psychotic basically lacks (see PSYCHOSIS).

OPTIMISM AND PESSIMISM   According to Frieda Goldman Eisler (1953), quoted by Carstairs in his 1963 Reith Lectures, optimism is significantly associated with prolonged breast-feeding and pessimism with early weaning. Clinically, optimism, in the sense of under-estimating obstacles, tends to be regarded as a manic trait (see MANIC-DEPRESSIVE PSYCHOSIS), and pessimism, in the sense of over-estimating obstacles, as a depressive trait (see DEPRESSION).

ORAL   Appertaining to the mouth. Hence:

Oral character   CHARACTER displayed by persons with FIXATIONS at the oral stage (see below). Typical oral character traits are OPTIMISM AND PESSIMISM, generosity, moodiness, DEPRESSION, ELATION, talkativeness, greed, and the tendency to engage in wishful thinking.

Oral erotism   Sensuous pleasure derived from the mouth.

Oral sadism   Pleasure in hurting by biting. Pleasure in PHANTASIES of biting and eating destructively (cannibalism). According to Abraham (1927), there is an oral-sadistic phase of INFANTILE LIBIDINAL DEVELOPMENT which follows dentition.

Oral stage   In CLASSICAL THEORY, the first stage of both LIBIDINAL DEVELOPMENT and EGO DEVELOPMENT, in which the mouth is the main source of pleasure and hence the centre of experience. According to Abraham, the oral stage can be divided into two sub-stages, those of *oral sucking* and *oral biting*. The stage begins at birth, though it is not clear whether it ends with weaning or at whatever age it would be natural for the infant to wish to be weaned. Persons who are fixated at the *oral level* not only tend to retain the mouth as their primary (usually unconscious) EROTOGENIC ZONE and to be MOTHER-fixated (BREAST-fixated) but also to be prone to manic and depressive MOOD-swings (see MANIC-DEPRESSIVE PSYCHOSIS and DEPRESSION) and to *identify* with others rather than to relate to them as others. The reason for this is that the unconscious DEPENDENCE on the breast is associated with survival of primary IDENTIFICATION with it, as a result of which satisfying experiences are reacted to as though they confirmed the

PHANTASY of fusion with the mother (manic swing) and disappointments are reacted to as though they were loss of the mother (depressive swing). See Abraham (1927) for the seminal papers on the oral stage and its importance in the PSYCHOPATHOLOGY of mania and depression. See Lewin (1951) for a more recent exposition of the effects of the oral stage.

For historical reasons, OBJECT THEORY still uses the term oral stage to refer to the time at which 'the breast' and 'the mother' are the infant's primary object.

ORAL TRIAD   Term used by Lewin (1946) for the conjoined wishes to be suckled by, SLEEP with, and be devoured by the BREAST, wishes which, in his view, underlie the PSYCHOPATHOLOGY of MANIA. See ELATION; DREAM SCREEN.

ORECTIC   Adj. of desire or appetite. Occasionally used as an antonym of *cognitive*.

ORGANIC   Either relating to an organism, to a living, dynamic structure, or, as in *organic illness, organic symptom, organic origin*, to the bodily as opposed to the psychological. This latter usage is, strictly speaking, medical and not psychoanalytical. In *organic psychosis*, the differentiation is from *functional psychosis* and refers to the fact that the PSYCHOSIS is the result of disease of the brain.

ORGAN NEUROSIS   Term used in CLASSICAL THEORY for what is now more usually called PSYCHOSOMATIC illness.

ORGASM   The culminating-point in sexual intercourse; the moment at which TENSION-AFFECTS are replaced by DISCHARGE-AFFECTS. See AFFECTS; FORE-PLEASURE; END-PLEASURE. The word is occasionally used to refer to an equivalent moment in PRE-GENITAL acts, hence *gastro-intestinal orgasm* for satiation of the ORAL instinct; and, by still further extension, *pharmacotoxic orgasm* (Rado, 1933) for the response to addictive drugs.

ORTHOPSYCHIATRY   School of psychiatry concerned with healthy development and disturbances thereof.

OVER-   Since many psychiatric symptoms are the occurrence at a high degree of either intensity or frequency of experiences common to mankind, the prefix 'over-' is frequently used to designate behaviour which is considered pathological solely on account of its excessive frequency or intensity. Hence the *over-anxiety* of

PHOBICS, the *over-conscientiousness* of OBSESSIONALS, the *over-protectiveness* of MOTHERS who overwhelm their children with smother-love, etc. The concept implies that it is possible to establish a normal level of ANXIETY, conscientiousness, etc.

OVER-DETERMINATION   A symptom, dream-image, or any other item of behaviour is said to be over-determined if it has more than one MEANING or expresses drives and conflicts derived from more than one level or aspect of the personality; or, alternatively, and perhaps preferably, if it provides a 'final common pathway' to a number of convergent tendencies. Since psychoanalysis assumes the presence of a residuum of wishes dating from the past and that the various stages of DEVELOPMENT are superimposed on one another in layers, all behaviour is regarded as over-determined in the sense that it is possible to interpret it as the result of simultaneous activity at several levels.

P

PAEDERASTY   Sodomy. See HOMOSEXUALITY.

PAEDOPHILIA   Lit., love of children, but in practice reserved for the tendency to commit sexual offences against them. No psychoanalytical studies of paedophilia exist, but the sociological evidence suggests (a) that it is only rarely associated with violence towards the victim, (b) that it is not a PERVERSION in the sense of being the subject's *preferred* form of sexual behaviour, and (c) that the 'victim' is not infrequently a willing one. See Mohr *et al* (1965).

PAIN   According to context, 'pain' refers *either* to the familiar physical sensation *or* to distress associated with instinctual TENSION, the latter being, according to the PLEASURE-PAIN PRINCIPLE, the condition which instinctual action attempts to relieve. In Freud's writings, physical pain is '*Schmerz*' and mental pain due to tension is '*Unlust*' which Strachey translates as 'UNPLEASURE'. Other translations, however, use 'pain' for both German words.

PARAMETER   Term borrowed from mathematics to describe

those aspects of psychoanalytical technique which can (arguably) be modified to meet the needs of particular classes of patients. Frequency of attendance, length of sessions, degree of management of, and interference in, the patient's life, insistence or not on the use of the couch, are all parameters which may be varied to meet the clinical needs of adolescents, PSYCHOTICS, children, or other patients who do not belong to the categories for which CLASSICAL ANALYTICAL TECHNIQUE was designed.

PARANOIA Functional PSYCHOSIS characterized by DELUSIONS of grandeur and persecution, but without intellectual deterioration. In classic cases of paranoia, the delusions are organized into a coherent, internally consistent delusional system on which the patient is prepared to act. This consistency differentiates from *paranoid schizophrenia*. See SCHIZOPHRENIA.

PARANOID 1. Relating to PARANOIA (see above). 2. Tending to use projective mechanisms (see PROJECTION). 3. Loosely: touchy, suspicious. The contemporary tendency to use 'paranoid' to describe persons who use projection as a DEFENCE arises from two sources: (a) Freud's INTERPRETATION of delusions of persecution (see under DELUSION) as projections of unconscious HOMOSEXUAL wishes; and (b) Melanie Klein's concept of the PARANOID-SCHIZOID POSITION, during which, in her view, the infant deals with his innate destructiveness by attributing it to (projecting it on) the BREAST by which it feels persecuted (see also KLEINIAN).

PARANOID ANXIETY Dread of being attacked by 'BAD' OBJECTS, either internal, projected internal (see PROJECTION), or external. When used in its strict, KLEINIAN sense it refers to ANXIETY inferred to be the result of the patient projecting on to objects his own denied (self-)destructive impulses. See PARANOID-SCHIZOID POSITION.

PARANOID-SCHIZOID POSITION Psychic configuration postulated by Melanie Klein in which the individual deals with his innate destructive impulses by (a) SPLITTING both his EGO and his OBJECT-REPRESENTATIONS into GOOD and BAD parts, and (b) projecting (see PROJECTION) his destructive impulses on to the bad object by whom he feels persecuted. According to Klein, the paranoid-schizoid position constitutes the infant's first attempt to master its DEATH INSTINCT and precedes the DEPRESSIVE

POSITION. Failure to leave the paranoid-schizoid position (i.e. to reach the depressive position) is responsible, in Klein's view, not only for many SCHIZOID and PARANOID disorders, but also for obsessional difficulties (see OBSESSIONAL NEUROSIS) (in which the 'persecuting bad object' is introjected (see INTROJECTION), forming the core of the SUPER-EGO. See Segal (1964).

PARANOID TECHNIQUE One of the four TECHNIQUES described by Fairbairn in his *A Revised Psychopathology of the Psychoses and Psychoneuroses* (see FAIRBAIRN'S REVISED PSYCHOPATHOLOGY). These techniques are used by the subject to effect the transition from INFANTILE to mature DEPENDENCE (see also MATURE AND IMMATURE). According to Fairbairn, the infant constructs two images of the MOTHER (BREAST) on whom he is originally dependent, one being that of her as a GOOD, satisfying object, the other being that of her as a BAD, frustrating object, and the four techniques differ in where the subject locates these two objects. In the paranoid technique he locates the good object inside himself and the bad one outside himself – in Fairbairn's terminology, he internalizes the accepted object and externalizes the rejected object (see INTERNALIZATION and EXTERNALIZATION) – identifying with the good object (see IDENTIFICATION) but conceiving himself to be subject to PERSECUTION by objects external to himself. By use of this manoeuvre, the subject achieves 'QUASI-INDEPENDENCE' of the mother at the price of being subject to paranoid anxiety. Since this technique, like the other three, can be regarded as a DEFENCE against SEPARATION ANXIETY, it tends to be called the *paranoid defence*, but it is clear from Fairbairn's own text that he regarded it as a normal developmental process. See Fairbairn (1952). See INSTINCT THEORY AND OBJECT THEORY.

PARANOSIC This is encountered only in the phrase *paranosic* gain, which is synonymous with 'primary gain'. See GAIN, PRIMARY AND SECONDARY.

PARAPRAXIS A faulty action due to the interference of some unconscious wish, conflict, or train of thought. Slips of the tongue and pen are the classic parapraxes. See Freud's *The Psychopathology of Everyday Life* (1901), where he uses parapraxes to demonstrate the existence of unconscious mental processes in the healthy.

PARRICIDE Murder of one's father. In the analytical literature it occurs in connexion with either the individual's OEDIPUS COMPLEX and the resulting death wishes towards the father or the murder of the PRIMAL FATHER in the PRIMAL HORDE. See also TOTEM.

PART INSTINCT See INSTINCT, COMPONENT.

PART OBJECT See OBJECT; WHOLE AND PART OBJECT.

PASSIVE 'Suffering action. acted upon' – *C.O.D.* When applied to a person: unwilling to initiate action, prone to become dependent (see DEPENDENCE) on someone else, seeking relationships in which he can become *passive-receptive* or *passive-dependent*. When applied to sexual behaviour: either those roles which are contingent on the activity of the other, e.g. passive HOMOSEXUALITY or female HETEROSEXUALITY, or those roles which can be interpreted as REVERSALS of the subject's own active instincts, e.g. MASOCHISM and EXHIBITIONISM, both of which are, according to CLASSICAL THEORY, passive forms of the subject's own SADISM and VOYEURISM. See ACTIVE AND PASSIVE for the use made by classical analysis of the concepts active and passive.

PATHOBIOGRAPHY Psychoanalytical study of a historical character based on the available biographical evidence and not on direct clinical observation. This genre, of which Freud's *Leonardo da Vinci* is a good example and Freud and Bullitt's study of Wilson (1967) a bad one, suffers from the grave limitation that one of the clinical criteria of correct INTERPRETATION, the patient's (ultimate) agreement with it, is not forthcoming.

PATHOLOGY See PSYCHOPATHOLOGY. See also AETIOLOGY AND PATHOLOGY.

PATHONEUROSIS NEUROSIS, the symptoms of which are localized in a part of the body previously affected by ORGANIC disease.

PENIS AND PHALLUS Strictly speaking, the *penis* is an anatomical term referring to the male generative organ, the *phallus* an anthropological and theological term referring to the idea or image of the male generative organ, i.e. the penis is an organ with biological functions, the phallus is an idea venerated in various religions as a SYMBOL of the power of nature. Hence Jung's (probably apocryphal) remark that the penis is only a phallic symbol.

The psychoanalytical literature uses both 'the penis' and 'the phallus' to refer to the idea (mental REPRESENTATION) of the penis, but prefers the adjectival 'phallic' to 'penile'. For instance, boys are said to go through a PHALLIC PHASE during which they are not only preoccupied with their penis but also with the idea of potency, virility, manliness, and strength and power generally.

PENIS AWE   Term used by Phyllis Greenacre to describe the emotion evoked by the sight of the penis in certain patients, some of whom described it as being surrounded by a halo. See Greenacre (1953).

PENIS ENVY   ENVY of the penis occurring either in women in respect of men generally or in boys in respect of adult males. According to Freud, penis envy is universal in women, is responsible for their CASTRATION COMPLEX, and occupies a central position in the psychology of women. Freud's tendency to interpret the psychology of women negatively as a response to the discovery of not having a penis, i.e. to regard them as *hommes manqués*, was stigmatized by Jones as 'PHALLO-CENTRIC'. Jones himself interpreted the girl's wish to have a penis as itself a DEFENCE against ANXIETY concerning *feminine* wishes towards the FATHER. See also ACTIVE AND PASSIVE.

PERCEPTION   The process of becoming aware of something. Psychoanalysis distinguishes between *external* and *internal perception*, the former being based on SENSATIONS derived from sense-organs, the latter being based on CONSCIOUSNESS becoming aware of 'internal' mental processes. This usage derives from the fact that Freud regarded consciousness as a sense-organ capable of being directed in two ways: inwards towards mental activity, outwards towards the ENVIRONMENT. In general, perception needs to be distinguished from *sensation*, the process of becoming aware of sense-data, i.e. of stimulation of those sense-organs which give rise to sensations of touch, heat, light, sound, etc.; from *apperception*, the process of recognizing or identifying what has been perceived; and *conception*, the process of forming general ideas (CONCEPTS) based on recognition of the features common to a number of objects which have been perceived over a period of time.

The psychoanalytical theory of DEFENCE involves the assumption of UNCONSCIOUS perception in respect of both internal and external perceptions, since it asserts that defences are instituted to prevent IMPULSES, MEMORIES, etc., becoming conscious. This implies that the mental agency initiating defence must perceive the threatening percept before it becomes perceptible to consciousness. This is one of the reasons which led Freud to replace the 'the Conscious' by 'the EGO'. Prior to this change in terminology, it had been necessary to assert that the Conscious was unconsciously conscious of some forbidden impulse. The Ego, however, is defined as being partly unconscious and is held capable of making automatic, unconscious adjustments to changes in internal TENSION. It is, however, not difficult to find analytical writings which fall into the trap of asserting that a patient was unconsciously conscious (or aware) of something.

PERSECUTION   Delusions of being persecuted occur in PARANOIA and paranoid SCHIZOPHRENIA. *Persecutory ideas* are suspicions of being persecuted not amounting to fixed beliefs. *Persecutory anxiety* is synonymous with PARANOID ANXIETY. *Persecution mania* is an obsolete term for paranoia.

PERSONA   JUNGIAN term for 'the demeanour which correspond(s) with the requirements of the individual's everyday life'. See Bennet (1966). The word literally means a mask.

PERSONALITY DISORDER   See BEHAVIOUR DISORDER.

PERSONALITY TYPES   For Jung's and Eysenck's views on personality types, see EXTRAVERSION AND INTROVERSION. The psychoanalytical literature discusses personality typing under the heading of CHARACTER and uses two systems of classifying it, clinical and developmental. Clinical character types are labelled by reference to the psychiatric condition to which they are inferred to be analogous or which they most resemble, hence HYSTERICAL, OBSESSIONAL, PHOBIC, SCHIZOID, DEPRESSIVE, MANIC characters. Developmental character types are labelled by reference to the stage of LIBIDINAL DEVELOPMENT from which the characteristics are inferred to derive; hence ORAL, ANAL, PHALLIC, GENITAL characters.

PERSONOLOGY   Term borrowed by Marjorie Brierley from General Smuts to describe the study of the personality 'not as an abstraction or bundle of psychological abstractions, but rather as a vital organism, as the organic psychic whole which *par excellence* it is' (Smuts), and used by her to distinguish the science of personality from METAPSYCHOLOGY, the two differing in that the former retains the person and his experience while the latter conceives of it as the result of the interaction of impersonal structures.

PERVERSION, SEXUAL Any form of adult sexual behaviour in which heterosexual intercourse is not the preferred goal. The psychoanalytical literature prefers 'perversion' to 'deviation' or 'anomaly' on the ground that such behaviour is the result of perversion and distortion of both LIBIDINAL and EGO DEVELOPMENT, i.e. on the ground that they are perversions of DEVELOPMENT. As a result, psychoanalysis holds that the sexual perversions have a defensive function (see DEFENCE) and enable the subject to avoid or master ANXIETY, the source of the anxiety varying from one perversion to another. According to Freud (1916), the perversions are the negative of the NEUROSES, inasmuch as the pervert enacts impulses which the neurotic represses (see REPRESSION). An alternative formulation is that the pervert regresses to INFANTILE SEXUALITY (see REGRESSION), whereas the neurotic uses other defences either instead of or after regression, both formulations implying that perverse behaviour in adult life is a revival of one or other of the COMPONENT-INSTINCTS which comprise infantile sexuality and out of which the adult heterosexual instinct develops. Another way of putting this is the formulation that the infant is polymorphously perverse (see POLYMORPHOUS PERVERSITY) and that the perversions represent regressions to one or other of the perverse propensities of infantile sexuality. See Freud (1905, 1916). Despite these and other formulations of the difference between neurosis and perversion, no satisfactory account exists as to why some individuals become perverts while others develop neuroses, or, in particular, while some 'capitalize', as Fairbairn (1952) puts it, precisely those propensities which others strive hardest to repress. Male HOMOSEXUALITY is the only perversion for which constitutional factors have been seriously adduced as an explanation.

Contemporary psychiatry classifies the perversions as BEHAVIOUR DISORDERS on the grounds that the 'symptoms' are behaviour which the patient claims to enjoy rather than disabilities which themselves cause him suffering. The claim to enjoy behaviour which PSYCHOPATHOLOGY considers defensive raises problems as to the authenticity of perverse behaviour and relationships (see AUTHENTIC AND INAUTHENTIC). For the specific perversions, see HOMOSEXUALITY; EXHIBITIONISM; VOYEURISM; NARCISSISM; SADISM; MASOCHISM; PAEDOPHILIA.

PESSIMISM See OPTIMISM.

PETRIFICATION Term used by Laing (1960) to describe one of the processes by which persons who lack PRIMARY ONTO-LOGICAL SECURITY defend themselves against threats to their IDENTITY. He uses the term to include *both* depersonalizing one-self (turning oneself to stone) to prevent oneself being over-powered by the other, and depersonalizing the other to prevent him affecting one. The term has relations to the psychiatric terms DEPERSONALIZATION and DEREALIZATION.

PHALLIC See PENIS AND PHALLUS. Hence:

Phallic character Person who displays COMPULSIVE character traits referable to the PHALLIC PHASE (see below); more specifically, a person who conceives of sexual behaviour as a display of potency, in contrast to the GENITAL CHARACTER, who conceives of it as participation in a relationship.

Phallic phase Stage of infantile LIBIDINAL DEVELOPMENT (see also INFANTILE) in which the child is preoccupied with his PENIS, its functions, and the idea of potency generally. It succeeds the ANAL and precedes the OEDIPAL phases.

Phallic woman 1. The idea of woman with phallic attributes, usually either an INFANTILE conception of the MOTHER during the PRE-OEDIPAL phases of LIBIDINAL DEVELOPMENT, or a neurotic conception of woman found in men with an aversion to women or with a masochistic, submissive attitude towards them (see MASO-CHISM, SUBMISSION). The concept is also encountered in primitive religions, mythology, and folklore. 2. A woman who is conceived by others, or by herself, to be the incarnation of such an idea. In both usages it is unclear whether the woman should be regarded as masculine or hermaphroditic.

PHALLO-CENTRIC Term used by Jones to describe the tendency of CLASSICAL THEORY to attach excessive importance to the PENIS and, in particular, to explain the psychology of women as a reaction to their discovery that they lack a penis. See ACTIVE AND PASSIVE; CASTRATION; ENVY; PENIS ENVY.

PHANTASY   The psychoanalytical concept of phantasy shares the ambiguities inherent in the everyday use of the word. In one sense, phantasy refers to imagining, daydreaming, fancying, as contrasted with adaptive thought and behaviour (see ADAPTATION). In this sense it is synonymous with neurotic daydreaming. In another sense it refers to the imaginative activity which underlies all thought and feeling. In theoretical writing the latter sense is usually intended; hence the spelling 'phantasy' adopted by English but not by American writers. (See FANTASY.) All schools agree that conscious mental activity is accompanied, supported, maintained, enlivened, and affected by UNCONSCIOUS phantasy, which begins in childhood, is primarily (originally) concerned with biological processes and relations, and undergoes symbolic elaboration (see SYMBOL). There is, however, considerable difference of opinion as to the practical value of making INTERPRETATIONS in terms of unconscious phantasy, KLEINIANS holding that such interpretations are alone effective, the ego psychologists (see EGO PSYCHOLOGY) believing that they are likely to be 'wild' (i.e. to be dramatic statements about, say, wishing to attack the BREAST or PENIS, which make little sense to the adult patient's EGO). Kleinian theory uses 'unconscious phantasy' as a bridge concept between INSTINCT and thought. 'On the views here developed: (a) Phantasies are the primary content of unconscious mental processes. (b) Unconscious phantasies are primarily about bodies, and represent instinctual aims towards objects. (c) These phantasies are, in the first instance, the psychic representatives of *libidinal* and destructive instincts. . . . (j) ADAPTATION to REALITY and reality-thinking require the support of concurrent unconscious phantasies . . .' – Susan Isaacs (1952). Classical theory makes much the same point by locating phantasy in the ID.

Phantasies may be DEEP or SUPERFICIAL, ORAL, ANAL, PHALLIC, GENITAL, CONSCIOUS or UNCONSCIOUS, LIBIDINAL or aggressive (see AGGRESSION), INFANTILE or adult, sadistic or masochistic (see SADISM and MASOCHISM), CREATIVE or NEUROTIC, HYSTERICAL, OBSESSIONAL, DEPRESSIVE, SCHIZOID, PARANOID, etc. See also IMAGINATION; SYMBOLISM.

PHENOMENOLOGY   The study of experience. Phenomenological studies (a) confine themselves to conscious experiences
without postulating that they are the effect of underlying processes,
without explaining them as the manifestations of noumena, essences, principles, etc., of which the senses have no knowledge;
(b) formulate their data from the SUBJECT's point of view.

Psychotherapists and philosophers who take a phenomenological standpoint usually reject the idea of the UNCONSCIOUS and also
those parts of psychoanalytical theory such as METAPSYCHOLOGY
which are formulated as though the subject can be observed from
the outside, i.e. without the observer identifying with the subject
(see IDENTIFICATION). See also EXISTENTIALISM; ESSENTIALISM;
ONTOLOGY; PERSONOLOGY.

PHOBIA   1. The symptom of experiencing unnecessary or excessive ANXIETY in some specific situation or in the presence of
some specific object. Hence *agoraphobia*: anxiety in open spaces
(see AGORAPHOBIA); *claustrophobia*: anxiety in an enclosed space
(see CLAUSTROPHOBIA); phobia of spiders, snakes, etc. 2. NEUROSIS
in which phobia in sense 1 is the predominant symptom. In this
sense synonymous with *phobic illness* and ANXIETY-HYSTERIA.
Hence:

Phobic anxiety   Anxiety provoked by some external object or
situation out of all proportion to its real dangerousness. See
PHOBIC DEFENCE.

Phobic character   Person who habitually deals with situations
that are likely to cause ANXIETY and CONFLICT by avoiding them,
typically by restricting his life and refusing to be parted from
an ideal, protecting parent or parent-figure. Hence *counter-phobic
character*: person who adopts a *counter-phobic attitude* towards
life, doing and taking pleasure in doing precisely those activities
which are dangerous and arouse anxiety in 'normal' persons. The
counter-phobic attitude is usually regarded as a form of MANIC
DEFENCE, the satisfactions of it deriving from the sense of triumph
and OMNIPOTENCE evoked by successful mastery of anxiety.

Phobic defence   The defensive manoeuvre (see DEFENCE) of
avoiding those objects and situations which give rise to phobic
anxiety. All schools agree that the *phobic object* (situation) arouses
anxiety not on its own account but because it has become a

SYMBOL of something else, i.e. because it represents some impulse, wish, INTERNAL OBJECT, or part of the SELF which the patient has been unable to face. CLASSICAL THEORY regards phobic illness as a form of HYSTERIA, hence its synonym, 'anxiety-hysteria', but contemporary psychiatric textbooks usually link it with OBSESSIONAL NEUROSIS. Behaviour therapists (see BEHAVIOUR THERAPY) regard it as a suitable condition for treatment by deconditioning, on the ground that the symptom is an isolated phenomenon which can be treated without reference to the patient's personality.

PHOBIC TECHNIQUE   One of the four techniques described in FAIRBAIRN'S REVISED PSYCHOPATHOLOGY. These techniques are used by the subject to effect the transition from INFANTILE to mature DEPENDENCE. According to Fairbairn, the infant constructs two images of the MOTHER (BREAST) on whom he is originally totally dependent, one being that of her as a GOOD, satisfying OBJECT, the other that of her as a BAD, frustrating OBJECT, and the four techniques differ in *where* the subject locates these two objects. In the phobic technique he locates both outside himself – in Fairbairn's terminology he EXTERNALIZES both the accepted and the rejected object – imagining himself to be protected by the good object but at risk from attacks by (the) bad object(s). As a result, he achieves a sense of security at the cost of PHOBIC ANXIETY. CONFLICT between this technique and the progressive urge to maturity leads to oscillation between wishes to escape from the suffocating protection of the good object (CLAUSTRO-PHOBIA) and wishes to return from it to escape from a world imagined to be peopled with bad objects (AGORAPHOBIA). See Fairbairn (1952). See also INSTINCT THEORY AND OBJECT THEORY.

PHYLOGENETIC   Relating to the evolution of the species. See ONTOGENY AND PHYLOGENY.

PLAY   Activity engaged in for its own sake, for the pleasure it gives without reference to serious aims and ends, typically contrasted with WORK or the performance of other socially or biologically necessary acts. Play is of interest to psychoanalysts on several counts. It is an activity which engages simultaneously functions which theory tends to oppose, since (a) the subject is simultaneously expressing PHANTASY and adapting to the external WORLD (see ADAPTATION), and (b) the subject's individual, private

IMAGINATION (PHANTASY) is engaged in communal activity (or at least, in the case of solitary play, activity which is observable by others). Being an activity which in some senses doesn't count (being 'pretend' or 'pretend real'), and in which the actions are 'acting' and not actual, censorship, INHIBITION, and GUILT are in partial abeyance; as a result, play affords evidence of wishes, ANXIETIES, etc., which are otherwise repressed (see REPRESSION). It is therefore used by child analysts as a substitute for FREE ASSOCIATION, the games the child makes up with the toys given it by the analyst being used as evidence for inferring the nature of its unconscious phantasies. Even the psychoanalysis of adults has resemblances to play inasmuch as the clinical situation is set apart from the rest of life, the patient's utterances are not acted upon by the analyst, and free association allows free play for the imagination. *Play therapy* usually refers to non-interpretative therapy of children. *Sexual play* is either a euphemism for petting or a description of pre-pubertal or childhood sexual behaviour.

PLEASURE PRINCIPLE According to Freud (1911, 1917), the psyche is initially actuated solely by the pleasure or pleasure-pain principle, which leads it to avoid PAIN or UNPLEASURE aroused by increases in instinctual TENSION and to do so by hallucinating (see HALLUCINATION) the SATISFACTION necessary to reduce the tension. Only later, after the EGO has developed, is the pleasure principle modified by the REALITY PRINCIPLE, which leads the individual to replace hallucinatory WISH-FULFILMENT by adaptive behaviour (see ADAPTATION).

Its usual, shortened form, 'pleasure-principle', is misleading since the concept does not imply that pleasure is positively pursued but that unpleasure is avoided. The concept can be regarded as analogous to Cannon's HOMEOSTASIS, since it postulates a built-in tendency to keep instinctual tension at an optimal or minimal level. (Freud sometimes wrote as though he meant 'minimal', but 'optimal' corresponds to most contemporary interpretations of the concept.)

For a summary of the difficulties involved in assuming that the pleasure and reality principles are always opposed to one another, or that the pleasure-principle alone is operative in infancy, see Rycroft (1962).

POLYMORPHOUS PERVERSITY According to CLASSICAL

THEORY, the human infant is *polymorphously perverse*, i.e. his INFANTILE sexual wishes are not canalized in any one direction and he regards the various EROTOGENIC ZONES as interchangeable. According to some versions of this concept, there is a specific polymorphously perverse stage of LIBIDINAL DEVELOPMENT, though it is not clear where this stage should be placed in the chronology of infantile development.

POSITION   Term used by KLEINIAN theory to describe certain configurations of OBJECT-RELATIONS and LIBIDO-distribution through which the individual passes during DEVELOPMENT. The two positions which have become established in Kleinian theory are the PARANOID-SCHIZOID and DEPRESSIVE, though references to a MANIC position also occur. The concept has affinities with the classical concept of 'stage of LIBIDINAL DEVELOPMENT', but differs in that it refers to complex patterns of PHANTASY and object-relationship rather than to attachment to one particular object and EROTOGENIC ZONE. Both positions occur in the first year of life, i.e. during the ORAL stage of CLASSICAL THEORY.

POSITIVE AND NEGATIVE   These are usually synonyms for loving and hating, but *positive Oedipus complex* refers to love of the parent of the opposite sex and rivalry with the parent of the same sex, while the *negative Oedipus complex* refers to love of the parent of the same sex and rivalry with the parent of the opposite sex. See also OEDIPUS COMPLEX; NEGATIVE THERAPEUTIC REACTION; NEGATIVISM.

POSTUROLOGY   The study of posture. In psychoanalysis the study of the ways in which character, defences, sexual attitudes, and conflicts are revealed in posture. See Deutsch (1947). Its logical companion, *gesturology*, does not occur.

PRE-CONSCIOUS   Adj. referring to thoughts which are UN-CONSCIOUS at the particular moment in question but which are not repressed (see REPRESSION) and are, therefore, capable of becoming CONSCIOUS (available to recall).

PRE-GENITAL   Adj. referring to those phases of infantile LIBIDINAL DEVELOPMENT (see also INFANTILE) which precede the GENITAL, and to IMPULSES and PHANTASIES derived therefrom.

PRE-OEDIPAL   Adj. referring to those stages of LIBIDINAL

DEVELOPMENT which precede the OEDIPAL, and to the relationship to the MOTHER during them.

PRIMACY   In analytical writings, this means prepotence not pre-eminence. A person is said to have achieved *genital primacy* (see GENITAL) if his capacity for heterosexual OBJECT-RELATION-SHIPS (see also HETEROSEXUAL) and for mental AUTONOMY is suffi-cient to withstand any regressive (see REGRESSION) or INFANTILE tendencies which may still be present, if his PRE-GENITAL, infantile component INSTINCTS have become subordinated to the genital sexual instinct, i.e. if they have been included in FORE-PLEASURE, or repressed or sublimated (see REPRESSION and SUBLIMATION).

PRIMAL   Primitive, primeval, primordial. Often referring to ideas which have a legendary or mythopoieic quality. The *primal scene* is the patient's (child's) conception of his parents having intercourse regarded as an idea around which PHANTASY has been woven rather than as a recollection of something actually per-ceived. The *primal horde* is Freud's term for the type of community which Darwin surmised, on the basis of reports about the habits of apes, to have been the original structure of human society, viz. a group consisting of a dominant male, the *primal father*, a number of females whom he reserved for himself, and a number of males whom he kept in subjection. Freud used this hypothesis to explain (a) the origin of EXOGAMY and the INCEST TABOO – the primal father kept the women to himself and forced other potent males out of the group; (b) the origin of GUILT – the sons combined, murdered the father, and divided the women among them, but felt and passed on to their descendants their guilt at having committed PARRICIDE and incest; and (e) totemism – the TOTEM animal symbolizes (see SYMBOL) the murdered FATHER. See ONTOGENY.

PRIMAL FATHER   See under PRIMAL.

PRIMAL HORDE   See under PRIMAL.

PRIMARY   When used as part of a technical term, 'belonging to first stage of DEVELOPMENT'. The *primary processes* were so called by Freud because he believed that they were more primitive and manifested themselves at an earlier stage of development than the secondary processes. See PROCESSES, PRIMARY AND SECONDARY. *Primary* or *automatic anxiety* is that form of ANXIETY which is evoked by the experience of SEPARATION from a necessary object or by dissolution of the EGO (from without, as in TRAUMA, or from within, as in a true NIGHTMARE) and to prevent which the mechanism of SIGNAL ANXIETY develops later.

The *primary object* is that OBJECT, i.e. the BREAST or the MOTHER, to which the infant initially relates. *Primary object-love* is the form of LOVE experienced by the infant in relation to its primary object. *Primary identification* is the infant's feeling of oneness with the mother before it has discovered the otherness of objects; in contrast to secondary identification, which occurs after the infant has learnt to distinguish between the SELF and the other. *Primary narcissism* is that form of self-love which is present at birth; in contrast to secondary NARCISSISM, which only occurs after OBJECT-LOVE has developed. *Primary gain* is the relief from anxiety and CONFLICT acquired by developing a NEUROSIS; in contrast to secondary gain, the advantages which can be extracted from the fact of having a neurosis.

PROCESSES, PRIMARY AND SECONDARY   Two types of mental functioning, the former being characteristic of UNCONSCIOUS mental activity, the latter being characteristic of CONSCIOUS thinking. *Primary process thinking* displays CONDENSATION and DISPLACEMENT, i.e. images tend to become fused and can readily replace and symbolize one another (see SYMBOL), uses mobile ENERGY, ignores the categories of space and TIME, and is governed by the PLEASURE-PRINCIPLE, i.e. reduces the unpleasure of instinctual TENSION by hallucinatory WISH-FULFILMENT (see also HALLUCINATION). In TOPOGRAPHICAL formulations it is the mode of THINKING operative in the ID. *Secondary process thinking* obeys the laws of grammar and formal logic, uses bound energy, and is governed by the REALITY-PRINCIPLE, i.e. reduces the UNPLEASURE of instinctual tension by adaptive behaviour (see ADAPTATION). Freud believed the primary processes to be ontogenetically (see ONTOGENY) and phylogenetically earlier than the secondary processes – hence the terminology – and regarded them as inherently maladaptive, all EGO DEVELOPMENT being secondary to their REPRESSION. The secondary processes, in his view, developed *pari passu* with the EGO and with adaptation to the external WORLD and have an intimate connexion with verbal thinking. The primary processes are exemplified in dreaming (see DREAMS), the secondary processes by thought. Day-dreaming, imaginative and creative activity (see IMAGINATION and CREATIVITY) and emotional thinking contain an admixture of the two processes. The two processes resemble the discursive and non-discursive symbolism described by Suzanne Langer (1951).

For a summary of some the objections to the view that the primary and secondary processes are mutually antagonistic, and that the primary processes are maladaptive, see Rycroft (1962).

See Freud (1900, 1911, 1917) for his own accounts of the two processes. See also VERBALIZATION; WORD-PRESENTATION.

PROCESS THEORY Statements that psychoanalysis is, or should be recognized as, a process theory are usually protests against TOPOGRAPHICAL and STRUCTURAL formulations which tend to imply that the mind is a thing with parts, e.g. a PSYCHICAL APPARATUS consisting of three bits, an ID, an EGO, and a SUPER-EGO, and pleas that psychoanalysis should be formulated in terms of mental processes and their organization. See PERSONOLOGY.

PROGNOSIS Prognostication; forecast of the course of an illness. Prognoses are of two kinds: estimates as to how a disease will run with and without treatment. Psychoanalysis assumes that the NEUROSES have a bad prognosis, i.e. that they are chronic illnesses that are unlikely to lead to spontaneous recovery, their origin in childhood being adduced as the theoretical reason for this assumption. Facts bearing on this assumption are, however, remarkably hard to come by and the issue is in any case bedevilled by the fact that psychiatric follow-ups (see PSYCHIATRY) record the course of symptoms while psychoanalysts think in terms of the patient's total personality. Loss of symptoms which psychiatric statistics record as recovery may be assessed by a psychoanalyst as the result of an insignificant shift in the patient's psychopathology. See Eysenck (1965), Malan (1963).

PROJECTION Lit. throwing in front of oneself. Hence its use in psychiatry and psychoanalysis to mean 'viewing a mental image as objective REALITY'. In psychoanalysis two sub-meanings can be distinguished: (a) the general misinterpretation of mental activity as events occurring to one, as in DREAMS and HALLUCINATIONS; and (b) the process by which specific IMPULSES, wishes, aspects of the SELF, or INTERNAL objects are imagined to be located in some

OBJECT external to oneself. Projection of aspects of oneself is preceded by DENIAL, i.e. one denies that one feels such and such an emotion, has such and such a wish, but asserts that someone else does. Sometimes the projected wish or emotion remains directed at its original object – 'I don't love (hate) X, but Y does'; but, perhaps more frequently it is accompanied by REVERSAL – 'I don't love (hate) X, but X loves (hates) me'. Projection of internal objects consists in attributing to someone in one's environment feelings towards oneself which derive historically from some past external object whom one has introjected (see INTROJECTION), e.g. imagining that X loves (hates) one the way one imagined Y did in the past. Since introjected objects may themselves be the depositories of projection, projection of internal objects may lead to endowing the recipient with aspects not only of one's past objects but also of one's past self.

Projection was first described in connexion with DELUSIONS of PERSECUTION, which Freud (1911) interpreted as being the result of denial, projection, and reversal, his hypothesis being that the PARANOID patient denied his HOMOSEXUAL feelings, projecting them on to someone else and then doubly reversing them, thereby transforming and disguising the homosexual impulse into the delusion that he was hated, i.e. he denied that he loved the male X, but asserted instead that X hated him. Of recent years, largely owing to the influence of Melanie Klein (see KLEINIAN), projection has been accepted as a normal developmental process (see DEVELOPMENT) and most accounts of INFANTILE development assume that the infant regularly attributes to its objects impulses that are in fact its own and then introjects objects distorted by these projections, thereby acquiring internal objects possessing its own qualities. According to Klein, indeed, all fear of the MOTHER in infancy and all paranoid ideas in later life ultimately stem not from any actual experience of being hated, rejected, or maltreated, but from projection on to the BREAST of the infant's own self-destructive DEATH INSTINCT. See PARANOID-SCHIZOID POSITION.

PROJECTIVE TESTS (or PROJECTION TESTS) Psychological tests which attempt to ascertain personality traits by inviting the subject to interpret pictures or indeterminate shapes such as ink-blots in the light of his imagination.

PSEUDO-   False or misleading. Hence:

Pseudocyesis   False pregnancy. Condition in which the patient believes herself to be pregnant, shows some of the signs of pregnancy, typically amenorrhoea and enlargement of the abdomen, but in fact is not pregnant.

Pseudologia fantastica   Condition in which the subject habitually tells circumstantial lies of a kind likely to enhance his own importance and interest to others.

Pseudo-mutuality   Phenomenon displayed by married couples and families in which the members are united by their capacity to satisfy each others' neurotic needs. See Wynne (1958).

PSYCHE   The mind. The psychoanalytical literature, following Freud, uses psyche and MIND (Seele) synonymously. Its two adjectives, *psychical* and *psychic*, are also synonymous with 'mental' (neither having any connexion with 'PSYCHICAL RESEARCH', in the sense of investigation into paranormal phenomena, extrasensory perception, etc.). However, whereas 'mind' tends to be used in contrast to 'body', 'psyche' is usually contrasted with 'SOMA'.

PSYCHESOMA   Since psychoanalytical writings conform to the convention of assuming that persons consist of two parts, a body (SOMA) and a mind (PSYCHE), *psychesoma* is sometimes used when it is necessary to assert the unity of the organism. See PSYCHOSOMATIC.

PSYCHIATRIST   A medical practitioner who specializes in PSYCHIATRY. A PSYCHOANALYST may or may not be a psychiatrist. LAY ANALYSTS are not psychiatrists, since they are not medically qualified. A medically qualified analyst is unlikely to claim also to be a psychiatrist unless he has also had experience in general psychiatry, i.e. in the treatment of forms of MENTAL ILLNESS for which psychoanalysis is not indicated.

PSYCHIATRY   That branch of medicine which is concerned with patients whose presenting symptoms are mental (see MENTAL ILLNESS), regardless of whether the symptoms are of physical or mental origin. The popular equation of psychiatry with psychoanalysis is unfounded for several reasons: (a) Psychiatric practice includes the treatment of a number of illnesses known to be of physical origin, e.g. general paralysis of the insane, senile

DEMENTIA, the organic PSYCHOSES, mental deficiency. (b) Its repertoire of treatments includes a number of techniques which are neither psychoanalytical nor psychotherapeutic, e.g. electroconvulsive therapy and the use of tranquillizers, anti-depressants, and sedatives. (c) Many psychiatrists are actively opposed to psychoanalysis and never recommend it even for those types of illness for which psychoanalysts consider it suitable. (d) The nature of the functional psychoses, SCHIZOPHRENIA and MANIC-DEPRESSIVE PSYCHOSIS, which between them are responsible for the bulk of admissions to mental hospitals, remains problematical, the *organic school* claiming that they are due to as yet undiscovered physical causes, the *dynamically-orientated school* claiming that they are PSYCHOGENIC (without, however, usually claiming that they are treatable by existing techniques of psychoanalysis or psychotherapy). (e) In this country at least, only a small proportion of psychiatrists have had any training in psychoanalysis.

PSYCHIC, PSYCHICAL   See PSYCHE; MIND.

PSYCHIC(AL) APPARATUS   This is the central concept of Freudian METAPSYCHOLOGY. 'We assume that mental life is the function of an apparatus to which we ascribe the characteristics of being extended in space and of being made up of several portions [viz. the ID, EGO, and SUPER-EGO]' – Freud (1940). Formulations which locate mental activity in some part of the apparatus are termed TOPOGRAPHICAL, those which define it in terms of the interaction of its portions or in changes in its shape are STRUCTURAL, while those which postulate the movement of ENERGY within it are termed ECONOMIC. Psychoanalysts differ sharply in their attitude towards the psychic apparatus, some taking joy in it, others finding it an embarrassment. The former regard it as the concept which justifies the claim of psychoanalysis to be an objective, impersonal SCIENCE as exact and precise in its formulations as longer- and better-established disciplines; the latter feeling that it eliminates the person and therefore achieves objectivity at the price of ignoring its own subject-matter. CLASSICAL THEORY and EGO PSYCHOLOGY use the concept; OBJECT THEORY rejects it while attempting to salvage many ideas classically formulated in terms of it; EXISTENTIALISM uses it as the starting-point of its criticisms of psychoanalysis. For Freud's own formulations, see Freud (1900, 1917, 1940). For sophisticated handling of the concept, see Rapaport (1951). For benevolent criticism of it, see Brierley (1951). For out and out rejection of it, see Guntrip (1961). It should perhaps be added that Freud was consistently clear that the concept is a FICTION. See INSTINCT THEORY AND OBJECT THEORY; ONTOLOGY; PERSONOLOGY; PROCESS THEORY; PHENOMENOLOGY.

PSYCHIC(AL) DETERMINISM See DETERMINISM, PSYCHIC

PSYCHICAL RESEARCH Parapsychology; the study of para-normal phenomena (extrasensory perception, psychokinesis). See Jones's biography, Vol. 3 (1957), for an account of Freud's life-long interest in psychical research and the occult and his AM-BIVALENCE towards them. 'The wish to believe fought hard with the warning to disbelieve.'

PSYCHOANALYSIS 1. The form of treatment of the NEUROSES invented by Freud in the 1890s and elaborated since then by himself, his disciples and followers. The key defining concepts are (a) FREE ASSOCIATION, which replaced HYPNOSIS; (b) INTERPRETA-TION, which replaced suggestion; and (c) TRANSFERENCE. *Psycho-analytical technique* consists essentially in instructing and helping the patient to associate freely, in interpreting both his associations and the obstacles he encounters in trying to associate, and in interpreting his feelings and attitudes towards the analyst. Forms of PSYCHOTHERAPY which use Freudian theory in combination with other techniques are, strictly speaking, *psychoanalytically orientated psychotherapy* and not psychoanalysis. 2. The psycho-logical theories of the origin of the neuroses and (later) of general mental DEVELOPMENT formulated by Freud, his disciples and fol-lowers concurrently with the invention and elaboration of psycho-analytical treatment. The key defining concepts are (a) the UNCONSCIOUS, the idea that there exists mental activity of which the subject is unaware but which none the less exerts a dynamic effect on his behaviour; (b) RESISTANCE, the idea that CONSCIOUS-NESS resists the emergence of UNCONSCIOUS tendencies into con-sciousness and does so by the use of DEFENCES; (c) TRANSFERENCE, the idea that the relationship of the subject to his present objects is unconsciously influenced by his relationship to past objects and that, in particular, the relationship of the patient to his analyst re-capitulates his childhood relationships with his parents. 3. Although 1 and 2 define psychoanalysis in terms what are (I hope) acceptable to Freudian analysts of all schools, the laity use the term in a much wider sense to include the theories and therapies of all PSYCHOTHERAPISTS who follow Freud, Jung, and Adler, this despite the fact that the JUNGIANS call themselves *analytical psychologists* and their theory analytical psychology and the ADLERIANS call themselves *individual psychologists*. For *existential psychoanalysis*, see EXISTENTIALISM.

PSYCHOANALYST   Any person who has received a training in PSYCHOANALYSIS at a recognized psychoanalytical institute and who practises psychoanalytical treatment.

PSYCHOBIOLOGICAL   1. Relating to psychological problems in biology or to problems which require both psychological and biological consideration. 2. Relating specifically to the psychobiological school of psychiatry founded in America by Adolf Meyer.

PSYCHODRAMA   Form of PSYCHOTHERAPY in which the patient is required to act a part in some drama constructed with special reference to his symptoms or problems, the other parts being taken by members of the therapeutic team.

PSYCHODYNAMICS   Either 1. the study of mental processes from a DYNAMIC point of view. Or 2. the theoretical formulation of the workings (dynamics) of some specific person's mind, without implying that the processes are abnormal.

PSYCHOGENESIS   The origin and development of mental processes.

PSYCHOGENIC   Qualifier of illnesses and symptoms assumed to be of mental origin.

PSYCHOLOGIST   Any person trained in or practising any form of PSYCHOLOGY.

PSYCHOLOGY   Traditionally defined as 'the science of mind', but of recent years, and increasingly, 'the science of behaviour'. This latter definition bypasses philosophical problems about the nature of mind but makes it necessary to regard THINKING as a form of behaviour. Qualifiers of 'psychology' refer either to specialized branches of the subject – *abnormal, normal, animal, human, child, genetic* (developmental), *industrial, social, clinical, academic, educational* – or to different systems of thought – *behaviouristic, Gestalt, psychoanalytical, Freudian, Jungian, Adlerian.* Freudian psychology is *psychoanalysis*; JUNGIAN psychology is *analytical psychology*; ADLERIAN psychology is *individual psychology.* See DEPTH PSYCHOLOGY; EGO PSYCHOLOGY.

PSYCHOMOTOR ACCELERATION Psychiatric term for the speeding-up of thought and action occurring in MANIA.

PSYCHOMOTOR RETARDATION Psychiatric term for gross slowing-down of both mental and physical processes occurring in deep DEPRESSION. Often regarded as evidence that the depression is ENDOGENOUS, i.e. of constitutional not psychogenic origin.

PSYCHONEUROSIS Technical psychoanalytical term for one group of the NEUROSES, viz. those in which the symptoms are interpretable as manifestations of CONFLICT between EGO and ID. Psychoneurosis differs from PSYCHOSIS in that REALITY-TESTING is unimpaired, i.e. the patient has INSIGHT into the fact that he is ill and that his symptoms are invalid; from the PERVERSIONS in that the symptoms are in themselves distressing and that the ego is intact; from CHARACTER neurosis in that the conflict has produced symptoms and not character traits; and from ACTUAL NEUROSIS in that the conflict dates from the past. The three subdivisions of psychoneurosis are *conversion hysteria, anxiety hysteria* (PHOBIA), and *obsessional neurosis.* They have in common not only the characteristics cited above but also that they are accessible to psychoanalytical treatment. (See ANXIETY HYSTERIA; CONVERSION HYSTERIA; OBSESSIONAL NEUROSIS.)

PSYCHOPATH Person whose behaviour makes him liable to the psychiatric diagnosis of PSYCHOPATHY.

PSYCHOPATHOLOGY *Either* 1. the study of abnormal mental functioning. *Or* 2. the theoretical formulation of the abnormal workings of some particular person's mind. Often used loosely to include PSYCHODYNAMICS.

PSYCHOPATHY Psychiatric and medico-legal term for what used to be called moral imbecility. It is defined by the Mental Health Act, 1959, as 'a persistent disorder or disability of mind (whether or not including subnormality of intelligence) which results in abnormally aggressive or seriously irresponsible conduct on the part of the patient, and requires or is susceptible to medical treatment'. 'Promiscuity or other immoral conduct' is specifically excluded from the forms of conduct which make a patient liable to the diagnosis. The concept is a logical hybrid since it combines medical and legal criteria, but it fulfils the useful function of enabling offenders to be treated in special hospitals. The concept is not recognized by Scottish law. Psychiatrically the condition is listed as one of the BEHAVIOUR DISORDERS.

PSYCHOSEXUAL   Relating to the mental aspects of SEXUAL phenomena. The literature frequently uses 'sexual' when 'psychosexual' is intended.

PSYCHOSIS   Both psychiatry and psychoanalysis use this term to describe those mental illnesses which are liable to render their victims *non compos mentis*; in contrast to NEUROSIS for those in which the patient's sanity is never in doubt. Psychiatric definitions are usually in terms of the patient's lack of INSIGHT into the fact that he is ill; psychoanalytical definitions usually include a reference to failure in REALITY-TESTING. Psychiatry distinguishes between the *organic psychoses*, which are due to demonstrable organic disease, usually of the brain, and the *functional psychoses*, in which no organic lesion is demonstrable. Controversy exists as to whether the functional psychoses are due to as yet undiscovered physical and constitutional causes or whether they are PSYCHOGENIC illnesses, differing from the neuroses only in their greater severity; this controversy is one of the issues which divide the ORGANIC and PSYCHODYNAMIC schools of psychiatry. Both psychiatry and psychoanalysis recognize three functional psychoses: SCHIZOPHRENIA, MANIC-DEPRESSIVE PSYCHOSIS, and PARANOIA (though the last is sometimes regarded as a variety of the first).

According to CLASSICAL THEORY, the psychoses, even if psychogenic in origin, are inaccessible to psychoanalytical treatment, the reason advanced being that they are narcissistic disorders (see NARCISSISM) in which the patient is incapable of forming a TRANSFERENCE. The small but heroic band of analysts who do attempt to analyse psychotics maintain, however, that they do form transferences, but that these transferences differ qualitatively from

PSY

neurotic transference; instead of regarding the analyst as an OBJECT (and, to some measure, a GOOD object), the psychotic regards him as a part of himself or as an enemy (identificatory and persecutory transference (see IDENTIFICATION and PERSECUTION)). Of recent years the theoretical distinction between psychosis and neurosis has become confused by the idea that psychotic processes form part of the PSYCHOPATHOLOGY of the neuroses and even that the normal infant passes through psychotic developmental stages. This idea, which forms an essential part of the KLEINIAN system of thought, derives in the first instance from the work of Abraham, who postulated that both SCHIZOPHRENIA and MANIC-DEPRESSIVE PSYCHOSIS were REGRESSIONS to the ORAL stage of LIBIDINAL and EGO DEVELOPMENT. See PARANOID-SCHIZOID POSITION; DEPRESSIVE POSITION.

PSYCHOSOMATIC Illnesses and symptoms are designated 'psychosomatic' if (a) the symptoms are accompanied by demonstrable physiological disturbances of function, and (b) the symptoms and the illness as a whole can be interpreted as a manifestation of the patient's personality, conflicts, life-history, etc. Condition (a) distinguishes from NEUROSIS, particularly CONVERSION HYSTERIA. Condition (b) distinguishes from ORGANIC disease pure and simple. Delimitation of the field of psychosomatic illness is bedevilled by two factors: the ease with which condition (b) can be fulfilled by enthusiastic speculation and the possibility that constitutional factors may predispose to specific types of both mental and physical illness. Much of the literature on psychosomatic illness consists of demonstrations that patients suffering from a particular physical illness share common features of personality. Perhaps bronchial asthma, peptic ulcer, and ulcerative colitis are the best-attested psychosomatic illnesses.

PSYCHOTHERAPIST Either 1. any person who practises PSYCHOTHERAPY of whatever kind regardless of whether he is LAY or medical or to which school he belongs. Or 2. any person who practises psychotherapy but who is not a PSYCHOANALYST. The latter illogical usage derives from two sources: (a) the existence of persons who practise psychotherapy, but who for whatever reason wish to make it clear that they are not psychoanalysts, and (b) the claim made by PSYCHOANALYSIS (and largely accepted) that it is a deeper, more intensive and thorough form of treatment than other

forms of psychotherapy and is therefore in a class of its own·
A *psychoanalytically orientated psychotherapist* is a person who
claims to use psychoanalytical theories and techniques without
making any claim to have been trained by a psychoanalytic
institute.

PSYCHOTHERAPY   Any form of 'talking cure' (in all forms of
psychotherapy one or other party talks and in most forms both).
Psychotherapy may be either *individual* or GROUP, superficial or
deep (see DEEP AND SUPERFICIAL), interpretative (see INTERPRETA-
TION), supportive, or suggestive, the latter three differing in the
intention underlying the therapist's utterances. *Intensive* refers
either to the frequency of the patient's attendances or to the zeal
displayed by the therapist. The term always differentiates from
physical treatment, but, according to context, either includes or
excludes PSYCHOANALYSIS (see PSYCHOTHERAPIST above), despite
the fact that psychoanalysis can correctly be described as long-
term, intensive, interpretative psychotherapy. See also FOCAL
THERAPY.

PUERPERIUM, PUERPERAL   (The weeks immediately) fol-
lowing childbirth. Hence as in *puerperal psychosis*, *puerperal depression*, for PSYCHOSIS and DEPRESSION following and, by inference,
caused or precipitated by childbirth.

PSYCHOTIC ANXIETY   Term used mostly by KLEINIAN
analysts to refer to DEPRESSIVE and PARANOID (persecutory)
ANXIETY. These two forms are deemed 'psychotic' on two grounds:
(a) they are held to stem from levels of the personality and stages of
DEVELOPMENT at which the PSYCHOSES originate, i.e. the DEPRES-
SIVE POSITION and PARANOID-SCHIZOID POSITION; and (b) the dread
is of total annihilation. Non-Kleinians using the phrase are likely
to be referring to dread of loss of IDENTITY.

PURPOSE   Although psychoanalysis maintains that much behaviour which appears accidental is in fact purposive, the concept
is not used theoretically. See PARAPRAXIS; WILL.

Q

Q. QUANTITY   In his *Project for a Scientific Psychology*, which was written in 1895 but only published posthumously in 1950, Freud used 'Q' to represent whatever it is that distinguishes activity from rest in the nervous system and which is capable of being quantified. Q was conceived as being attached to NEURONES and of being capable of passing from one neurone to another. It forms the forerunner of Freud's later concept of psychic ENERGY and is of interest in showing that this concept was originally conceived in neurological terms. See ENERGY; CATHEXIS.

QUANTUM   Lit. an amount, but usually, as in *quantum physics*, the discrete unit into which a quantifiable entity is divisible. (The quantum theory of physics asserts that in radiation the energy of electrons is discharged not continuously but in discrete quanta.) CLASSICAL THEORY postulates the existence of quanta of psychic ENERGY, which are generated in the ID, which are capable of being discharged in action, and of being bound (attached) to those mental structures which constitute the EGO. References to quanta of LIBIDO and AFFECT are also encountered in the literature. Since psychoanalysis has no means of measuring psychic energy, the idea that it consists of discrete quanta is a purely speculative notion – nor do analytical users of the word 'quantum' always wish to imply such a hypothesis. See also Q.

QUASI-INDEPENDENCE   The second of Fairbairn's three stages of development (see FAIRBAIRN'S REVISED PSYCHOPATHOLOGY). It succeeds INFANTILE DEPENDENCE, in which the infant is objectively dependent on the actual BREAST, and precedes mature dependence, in which the MATURE adult relates genitally (see GENITAL CHARACTER) to a person (a whole OBJECT). During the stage of quasi-independence the child achieves partial independence of the breast by means of one or other of the transitional TECHNIQUES which enable him to relate to an idea of the breast located either inside himself (PARANOID TECHNIQUE and OBSESSIONAL TECHNIQUE) or outside himself (HYSTERICAL TECHNIQUE and PHOBIC TECHNIQUE). This schema of development differs from that of CLASSICAL THEORY in that (a) the stages of development are defined in terms of the relation to an object and not in terms of EROTOGENIC ZONES, and (b) the various NEUROSES are regarded not as REGRESSIONS to different levels of LIBIDINAL DEVELOPMENT, but as alternative solutions to the problem of achieving detachment from the breast.

R

RAPPORT 'That mysterious affective contact' between analyst and patient, without which psychoanalytical treatment is impossible. It is perhaps characteristic of the intellectualist bias of psychoanalysis that rapport should appear to it to be mysterious. The concept implies that the natural attitude of one human being to another is to observe him with detachment as though he were a thing and that some mysterious extra process has to take place if they are to communicate (see COMMUNICATION). But perhaps it is really the other way round and rapport occurs naturally unless it is inhibited (see INHIBITION) by such factors as the absence of shared SYMBOLS, suspicion on the part of one or both parties, or lack of IMAGINATION on the part of the therapist. See AFFECT; EMPATHY.

RATIONALIZATION The process by which a course of action is given *ex post facto* reasons which not only justify it but also conceal its true motivation.

'RAT MAN' Nickname given in the analytical literature to the patient described by Freud in his paper *Notes Upon a Case of Obsessional Neurosis* (1909).

REACTION-FORMATION Defensive process (DEFENCE mechanism) by which an unacceptable IMPULSE is mastered by exaggeration (hypertrophy) of the opposing tendency. Solicitude may be a reaction-formation against cruelty, cleanliness against COPROPHILIA, etc. Reaction-formation is regarded in CLASSICAL

THEORY as an OBSESSIONAL DEFENCE and it is usually assumed that the UNCONSCIOUS, rejected impulse survives in its original, INFANTILE form. Sometimes, however, the possibility is envisaged of reaction-formation forming the basis of SUBLIMATION (in which case the infantile impulse is no longer repressed (see REPRESSION) but transformed).

REACTION TYPE Term used in psychiatric classificatory systems which attempt to define MENTAL ILLNESSES in terms of characteristic reactions to stress. In the *International Classification of Diseases* (1955), HYSTERIA features as 'hysterical reaction without mention of anxiety-reaction'.

REAL, REALITY Psychoanalysis combines allegiance to the common-sense or natural scientific view that a distinction can be made between external phenomena which are 'real' or 'really there' and mental phenomena which are subjective images, with the conviction that mental phenomena are of dynamic consequence and, therefore, in some other sense also real. As a result it uses 'real' to mean either objectively present or subjectively significant. It also assumes that all objective phenomena occupy a space external to the subject which is called *external reality* (or less frequently *objective reality*), and that images, thoughts, PHANTASIES, feelings, etc., occupy a space inside the subject which is called *internal reality* or *psychical reality* – internal and external reality both being realms in which things are and processes occur. The assumption of an inner realm of reality is a FICTION since mental processes can in no sense be considered spatially related to one another – their connexions are all temporal. Although the use of this fiction corresponds to general usage – we all locate our thoughts and feelings inside ourselves – it enables psychoanalysis to bypass problems of meaning by equating 'significant' and 'real' and to ignore the differences between man-created thoughts and external phenomena by treating them *both* as objects existing in space – a procedure which enables psychoanalysis to claim that it is a natural and not a moral SCIENCE.

Psychoanalysis, then, postulates two realms of reality: external (objective) reality and internal (psychical, subjective) reality. In the terms *reality-testing*, *reality-adaptation*, and *reality principle*, 'reality' means 'external reality'; *derealization*, however, refers to psychical reality, since patients with this symptom complain that, although they perceive the external world correctly, it no longer means anything to them, it seems 'unreal' (see DEREALIZATION).

The processes of INTERNALIZATION, INTROJECTION, and IN-CORPORATION are usually defined in a way that implies that objects can be transferred from external to internal reality, while PRO-JECTION and EXTERNALIZATION are defined in terms of movement of objects in the opposite direction, although in fact these terms refer to shifts in the amount of significance with which external objects (PERCEPTS) and mental images (CONCEPTS) are endowed.

See OBJECTIVE AND SUBJECTIVE; INTERNAL; MEANING; NEUROLOGY; ADAPTATION; and immediately below.

REALITY-ADAPTATION The process of becoming adapted to the external ENVIRONMENT. For the edge put on this concept by the assumption in CLASSICAL THEORY that the infant is totally maladapted and obeys the PLEASURE-PRINCIPLE without reference to external REALITY, see ADAPTATION.

REALITY PRINCIPLE According to Freud, mental activity is governed by two principles: the PLEASURE PRINCIPLE and the reality principle, the former leading to relief of instinctual TENSION by hallucinatory WISH-FULFILMENT (see also HALLUCINATION), the latter to instinctual gratification by accommodation to the facts of, and the objects existing within, the external WORLD. According to Freud's original formulations, the reality principle is acquired and learned during DEVELOPMENT, whereas the pleasure principle is innate and primitive.

REALITY-TESTING The capacity to distinguish between mental images and external PERCEPTS, between PHANTASY and external REALITY, to correct subjective impressions by reference to external facts. According to CLASSICAL THEORY, the infant lacks any capacity for reality-testing. DELUSIONS and HALLUCINATIONS occurring in PSYCHOSIS are defined as failures in reality-testing. See PLEASURE PRINCIPLE.

REFERENCE, IDEAS OF The symptom, often PSYCHOTIC, of interpreting indifferent phenomena as though they had reference to oneself.

REGRESSION In general, reversion to an earlier state or mode of functioning. Specifically, defensive process (see DEFENCE) by which the subject avoids (or seeks to avoid) ANXIETY by (partial or total) return to an earlier stage of LIBIDINAL and EGO DEVELOPMENT, the stage to which the regression occurs being determined by the existence of FIXATION-POINTS. The theory of regression presupposes that, except in ideal cases, INFANTILE stages of development are not entirely outgrown, so that the earlier patterns of behaviour remain available as alternative modes of functioning. It is, however, not maintained that regression is often a viable or efficient defensive process; on the contrary, it is usually a question of out of the frying-pan into the fire, since regression compels the individual to re-experience anxiety appropriate to the stage to which he had regressed. For instance, regression from the PHALLIC or OEDIPAL level to the ORAL level, undertaken as a defence against CASTRATION ANXIETY, lays the patient open to re-experiencing SEPARATION ANXIETY. As a result, regression tends to be followed by further defensive measures designed to protect the EGO from its effects.

SUBLIMATIONS may also undergo regression, i.e. they may revert to their infantile precursors, painting becoming smearing, intellectual curiosity becoming VOYEURISM or greed.

Controversy exists as to the value of *therapeutic regressions*, i.e. regressive behaviour occurring during treatment and in relation to it, typically with increased DEPENDENCE on the analyst. On the one hand, so it is argued, it may enable the analyst to gain access to early phases and levels of development and facilitate reorganization of the personality on a new pattern; on the other it may, it is also argued, create irreversible dependence on the analyst and militate against VERBALIZATION and sublimation of infantile tendencies. According to CLASSICAL THEORY, the relaxed position on the analytical couch and the opportunities provided for FREE ASSOCIATION provide as much regression as is necessary for the treatment of the PSYCHONEUROSES. See Balint (1952) and Winnicott (1958) for the case in favour of therapeutic regression in the treatment of CHARACTER disorders and BORDERLINE patients. (See BASIC FAULT; NEW BEGINNING; TRUE AND FALSE SELF.

'Regression' is also used in a rather specialized sense in the theory of DREAMS to provide an explanation of the fact that they are hallucinatory phenomena. The theory states the ENERGY which in waking life would go to the musculature and be discharged in action is compelled by the INHIBITIONS operative in SLEEP to 'regress' to the sense-organs, provoking HALLUCINATIONS. The underlying assumption here is that the psyche is constructed like a reflex arc with psychic impulses 'normally' moving from the sensory to the motor ends and only in sleep compelled to move in the opposite, regressive, direction.

REIFICATION   The process of treating CONCEPTS as though they were things (abstract nouns as though they were concrete nouns). Metapsychological STRUCTURAL concepts (see META-PSYCHOLOGY) lend themselves to reification by the unsuspecting, since it is easy to forget that the SUPER-EGO, EGO, and ID are concepts designed to explain processes and to discuss their physical attributes and spatial relations. Similarly, in OBJECT-THEORY, concepts like 'the good MOTHER' (see also GOOD) or 'the bad BREAST' (see also BAD) may be discussed as though they were objects or persons inhabiting the subject. See FICTION; MIND; PERSONOLOGY; PROCESS THEORY; PHENOMENOLOGY.

RELATION   For *object-relation*, see OBJECT. For *interpersonal relations*, see INTERPERSONAL. The *analytical relation(ship)* refers to the interpersonal relationship *between* patient and analyst in contrast to the patient's TRANSFERENCE on the analyst or the analyst's COUNTER-TRANSFERENCE. In *doctor–patient relation*, *mother–child relation*, etc., the relation refers to the transactions between the two parties and not to status or kinship relations, i.e. the word is being used psychologically and not sociologically.

RELIGION   For Freud's view that religious ideas are 'illusions, fulfilments of the oldest, strongest, and most urgent wishes of mankind', see his *The Future of an Illusion* (1927), where he interprets belief in God as a response to recognition of human helplessness: '. . . the terrifying impression of helplessness in childhood aroused the need for protection – for protection through love – which was provided by the father; and the recognition that this helplessness lasts throughout life made it necessary to cling to the existence of a father, but this time a more powerful one.' For his view that religious emotions are REGRESSIONS 'to an early phase of EGO-feeling', see his *Civilization and Its Discontents* (1930); also OCEANIC FEELING. For a Protestant psychoanalyst-pastor's views of Freud's attitude to religion, see *Psycho-analysis and Faith* (1963) (the letters of Sigmund Freud and Oskar Pfister). Since

Freud's time, psychoanalysis has become increasingly MOTHER-orientated and the new theologians have been busy eliminating the idea of God 'out there'; as a result, it is difficult to assess the relevance of Freud's writings to the contemporary religious scene.

For the parallels between religious and obsessional RITUALS (see also OBSESSION), see Freud's *Obsessive Actions and Religious Practices* (1907), where he wrote: 'In view of these similarities and analogies one might venture to regard obsessional neurosis as a pathological counterpart of the formation of a religion, and to describe that neurosis as an individual religiosity and religion as a universal obsessional neurosis.' See OBSESSIONAL NEUROSIS.

REPARATION The process (DEFENCE mechanism) of reducing GUILT by action designed to make good the harm imagined to have been done to an ambivalently invested object (see AMBIVALENCE); the process of re-creating an internal object which has in PHANTASY been destroyed. In KLEINIAN writings there is a tendency to regard all creative activity (see CREATIVITY) as reparative, and to consider reparation one of the normal processes by which the individual resolves his inherent ambivalence towards objects. See DEPRESSIVE POSITION.

REPETITION-COMPULSION Term used by Freud to describe what he believed to be an innate tendency to revert to earlier conditions. The concept was used by him in support of the DEATH INSTINCT concept. Since the animate develops out of the inanimate, there is, he believed, an innate drive, the death instinct, to return to the inanimate. The concept was also used to explain the general phenomenon of RESISTANCE to therapeutic change. According to Freud (1926), the compulsion to repeat operates as a 'resistance of the unconscious' which necessitates a period of 'WORKING THROUGH', even after the patient has acquired insight into the nature and functions of his DEFENCES and has decided to relinquish them. In this context the concept means little more than mental sluggishness. Nowadays working through tends to be regarded as analogous to MOURNING, inasmuch as all change involves abandoning attachments to objects, e.g. parental figures, and familiar patterns of behaviour.

REPRESENTATION That which enables the mind to present to itself the image of something not actually present. A *mental representation* is a relatively permanent image of anything that has previously been perceived (see PERCEPTION), or alternatively the process by which such images are constructed (acquired). It is synonymous with 'mental image', 'memory image', 'mnemic image', and with some usages of 'INTERNALIZATION'. An *object-representation* is the mental representation of any person who constitutes an OBJECT for the SUBJECT, i.e. to whom he is psychologically related. Strictly speaking all 'objects' are 'object-representations'. *Symbolic representation* is the process by which the mental image of one object comes to stand for (the mental image of) another one, the former becoming a SYMBOL of the latter.

REPRESSION The process (DEFENCE mechanism) by which an unacceptable IMPULSE or idea is rendered UNCONSCIOUS. Freud distinguished between *primary repression*, by which the initial emergence of an instinctual impulse is prevented, and *secondary repression*, by which derivatives and disguised manifestations of the impulse are kept unconscious. '*The return of the repressed*' consists in the involuntary irruption into consciousness of unacceptable derivatives of the primary impulse, not the dissolution of the primary repression. According to Freud, all EGO DEVELOPMENT and ADAPTATION to the ENVIRONMENT are dependent on primary repression, in the absence of which impulses are discharged immediately by hallucinatory WISH-FULFILMENT (see also HALLUCINATION). On the other hand, excessive secondary repression leads to defective ego development and the emergence of SYMPTOMS not SUBLIMATIONS. Repression presupposes a repressing agency, either the EGO or the SUPER-EGO, and a STIMULUS, which is ANXIETY, and it leads to division of the personality into two parts. In Freud's early writings the UNCONSCIOUS is sometimes called 'the repressed'. Repression differs from INHIBITION in that it presupposes the opposition of two QUANTA of ENERGY: that invested in the repressed impulse and striving for release, and that invested in the repressing agency (the COUNTER-CATHEXIS) striving to maintain the repression, i.e. repression resembles a dam holding back the flow of a river, whereas inhibition resembles switching off an electric light.

RESISTANCE When used as a technical term, the opposition encountered during psychoanalytical treatment to the process of making UNCONSCIOUS processes CONSCIOUS. Patients are said to be in a state of resistance if they oppose the analyst's INTERPRETATIONS and to have weak or strong resistances according as to whether they find it easy or difficult to allow their analyst to understand them. Resistance is a manifestation of DEFENCE, with the possible exception of 'the resistance of the unconscious', REPETITION-COMPULSION.

RESTITUTION   Either 1. the defensive process (see DEFENCE) of reducing GUILT by making amends to an ambivalently (see AMBIVALENCE) invested object. (See REPARATION.) Or 2. the process by which a SCHIZOPHRENIC or PARANOID patient constructs DE-LUSIONS which restore to him a sense of significance. According to Freud (1911), the paranoid experiences an internal catastrophe, often symbolized (see SYMBOL) by the idea of a WORLD-CATAS-TROPHE, as a result of which everything becomes indifferent and irrelevant to him. He then constructs delusions which restore meaning to the world. 'The delusional formation, which we take to be the pathological product, is in reality an attempt at recovery, a process of reconstruction.'

RETARDATION   Symptom of DEPRESSION in which the patient's thought-processes and physical movements are greatly slowed down. Sometimes used to differentiate ENDOGENOUS and EXOGENOUS depression, it being claimed that retardation is evi-dence that the depression has a physiological cause. See MANIA; MANIC-DEPRESSIVE PSYCHOSIS; PSYCHOMOTOR ACCELERATION.

REVERSAL   1. An instinctual vicissitude. According to CLAS-SICAL THEORY, instincts are capable of undergoing reversal so that SADISM can change into MASOCHISM, VOYEURISM into EXHIBITION-ISM, etc., the reversal being usually, though not always, from ACTIVE to PASSIVE. 2. DEFENCE mechanism which exploits the possibility of reversal 1. According to Anna Freud, REACTION-FORMATION is a defence in which 'the ego avails itself of the instinct's capacity for reversal' – A. Freud (1937).

RITUAL   Originally a religious or magical ceremony or pro-cedure; borrowed by both psychiatry and psychoanalysis to describe a form of behaviour displayed by patients suffering from OBSESSIONAL NEUROSIS, in which the patient attempts to reduce ANXIETY by carrying out a more or less complex and stereotyped series of actions. Obsessional rituals can be regarded as a privately constructed system of counter-MAGIC by which the patient attempts to ward off fantastic fears by equally fantastic actions, the logic of both being animistic and dependent on PRIMARY PROCESS thinking. In *washing rituals*, patients feel compelled to wash themselves according to a rigidly prescribed and complex routine in order to allay a dread of being infected or of infecting others, the fear of infection being one which their own intelligence does *not* endorse. In this respect, obsessional rituals differ sharply from the rituals of the ignorant, superstitious, and religious. They also differ from religious rituals in being private and solitary. See RELIGION.

ROLE DIFFUSION   See IDENTITY *v*. ROLE DIFFUSION.

RORSCHACH TEST   Probably the most sophisticated PROJECTIVE TEST, in which the subject is invited to describe what he can see into a series of symmetrical ink-blots, some of which are coloured, his answers being used as evidence of his phantasy life, personality structure, psychiatric diagnosis, and even intelligence. Designed in the 1920s by Rorschach, a Swiss psychoanalyst.

S

SABOTEUR, INTERNAL   Term used by Fairbairn (see FAIRBAIRN'S REVISED PSYCHOPATHOLOGY) to describe what he also calls the anti-libidinal EGO, one of the three part-egos into which the original unitary ego becomes split (see SPLITTING), the other two being the central ego (the self) and the LIBIDINAL ego. According to Fairbairn, the inevitable disturbance of the infant's original solely libidinal attitude towards the MOTHER leads first to AMBIVALENCE towards her and then the splitting off from his ego of two parts: one libidinal, which is attached to a GOOD or 'accepting' image of the BREAST, the other aggressive (anti-libidinal, see also AGGRESSION), which is attached to a BAD or 'rejecting' image of the breast. Fairbairn's libidinal ego corresponds to Freud's ID, while the Internal Saboteur contributes to the formation of the SUPER-EGO. See PARANOID-SCHIZOID POSITION; SCHIZOID POSITION.

SADISM 1. Sexual PERVERSION in which the subject claims to get erotic pleasure from inflicting pain on his object. 2. Pleasure in cruelty. 3. *Oral sadism*: pleasure in biting (see also ORAL). 4. *Anal sadism*: pleasure in cruelty of a kind theoretically associated with the ANAL phase of LIBIDINAL DEVELOPMENT. It is unclear whether sadism is an infantile COMPONENT-INSTINCT pure and simple, or whether it is a fusion of libidinal and aggressive impulses (see AGGRESSION); or whether, if the latter, the aggressive element in it is a manifestation of innate aggressive or destructive tendencies or a response to FRUSTRATION and/or humiliation. It is also unclear whether the 'pleasure' derived from sadistic activity resides in the sight of the other's pain or in the sense of power in being able to inflict pain.

According to Freud prior to 1920, sadism is capable of REVERSAL into MASOCHISM, but later he used masochism as evidence in favour of the DEATH-INSTINCT and held that masochism was the primary tendency and that it underwent reversal into sadism. See ACTIVE AND PASSIVE.

SADNESS A quiet mood, resembling SORROW and GRIEF, provoked either by acceptance that some loss has occurred or by recognition of the transcience of all sources of satisfaction. It differs from DEPRESSION in that conflict forms no part of it.

SADO-MASOCHISM See SADISM; MASOCHISM.

SANITY AND INSANITY These are popular and medico-legal terms, which PSYCHIATRISTS and PSYCHOANALYSTS only use when they have dealings with the law, a sane person being someone who is *compos mentis* and fit to plead in a court of law, an insane person someone who is unfit to plead. There is, however, a tendency to equate insanity and PSYCHOSIS.

SATISFACTION The emotion accompanying the achievement of a goal. *Instinctual satisfaction*: the emotion accompanying discharge of an instinctual IMPULSE. Classical INSTINCT THEORY (see also CLASSICAL THEORY) is compelled by its adherence to the PLEASURE PRINCIPLE to define satisfaction in terms of diminution of instinctual TENSION. See INSTINCT; FORE-PLEASURE AND END-PLEASURE.

SCHIZOID Adj. 1. Originally, referring to persons in whom there is a divorce between the emotional and intellectual functions.

145

The usage derives from Bleuler, who held that this divorce was the essential disturbance in SCHIZOPHRENIA and in schizoid types of personality. **2.** By extension, referring to anyone whose character suggests comparison with schizophrenia or who (if he did become PSYCHOTIC) would be more likely to develop schizophrenia than MANIC-DEPRESSIVE PSYCHOSIS. **3.** Hence, by further extension, withdrawn, suspicious, tending to have a vivid PHANTASY life. **4.** Referring to persons whose PSYCHOPATHOLOGY includes the use of DEFENCES such as SPLITTING, DENIAL, INTROJECTION, and PROJECTION, which enable GUILT and DEPRESSION to be denied. **5.** Used to describe these defences and to describe the position in infancy from which the use of these defences derives.

Usages **4** and **5** derive from an assumption made by OBJECT THEORY that everyone is either schizoid or DEPRESSIVE, the difference being determined by vicissitudes of development occurring during the PARANOID-SCHIZOID (Klein, see KLEINIAN) or schizoid (Fairbairn, see FAIRBAIRN'S REVISED PSYCHOPATHOLOGY) and DEPRESSIVE POSITIONS. Hence:

Schizoid character Either **1.** a person who is detached, withdrawn, or whose intellectual and emotional functions seem divorced. Or **2.** a person whose introjections of GOOD objects and projections of BAD objects (see also OBJECT) and parts of the self renders him relatively independent of others and free of guilt at the price of distrust of others and over-estimation of himself.

Schizoid defences This term refers to the combined use of introjection of good objects and denial, splitting, and projection of bad aspects of the self as a defence against guilt, anxiety, and depression.

Schizoid position Term used by Fairbairn to describe the situation occurring in early infancy in which the infant interprets rejection and FRUSTRATION as evidence that his love is destructive and responds by splitting of the EGO into three parts – the central ego (self), the libidinal ego, which is attached to a good 'accepting' image of the BREAST, and the anti-libidinal ego (INTERNAL SABOTEUR), which is attached to a bad 'rejecting' image of the breast. The concept resembles Klein's paranoid-schizoid position, but makes no use of the idea of a DEATH INSTINCT.

The difficulties surrounding the concept of 'schizoid' derive from two sources: (a) it is used in both descriptive and psychopathological senses; (b) the psychopathological usage is confused because it derives from two different versions of object theory: those of Klein and Fairbairn, which agree in thinking it legitimate to correlate INFANTILE developmental stages (see also LIBIDINAL DEVELOPMENT) and psychotic processes but differ in their basic assumptions about the nature of INSTINCT, Klein using Freud's theory of a LIFE INSTINCT and a death instinct, Fairbairn conceiving of AGGRESSION as a response to frustration and rejection.

SCHIZOPHRENIA   Term invented by Eugen Bleuler to describe the mental illness previously known as DEMENTIA PRAECOX and now used generally by PSYCHIATRY to describe functional PSYCHOSES in which the symptoms are withdrawal and poverty of affect (in contrast to both the capacity for RAPPORT displayed by the healthy and ˙NEUROTIC, and the DEPRESSION or ELATION displayed by the MANIC-DEPRESSIVE), DELUSIONS, HALLUCINATIONS, confusion, AUTISTIC and schizophrenic THINKING (in which syntax is disrupted) and disturbances in the sense of IDENTITY. For Bleuler, the essence of schizophrenia was divorce between the intellectual and emotional functions, as exemplified by the phenomenon known as 'incongruity of affect', in which the idea expressed and the emotion accompanying it are incompatible. Descriptive psychiatry distinguishes three varieties of schizophrenia: HEBEPHRENIA, CATATONIA, and PARANOID schizophrenia.

For the attitude of both CLASSICAL THEORY and OBJECT THEORY to the problem of schizophrenia, see PSYCHOSIS. For the theory that schizophrenia is the result of disturbed INTER-PERSONAL relations within the family, see DOUBLE BIND. For detailed accounts of the psychoanalysis of schizophrenia, see Searles (1965), which includes an exhaustive bibliography.

SCHIZOPHRENOGENIC   Adj. applied usually to parent, typically MOTHER, whose personality and behaviour is held (by user) capable of inducing SCHIZOPHRENIA in her children. Also applied to families and situations. See DOUBLE BIND.

SCIENCE   Since critics of psychoanalysis (e.g. Eysenck, 1965) often dismiss it on the ground that it is unscientific, and since an occasional psychoanalyst (e.g. Home, 1966) argues that psychoanalysis is not a science but a Humanity, it needs to be pointed out that the proposition 'psychoanalysis is not a science' can be made true or untrue by choosing the appropriate definition of science. If one defines science in a way that makes knowledge derived from experiment and measurement an essential part of the definition, psychoanalysis fairly obviously is not one. If one defines it in terms of the attempt to establish causal relationships between events, the question hinges on whether one believes that the laws of CAUSALITY (DETERMINISM) can be applied to living organisms capable of CONSCIOUSNESS – as Freud did and Home does not. If one defines it, as, for instance, the *C.O.D.* does, as 'systematic and formulated knowledge', psychoanalysis is a science, and the issue becomes one of deciding to what branch of science it belongs, i.e. whether it is a natural, biological, or moral science. See Rycroft (1966) for the idea that psycho-analysis constitutes a bridge between the biological sciences and the humanities, and Szasz (1951) for the view that it is a moral science.

SCOPOPHILIA   Pleasure in looking. Listed by classical theory as one of the infantile COMPONENT-INSTINCTS. The spelling 'scop*t*ophilia' dates from a mistake made by Freud's first trans-lators. See VOYEURISM.

SCOTOMIZATION   Defensive process (see DEFENCE) by which the subject fails (consciously) to perceive (see PERCEPTION) cir-cumscribed areas either of his environmental situation or of himself. (Derived from *scotoma*: a blank area in the visual field.) See DENIAL.

SCREEN MEMORY   A childhood memory which is in itself trivial but which can be treated as a DREAM, INTERPRETATION of its MANIFEST content revealing a significant LATENT content. Its aptness for symbolizing the patient's childhood situation is presumably responsible for it having been remembered and for it recurring sufficiently frequently in the patient's FREE ASSOCIATIONS to attract attention.

SEARCH FOR IDENTITY   See IDENTITY.

SECONDARY ELABORATION   The process by which a DREAM is modified by the dreamer's need to give it greater co-herence and internal consistency. It represents the contribution of the secondary processes to the text of a dream. See PROCESSES, PRIMARY AND SECONDARY.

SECONDARY GAIN   See GAIN, PRIMARY AND SECONDARY.

SECONDARY PROCESSES   See PROCESSES, PRIMARY AND SECONDARY.

SELF   1. When used by itself: the SUBJECT regarded as an AGENT, as being aware of his own IDENTITY and of his role as subject and agent. 2. As part of a hyphenated word: the subject regarded as the OBJECT of his own activity.

The self differs from the EGO of psychoanalytical theory in that (a) the self refers to the subject as he experiences himself while the ego refers to his personality as a structure about which impersonal generalizations can be made; and that (b) the ego, as defined by Freud, contains repressed (see REPRESSION), UNCONSCIOUS parts which cannot be recognized by the self as parts of itself. One of the existential criticisms (see EXISTENTIALISM) of CLASSICAL ANALYTICAL TECHNIQUE is that its theory, particularly its META-PSYCHOLOGY, leaves no room for the self (see ONTOLOGY). Hence:

Self-awareness   Awareness of oneself as the object of one's own experience.

Self-consciousness   Self-awareness, but also: awareness of the possibility that someone else is aware of oneself. When accompanied by embarrassment, this implies a defect in self-awareness. Either one fears that the other will perceive oneself in a way that is incompatible with one's image of oneself, or one fears that one's presentation of oneself is inadequate to the situation one is in. See IDENTITY; SHAME.

Self-esteem   The value put on oneself by oneself. See NARCISSISM.

Self-love   Love of oneself. See NARCISSISM.

Self-observation   Observation of oneself. Listed by Freud as a SUPER-EGO function on the ground that it arises by INTROJECTION of the experience of being observed by others and that it is, in the first instance, moralistic. See INTROSPECTION.

Self-preservation   Prior to the 1920s, Freud's theory of instincts (see INSTINCT THEORY) ran parallel with contemporary biological views on instinct, his EGO-INSTINCTS corresponding with the self-preservative instinct, and his sexual instincts corresponding with the reproductive instinct.

Self-punishment See MASOCHISM.

Self-reproaches Self-reproaches and self-accusations occur in DEPRESSION and the DEPRESSIVE phase of MANIC-DEPRESSIVE PSYCHOSIS, often in delusional and bizarre forms.

SEMANTIC(S) Originally, that branch of philology which is concerned with the meaning of words. Nowadays, often, the study of MEANING in general. According to Szasz (1961), Home (1966), Rycroft (1966), psychoanalysis, or at least some parts of it, is a semantic theory since it shows that DREAMS and neurotic SYMPTOMS have meaning.

SENSATION The irreducible elements of experience out of which PERCEPTIONS and conceptions are constructed, e.g. light, sound, smell, touch, taste, pain, heat, cold. Sensations depend on the organ stimulated not on the object stimulating it.

SENSUAL AND SENSUOUS In non-analytical writings, *sensual* usually refers to taking an excessive or greedy pleasure in the senses, while *sensuous* lacks moral overtones. The psychoanalytical view that all pleasure is, in some sense, SEXUAL confuses this distinction; this despite the fact that the theory of SUBLIMATION includes the idea that the pleasure derived from sublimated and unsublimated activities differ in quality.

SENTIMENT 'An organized system of emotional dispositions centred about the idea of some object' – McDougall (1908), according to whom there are three sentiments: love, hate, and self-regard. See LOVE, HATE, AFFECT, and EMOTION, for some of the consequences of psychoanalytical theory's assumption that love and hate are instincts and not 'organized system(s) of emotional dispositions'.

SEPARATION ANXIETY ANXIETY at (the prospect of) being separated from someone believed to be necessary for one's survival. Separation anxiety may be objective, as in infancy or in adult invalids, or neurotic, when the presence of another person is used as a DEFENCE against some other form of anxiety. In both cases two factors are involved: dread of some unspecified danger, either from the outside or from mounting internal TENSION, and dread of losing the object believed capable of protecting or relieving one. INSTINCT THEORY tends to emphasize the connexions between separation-anxiety and instinctual tension, OBJECT THEORY the dread of losing contact with objects.

SEPARATION, MOTHER–CHILD During the last twenty years, largely as a result of the work of Bowlby and Winnicott, the idea that much psychiatric illness is due to separation from the MOTHER during infancy and childhood has achieved considerable currency. The hypothesis is not simply that separation causes distress at the time or even unhappiness later, but that it is the cause of specific MENTAL ILLNESSES, notably PSYCHOPATHY, PHOBIA, and DEPRESSION. Explanations as to *how* separation produces these effects vary in sophistication and complexity, e.g. (a) it causes insecurity; (b) it increases hostility and AMBIVALENCE; (c) it interferes with introjective and identificatory processes (see INTROJECTION and IDENTIFICATION) and thereby interferes with EGO-DEVELOPMENT; and (d) it institutes MOURNING processes at an age when the child is too immature to complete them, leaving him, as it were, 'stuck' in the phase of DESPAIR or DEPRESSION. Hypothesis (d), which is Bowlby's, has the advantage that it is capable of subsuming the others.

The hypothesis is a rarity among psychoanalytical concepts in that it is capable of statistical handling, since the most obvious causes of gross mother–child separation – hospitalization of either mother or child, death of the mother, desertion by the mother – are ascertainable facts. It appears, however, that the statistical findings are not sufficiently clear-cut to command universal assent. (See 'Parental Deprivation and Mental Health', leader in the *Lancet*, 6 August 1966, for a review of the literature.) The concept of separation is less straightforward than it seems since (a) only gross separation can be clearly distinguished from maternal DEPRIVATION, which can, of course, occur without physical separation; and (b) it involves consideration of two variables: the age of the child at which separation occurs and the duration of the separation. See SEPARATION ANXIETY. See Bowlby (1951, 1961).

SEX, SEXUAL 1. Biologically: all organisms, except the most simple and primitive, exist in two forms (sexes), one male, the other female, new members of the species arising by fusion of two sex cells, one produced by a male, the other by a female. Hence *sexual reproduction*, *sexual intercourse*, *sexual organs*, all referring to structures and functions necessary for the creation of new individuals. *Sexual characteristics* are those which enable sex to be identified; they are either *primary*, those directly related to reproduction, or *secondary*, those usually associated with one sex but not directly involved in reproduction. 2. Psychologically: *sexual* refers to drives, behaviour patterns, emotions, and sensations observed or inferred to be intrinsically connected with reproductive activity (or with the use of the reproductive organs as a source of sensations). 3. Psychoanalysis has upset traditional concepts of sex by asserting (a) that adult sexual behaviour has INFANTILE precursors – INFANTILE SEXUALITY, ORAL and ANAL erotism (see EROTIC), COMPONENT INSTINCTS, etc., – which play a part in the development of not only the adult sexual instinct but also of the personality as a whole; and (b) that infantile and adult sexual drives have effects on non-sexual behaviour, these effects being mediated by SYMBOLIZATION and SUBLIMATION. As a result, the psychoanalytical literature uses 'sex', 'sexual', and 'sexuality' to refer to phenomena which are manifestly non-sexual but are latently (or inferentially) derivatives or analogues of sexual phenomena (see MANIFEST AND LATENT). Ernest Jones recommended that the confusions created by this extension of the concept 'sex' should be guarded against by using 'sex' in its restricted, traditional sense and 'sexuality' for the wider range of phenomena.

Hence, according to context, 'sexual' means 'relating to the male–female differentiation'; 'relating to reproductive behaviour, instincts or organs'; 'erotic, pleasurable'.

SEXUALITY   See SEX.

SEXUALITY, INFANTILE   This term embraces not only manifestly SEXUAL behaviour occurring in childhood, but also all pleasure derived from the EROTOGENIC ZONES and all manifestations of the COMPONENT INSTINCTS.

SHAME   Shame is the Cinderella of the unpleasant emotions, having received much less attention than ANXIETY, GUILT, and DEPRESSION. Freud (1896) interpreted it as fear of ridicule, while Piers (1953) interprets it as the response to failure to live up to one's EGO IDEAL (i.e. whereas guilt occurs if we transgress an injunction derived from outside ourselves but represented in the

SUPER-EGO, shame occurs if we fail to achieve an ideal of behaviour we have set ourselves). According to Lynd (1958), who is not a psychoanalyst, shame has a close connexion with the sense of IDENTITY and with INSIGHT. It is provoked by experiences which call into question our preconceptions about ourselves and compel us to see ourselves through the eyes of others – and to recognize the discrepancy between their perception of us and our own over-simplified and egotistical conception of ourselves. If faced up to, shaming experiences increase insight and SELF-AWARENESS; if denied, they provoke the development of a defensive carapace. See Rycroft (1968) for the suggestion that shame as a persistent neurotic symptom occurs in SCHIZOID individuals who both over-value (fancy) themselves and possess insight into the fact that their self-overevaluation is not shared by others.

Sociologists distinguish between guilt and shame cultures, Judaeo-Christian Western civilization being an example of the former, traditional Japanese culture and that of the European aristocratic–military classes being examples of the latter.

Shame differs from guilt in being more closely connected with bodily sensations, e.g. blushing, and in being, as Lynd points out, more readily evoked by failures to conform to non-codifiable social rules. Whereas transgressions of moral codes and laws produce guilt, tactlessness and errors in taste induce shame.

SHELL SHOCK   Obsolete term for TRAUMATIC NEUROSIS.

SHOCK   **1.** *Physiological shock*: state of collapse, pallor, de-pressed blood pressure, etc., occurring as (immediate) response to bodily trauma (injury, wound, major surgery, etc.). **2.** *Psychological shock*: the response to a totally unexpected experience, for which one has not been prepared by VIGILANCE or ANXIETY, and which compels one to reorientate oneself. Unpleasant shocks of sufficient severity to cause symptoms or, if occurring in childhood, to disturb DEVELOPMENT are known as TRAUMATA.

SIB, SIBLING   Old English words for relatives or kin, revived by psychologists and sociologists to avoid the necessity for speci-fying the sex of the subject's brothers and sisters. Hence *sibling-rivalry*: rivalry with brothers and/or sisters. A *sibship* is a set of brothers and/or sisters.

SIGN, SYMPTOM, AND SYMBOL   A   sign   indicates   the

presence of some process or phenomenon. It requires differentiation from SYMPTOM and SYMBOL. In medicine, a *sign* is a phenomenon observed by the examining physician which indicates to him the presence of some pathological process, which enables him to assert that the patient has (or has not) the signs of such-and-such a disease; whereas a *symptom* is a phenomenon which causes the patient distress and of which he asks to be relieved. A sign may or may not be perceptible to the patient, and if perceptible may or may not cause him distress. A symptom may or may not also be a sign. In CONVERSION HYSTERIA, the patient complains of physical symptoms but the physician fails to discover any signs of physical illness – but, if fortunate, he will discover signs of neurotic illness. A *pathognomonic sign* indicates by itself the presence of some particular illness.

In psychoanalytical theory, a sign indicates the presence of something, whereas a symbol refers to something other than itself and derives its significance from that something else. Inarticulate cries, unlearned gestures and expressions, and the physical manifestations of ANXIETY are signs of what the subject is experiencing, whereas DREAM-images, neurotic CONVERSION-symptoms are symbols, since their referents can only be arrived at by INTERPRETATION. Signs reveal their meaning directly (to members of the same species), symbols require decoding. According to general usage, but not according to CLASSICAL THEORY, which defines symbols in a special sense (see SYMBOLISM), WORDS, national flags, and emblems are symbols since they derive their significance solely from the learned knowledge that they refer to something other than themselves.

SIGNAL ANXIETY One of the two forms of ANXIETY described by Freud (1926) in his third and last theory of anxiety, the other being PRIMARY (or automatic) ANXIETY. In Freud's formulation it is the response of the EGO to internal danger and the stimulus to the formation and use of DEFENCE-mechanisms. In ordinary language it is that form of apprehensiveness which alerts one to internal changes which might disturb one's equanimity and which, for instance, normally wakes one up before a DREAM can develop into a NIGHTMARE. It can be regarded as an inturned form of VIGILANCE, the scanning alertness which prevents one being taken by surprise by changes in one's environment.

SLEEP   Although Freud's own writings take sleep for granted, merely assuming that there is a physiological need for it and that the function of DREAMS is to prevent UNCONSCIOUS, repressed tendencies (see REPRESSION) from disturbing it, the work of Lewin and others suggests that it may itself have a PSYCHOPATHOLOGY deriving from an unconscious equation of sleep with fusion with the BREAST (primary IDENTIFICATION with the MOTHER). As a result of this equation, excessive sleeping may be manifestation of REGRESSION to the ORAL level and insomnia may be due either to AMBIVALENCE towards the (internal) mother and dread of fusing with her (it), or, as in MANIA, to the presence of a PHANTASY of being fused with the mother which renders sleep (psychologically) superfluous.

Recent physiological research has shown that there are two kinds of sleep: normal, or orthodox, and dreaming, or paradoxical; and also that dreaming only occurs in the latter form, which can be identified by, *inter alia*, movements of the eye (without opening of the lids) and slow voltage electroencephalic (brain) waves. It also seems likely that the function of dream-sleep is to enable the brain to process the intake of the previous day – the analogy is with a' computer, the brain being programmed during the day. If this is correct, Freud's idea that we dream in order to preserve sleep needs reversing – we sleep in order to dream. His theory that INFANTILE tendencies express themselves in dreams is reconcilable with these physiological ideas if one assumes that repressed wishes, phantasies, etc., constitute a backlog of material striving for processing – an assumption which is in line with Freud's own ideas on the role of TRAUMA, traumatic experiences being ones which the subject is incapable of assimilating as they occur. See Oswald (1966).

SLIPS OF THE TONGUE   See PARAPRAXES.

SOCIAL PSYCHIATRY   That branch of psychiatry which is concerned with the social aspects of mental illness and with the conversion of mental hospitals into therapeutic communities – as opposed to places where individuals are treated separately. See Martin (1963).

SOLIPSISM   Correctly, philosophical theory that only the self is knowable or that the apparent external world consists of our own thoughts. Sometimes used, notably by Suttie (1935), to describe what CLASSICAL THEORY calls the NARCISSISM of the infant, i.e. the assumption that the external world exists solely to satisfy its wishes and its failure to appreciate that its objects are persons with *their* wishes and needs.

SOMA, SOMATIC   The body, bodily. Usually, in contrast to the PSYCHE, psychological; but very occasionally, all the cells of the body with the exception of the germ cells, i.e. that part of the body which constitutes the mortal individual, in contrast to that part which ensures the continuance of the species. *Somatic compliance* refers to some physical factor which determines the site of a neurotic symptom, e.g. the location of a CONVERSION SYMPTOM in an organ previously affected by a physical illness.

SORROW   According to McDougall (1908), sorrow is 'a derived emotion, one of the retrospective emotions of desire; [that], in short, it is a special form of regret, essentially a regret that springs from the sentiment of love, and therefore a tender regret.' See SADNESS; GRIEF; MOURNING.

SPHINCTER   Ring-shaped muscle controlling a bodily opening. References to the acquisition or loss of *sphincter control* are to the sphincters controlling defaecation and urination.

SPLITTING   Process (DEFENCE mechanism) by which a mental structure loses its integrity and becomes replaced by two or more part-structures. Splitting of both EGO and OBJECT is described. After splitting of the ego, typically only one resulting part-ego is experienced as 'SELF', the other constituting a (usually) unconscious 'split-off part of the ego'. After splitting of an object, the emotional attitude towards the two part-structures is typically antithetical, one object being experienced as 'GOOD' (accepting, benevolent, etc.), the other as 'BAD' (rejecting, malevolent, etc.). Splitting of both ego and object tends to be linked with DENIAL and PROJECTION, the trio constituting a SCHIZOID defence by which parts of the self (and of INTERNAL OBJECTS) are disowned and attributed to objects in the environment. The phrase '*splitting of the ego*' is used in four confusingly different senses: (a) To describe gross splitting of the personality into two parts as in dual or multiple personality. In this sense it is synonymous with 'DISSOCIATION'. (b) To describe the EGO in the sexual PERVERSIONS, particularly

FETISHISM. According to Freud (1927, 1938), the ego of the fetish-ist is split inasmuch as his attitude towards his object enables him to disavow CASTRATION ANXIETY which another part of his ego admits. (c) To describe reflective SELF-AWARENESS. According to Sterba (1934) psychoanalytical treatment requires the patient to split his ego, one part identifying with the analyst (see IDENTIFI-CATION) and observing and reflecting on the FREE ASSOCIATIONS produced by the other. In this sense, splitting, so far from being a pathological phenomenon, is a manifestation of self-awareness. (d) To describe the developmental and defensive process described above.

STAGES OF MAN According to Erikson (1963), there are eight stages of man, during each of which the individual displays (or fails to display) 'ego-qualities – criteria by which the individual demonstrates that his EGO, at a given stage, is strong enough to integrate the timetable of the organism with the structure of social institutions'. The eight stages are: TRUST *v.* BASIC MISTRUST, corresponding to the ORAL phase of CLASSICAL THEORY; AUTONOMY *v.* SHAME AND DOUBT, corresponding to the ANAL phase of classical theory; INITIATIVE *v.* GUILT, corresponding to the PHALLIC and OEDIPAL phases of classical theory; INDUSTRY *v.* INFERIORITY, corresponding to the LATENCY PERIOD of classical theory; IDENTITY *v.* ROLE DIFFUSION, corresponding to adolescence and early man-hood; INTIMACY *v.* ISOLATION, corresponding to 'the prime of life'; GENERATIVITY *v.* STAGNATION, corresponding to middle age; and EGO INTEGRITY *v.* DESPAIR, corresponding to old age.

STEREOTYPE Sociological term for the popular or conven-tional idea of how any particular class of person behaves, looks, etc. The idea that all Jews are hook-nosed and avaricious and that madmen are violent are obvious stereotypes; more subtle are the various preconceptions about kinds of behaviour appropriate to men and women, the young and old, etc., which imply that deviations from them are unnatural. See ACTIVE AND PASSIVE; MASCULINE; FEMININE.

STIMULUS That which evokes a response or reaction in living tissue. According to Freudian METAPSYCHOLOGY, stimuli are either INTERNAL or external, the former being instinctual IMPULSES coming from within the organism but impinging on the PSYCHIC

APPARATUS, the latter being sensory impressions derived from the ENVIRONMENT. Stimuli heighten TENSION, produce UNPLEASURE (PAIN), which is relieved by DISCHARGE according to either the PLEASURE or the REALITY PRINCIPLES. The *stimulus barrier* is that part of the psychic apparatus which protects the EGO from excessive stimulation; it is directed against both internal and external stimuli. According to some accounts, traumatic experiences (see TRAUMA) disrupt the stimulus barrier. *Stimulus hunger* is craving for stimulation; the assumption underlying the concept being that organisms require and seek an optimal quantity of stimulation. *Sign-stimulus* is an ethological term (see ETHOLOGY); it refers to behaviour which acts as a stimulus to complementary behaviour in another member of the same species. Smiling and crying are sign-stimuli.

STRATA   Geological metaphor by which memories, phases of DEVELOPMENT, etc., are conceived to have been deposited one on another in such a way that earlier MEMORIES and phases are deeper down than later ones. The metaphor insinuates the idea that early 'MATERIAL' is more inaccessible than later, and that severe, intractable illnesses are earlier in origin than milder ones. When, as can happen, early 'material' turns out to be easily accessible, recourse can be taken to a further geological metaphor, that of 'faulting'.

STRUCTURAL   Structural formulations describe mental activity in terms of the interaction of psychic structures such as EGO, SUPER-EGO, and ID. 'INTERNAL OBJECTS' are also structures, since they are conceived of as relatively permanent parts of the mind. Structural concepts seem to be unavoidable in psychological theories which relate past and present experience and which take cognizance of CONFLICT. See PSYCHIC APPARATUS; CONCEPT; DYNAMIC.

SUBCONSCIOUS   Synonym for UNCONSCIOUS never used in psychoanalytic writings.

SUBJECT   The person whose experience and behaviour is under consideration. All psychoanalytical writings, even the most abstract, are ultimately about some one person, who is the subject, all other persons who are mentioned being his OBJECTS. In theoretical writings, this one person is an abstraction, referred to as 'the subject', 'the individual', 'the patient', 'the infant', who is conceived of being related to, or as having impulses directed towards, various objects such as 'the BREAST', 'the MOTHER', 'the parents', etc. The parallel with grammar is exact: the subject is the person whom the sentence, generalization, or theory is about; the verb (plus adverb) describes the nature of the IMPULSE (INSTINCT) or relationship under discussion; and the object is the person with whom the subject has (wishes to have) dealings.

SUBJECTIVE Pertaining to the SUBJECT. See OBJECTIVE AND SUBJECTIVE.

SUBLIMATION Developmental process (see DEVELOPMENT) by which instinctual ENERGIES (see INSTINCT) are discharged (see DISCHARGE) in non-instinctual forms of behaviour. The process involves (a) displacement of energy from activities and objects of primary (biological) interest on to those of lesser instinctual interest; (b) transformation of the quality of the EMOTION accompanying the activity such that it becomes 'desexualized' and 'deaggressified' (see DESEXUALIZATION and DEAGGRESSIFICATION); and (c) liberation of the activity from the dictates of instinctual TENSION. Some definitions include a social element, viz. that true sublimations are socially acceptable. Intellectual curiosity is regarded as a sublimation of SCOPOPHILIA in so far as (a) it is directed towards non-sexual topics; (b) the pleasure accompanying it is not sexual; and (c) its variations in intensity are independent of instinctual tension. The concept seeks to explain the evolution of 'higher functions' from lower ones. The evidence on which it is based is of two kinds: first, the emergence of new interests and gifts during the course of psychoanalytical treatment; secondly, the emergence of 'regressive' symptoms (see REGRESSION) in persons having a neurotic breakdown. In the example of intellectual curiosity, sublimation means the increase in intellectual curiosity following analysis of childhood inhibitions of sexual curiosity, and the recrudescence of voyeuristic ('Peeping Tom', see VOYEURISM) tendencies or of over-eating in a patient who, prior to his breakdown, had an inquiring mind.

All sublimations depend on SYMBOLIZATION and all EGO-DEVELOPMENT depends on sublimation. Most accounts of the concept assert that the instincts available for sublimation are the pre-genital COMPONENT INSTINCTS (see also PRE-GENITAL) rather than the adult sexual instincts. In other words, the concept is developmental and evolutionary. Anna Freud (1937) lists sublimation as a DEFENCE (but one 'which pertains rather to the study of the normal than to that of neurosis') on the ground that it provides a progressive solution of infantile CONFLICTS (see also INFANTILE) which might otherwise lead to NEUROSIS.

SUBMISSION, SUBMISSIVENESS The act of yielding to others. The analytical literature tends to subsume submissive behaviour under the headings of PASSIVITY and MASOCHISM. According to the ethologists (see ETHOLOGY), submissive gestures automatically inhibit the aggressive threats (see AGGRESSION) of other members of the same species. See ACTIVE AND PASSIVE.

SUICIDE 1. Person who intentionally kills himself. 2. The act of so doing. According to Stengel (1964), 'on the average one third of the people who commit suicide have been suffering from a NEUROSIS or PSYCHOSIS or a severe PERSONALITY DISORDER', DEPRESSIVE illness or MELANCHOLIA being the mental disorder with the highest suicidal risk. He distinguishes between *suicide*, in which self-destruction is the only or main intention, and *attempted suicide*, into other which motives enter. 'Some warning of suicidal intention has almost invariably been given. Those who attempt suicide tend, in the suicidal act, to remain near or move towards other people. Suicidal attempts act as alarm signals and have the effect of an appeal for help, even though no such appeal may have been consciously intended.' It is estimated that attempted suicide is six to eight times commoner than successful suicide. Psychoanalytical theories of suicide interpret the urge to self-destruction either as an attack on an introjected object (see DEPRESSION) or as a derivative of the DEATH INSTINCT. (See also INTROJECTION.)

SUPER-EGO That part of the EGO in which SELF-OBSERVATION, self-criticism, and other reflective activities develop. That part of the ego in which parental introjects (see INTROJECTION) are located. Since Freud maintained that self-observation is dependent on INTERNALIZATION of the parents, these two definitions tally. The super-ego differs from the CONSCIENCE in that (a) it belongs to a different frame of reference, i.e. METAPSYCHOLOGY not ethics; (b) it includes UNCONSCIOUS elements; and (c) injunctions and inhibitions emanating from it derive from the subject's past and may be in CONFLICT with his present values. It is not maintained that the super-ego is an accurate replica of the parental figures who have been introjected, since the relevant internalizations are held to occur early in childhood, when the infant endows his objects with his own characteristics. As a result, the severity or intolerance of the super-ego derives (in part at least) from the violence of subject's own feelings in infancy. It is also assumed that the energies of the super-ego derive from the ID, i.e. that the self-attacking tendency of the super-ego provides an outlet for the subject's own aggressive impulses (see AGGRESSION). This is an example of TURNING AGAINST THE SELF. Although earlier formulations gave the FATHER the central role in the formation of the super-ego, most contemporary accounts postulate precursors of the super-ego occurring in the PRE-OEDIPAL phases of DEVELOPMENT, these precursors being the 'INTERNAL OBJECTS' of OBJECT THEORY. The concept first appears in Freud's *The Ego and the Id* (1923), and most descriptions of it are coloured by Freud's preoccupation with OBSESSIONAL NEUROSIS which permeates that book.

Some accounts of psychoanalytical treatment give as one of its aims modification of the super-ego in the direction of greater tolerance and realism, while others describe the transfer of its functions to the ego. This ambiguity derives from the fact that the concept includes disparate elements, the 'archaic' element of INFANTILE introjects and the sophisticated element of reflective SELF-AWARENESS. In other words, it is both a container of the past and a higher level of (ego) functioning.

Corruption of the Super-ego refers to the attempt to diminish GUILT by seducing or corrupting some figure identified (see IDENTIFICATION) with one's super-ego, i.e. to reduce one's own sense of unworthiness by bringing a super-ego figure down to one's own level. *Super-ego lacunae* are gaps in a patient's moral sense.

SUPPRESSION   Suppression usually refers to CONSCIOUS, voluntary INHIBITION of activity in contrast to REPRESSION, which is UNCONSCIOUS, automatic, and instigated by ANXIETY not by an act of WILL.

SYMBIOSIS   In biology, 'permanent union between organisms each of which depends for its existence on the other' – *C.O.D.* Mahler's *symbiotic psychosis* occurs in children and is characterized by total and exclusive dependence on the MOTHER; the implication of the name is that the mother needs the dependence as much as the child. The mother–infant relationship, particularly during the first few weeks, is sometimes described as symbiotic on the ground that the mother needs the infant as much as the infant needs the mother. Relationships displaying pseudo-mutuality (see under PSEUDO-) are sometimes described as symbiotic, though they are really cross-parasitic.

SYMBOL, SYMBOL-FORMATION, SYMBOLIZATION, SYMBOLISM   In general, a symbol is something that refers to or represents something else, in contrast to a SIGN, which indicates the presence of something. In this sense, WORDS, emblems, badges are all symbols since they derive their significance from the fact that they refer to something else, their referent, the connexion between them and their referents being based on association of ideas and, usually, established by convention. In all these instances, however, the connexion between symbol and referent is CONSCIOUS, whereas the psychoanalytical theory of symbolism concerns itself with the UNCONSCIOUS substitution of one image, idea, or activity for another. Jones (1916) distinguished between 'true' symbolism and 'symbolism in its widest sense', and wrote, 'If the word symbolism is taken in its widest sense, the subject is seen to comprise almost the whole development of civilization. For what is this other than a never-ending series of evolutionary substitutions, a ceaseless replacement of one idea, interest, capacity, or tendency by another?' True symbolism, on the other hand, 'arises as the result of intrapsychic CONFLICT [see also INTRAPSYCHIC] between the repressing tendencies [see REPRESSION] and the repressed . . . only what is repressed is symbolized; only what is repressed needs to be symbolized. . . . The two cardinal characteristics of symbolism in this strict sense are (1) that the process is completely unconscious . . . and (2) that the affect investing the symbolized idea has not, in so far as the symbolism is concerned, proved capable of that modification in quality denoted by the term "SUBLIMATION".' According to this definition of symbolism, the substitutions involved in the creation of DREAM images and SYMPTOMS are examples of symbol-formation, while those involved in sublimation are not. 'True' or psychoanalytical symbolism, in fact, resembles dreaming and symptom-formation in that they are private constructions, the meaning of which is discoverable only in terms of the individual experience of the subject and not by reference to dictionaries or social conventions. The apparent exceptions to this, the so-called *universal symbols*, encountered in dreams, mythology, and folk-lore, are explained by reference to 'the uniformity of the fundamental and perennial interests of mankind' and to the uniformity of the human capacity for seeing resemblances between objects.

Symbolization is usually listed as one of the PRIMARY PROCESSES governing unconscious THINKING as exemplified in dreams and symptom-formation, though not by Freud himself (see Freud, 1900, 1917, 1940), presumably on the ground that the processes involved in symbol-formation are DISPLACEMENT and CONDENSA- TION. He would also, it seems, not have agreed with the idea that words are not 'true' symbols, since in his last work (1940) he wrote: 'Dreams make an unlimited use of linguistic symbols, the meaning of which is for the most part unknown to the dreamer. Our experience, however, enables us to establish their sense. They probably originate from earlier phases in the development of speech.' In his *Introductory Lectures* (1916) he also described symbolism as an 'ancient but obsolete mode of expression'. For the theoretical assumptions underlying both statements, see ONTOGENY AND PHYLOGENY. Jones's is, however, the 'classical' analytical theory (see CLASSICAL THEORY) of symbolism. See Rycroft (1956), for an attempt to reconcile the analytical and non-analytical usages on the basis of primary and secondary process symbolism, and Segal (1957), for the distinction between symbols which rep- resent instinctual processes and those which substitute for them.

Psychoanalytical theory asserts that the object or activity sym- bolized is always one of basic, instinctual, or biological interest, the substitution or displacement always being away from the body, i.e. and e.g. knives, aeroplanes, guns can be interpreted as *phallic symbols*, but the penis could never be a knife symbol. Displacements in the opposite, centripetal direction are 'REGRES- SIONS'. An exception is the *functional symbolism* of Silberer, which occurs when a fatigued or sleepy person sets out to think about abstractions and instead finds visual images coming to mind.

SYMPTOM Any deviation from HEALTH of which a patient complains.

Symptom-formation CLASSICAL THEORY regards NEUROTIC symptom-formation as analogous with dream-work (see under DREAM) the symptom effecting a COMPROMISE between the repressed wish (see REPRESSION) and the dictates of the repressing agency. See also SIGN, SYMPTOM, AND SYMBOL.

SYNDROME A group of SIGNS and SYMPTOMS known to occur together, but not in themselves constituting a disease, either because the connexions between the items composing it are unknown or because it may be a manifestation of a variety of diseases. *Effort syndrome* is an obsolescent term for a variety of NEUROSIS in which the patient complains of fatigue and breathlessness following exertion but has no physical signs to support his conviction that he suffers from heart disease.

SYNTHETIC 'Synthesizing', not 'artificial', is always intended. The 'synthetic functions of the ego', described by Hartmann (1958), are all concerned with INTEGRATION.

T

TABOO (TABU) 1. Anthropological term for the setting apart of an object or person or for the absolute prohibition of some class of acts on the ground that it would be a violation of the culture's whole system of thought (WELTANSCHAUUNG); i.e. an object is taboo if it is untouchable, an act is taboo if it is 'unthinkable' in terms of the culture's structure. 2. Hence, by extension, any action which is prohibited by authority or by social pressure can be described as 'taboo'. In the psychoanalytical literature, the taboos most frequently mentioned are those on INCEST and on killing the TOTEM animal except on ceremonial occasions. See Freud's *Totem and Taboo* (1913), in which he speculated that the incest taboo arose as result of the need of the males of the PRIMAL HORDE to prevent fighting among themselves after they had murdered the PRIMAL FATHER, who, prior to his murder, had kept all the females for himself. The theory assumes that the taboo prevented the sons from possessing precisely those females they had murdered the father to acquire. See ONTOGENY AND PHYLOGENY for the general biological theory which led Freud to believe such speculative theories were legitimate. See also OEDIPUS COMPLEX.

TECHNIQUE This term used in a somewhat special sense by Fairbairn (1952) to describe processes very similar to DEFENCES but which he regarded as normal adaptive processes during his second stage of development, that of transition or QUASI-INDE-PENDENCE. See HYSTERIA; OBSESSIONAL TECHNIQUE; PHOBIC TECH-NIQUE; PARANOID TECHNIQUE; FAIRBAIRN'S REVISED PSYCHO-PATHOLOGY.

TELEPATHY Communication at a distance and independently of all known sensory channels. See PSYCHICAL RESEARCH.

TENSION For *tension-affects*, see AFFECT; FORE-PLEASURE. *Tension state* is a psychiatric diagnostic term for a condition in which the patient is tense, under strain, etc., whether as a result of ex-ternal stress or of internal CONFLICT. Freud's conceptions of the CONSTANCY and PLEASURE PRINCIPLES make *instinctual tension* the prime mover of all behaviour. See CONSTANCY PRINCIPLE; INSTINCT.

TERRITORIALITY Ethological concept (see ETHOLOGY) re-ferring to the fact that in many species of animals, individuals establish areas which they defend against intruding members of their own species. This behaviour-pattern presumably fulfils two functions: spreading of the species over the available ENVIRON-MENT, and reducing the occasions for fighting between members of the same species (control of intra-specific AGGRESSION). Psycho-analysis tends to interpret behaviour in human males which is (arguably) territorial as being SEXUAL and OEDIPAL in origin.

THANATOS Greek God of Death used by Freud to personify the DEATH INSTINCT. Cf. EROS and the LIFE INSTINCT.

'THE' 'The FATHER', 'the MOTHER', usually, and 'the BREAST 'and 'the PENIS' always refer to the ideas of these persons or organs existing in the subject's mind and not to the actual, external object, i.e. they are 'INTERNAL OBJECTS' which form part of the subject's psychic structure.

THERAPY The process of treating a patient. To be distin-guished from *therapeutics*, that branch of medicine which is concerned with the theory of treatment, with the mode of action of agents and procedures used in treatment. Hence PSYCHO-THERAPY, physiotherapy, radiotherapy, occupational therapy, etc.

THINKING 1. Any form of mental activity in which ideas are involved. 2. More specifically, mental activity which is concerned with the solution of problems. Psychoanalysis's main contribution to the psychology of thinking is Freud's (1900, 1911, 1917) distinction between the PRIMARY AND SECONDARY PROCESSES, the former being that form of thinking (mental functioning) characteristic of the UNCONSCIOUS (ID), the latter being that characteristic of CONSCIOUSNESS (the EGO).

Autistic thinking is wish-fulfilling (see WISH-FULFILMENT), egocentric, and oblivious of the categories of space and TIME. *Obsessional thinking* (see OBSESSION) is riddled by AMBIVALENCE, with resulting attempts to reconcile contradictory propositions and to avoid coming down firmly on one side of the fence; manifesting itself in speech and writing by a high incidence of 'buts' and 'ifs'. *Schizophrenic thinking* (see SCHIZOPHRENIA) shows gross interference of secondary process thinking by irruptions of primary process and autistic thinking, leading to frequent ellipses and neologisms, disruption of syntax, and bizarre jumps in subject-matter – typically 'knight's moves', i.e. themes following one another in such a way that the listener senses that they are connected but is unable to see in what way. It seems probable that all the NEUROSES and PSYCHOSES show specific disturbances in thinking, these being revealed in characteristic grammatical and syntactical habits, but only the above-mentioned pathological types of thinking are generally recognized. See Lorenz and Cobb (1953), Lorenz (1953). See also SYMBOL.

THRESHOLD (or LIMEN) In physiology and psychology, that intensity of stimulation which just evokes a response, gives rise to a SENSATION; lower intensities being *subliminal*, higher intensities being *supra-liminal*. Psychoanalytical theories of IN-STINCT, ANXIETY, FRUSTRATION, etc., imply (usually without stating it) the idea of threshold, e.g. instinctual TENSION causes UNPLEASURE, leading to DISCHARGE according to either the PLEASURE or REALITY PRINCIPLE only if the tension has passed a certain threshold. Frustration only causes anxiety or AGGRESSION if it is above a certain intensity or lasts longer than a certain length of time. Only anxiety beyond a certain threshold of intensity leads to the activation of DEFENCE-mechanisms.

TIME   Time, and the philosophical puzzles associated with it, impinges on psychoanalytical theory at three specific points: (a) The distinction between the PRIMARY and SECONDARY PROCESSES is made partly on the basis that the former disregards the category of time whereas the latter takes cognizance of it. Since, according to some theories of the origin of the sense of time, it arises as a result of experiencing delay between desire and SATISFACTION, the wish-fulfilling propensities (see WISH-FULFILMENT) of the primary processes deny time, whereas the adaptive propensities (see ADAPTATION) of the secondary processes lead to the discovery of time. (b) Freud's theory of MEMORY assumes that all past experiences are represented in the present and are capable of exerting an effect on the present. (c) All definitions of the SELF and of the sense of IDENTITY inevitably include a reference to time. See Whitrow (1961) for the philosophy of time.

TOPOGRAPHICAL   Adj. for concepts and formulations which utilize the FICTION of a PSYCHIC APPARATUS extended in space, i.e. describable by a diagram on which mental processes can be located. See METAPSYCHOLOGY.

TOTEM   Anthropological term for animal, plant, or other object which is venerated by a particular tribe or community and which it treats as a symbol of itself or as its protector. See Freud's *Totem and Taboo* (1911) for his speculative theory that the totem symbolizes the PRIMAL FATHER who was murdered when his sons rebelled against his mastery of the PRIMAL HORDE. See also OEDIPUS COMPLEX.

TRAINING ANALYSIS   The psychoanalytical treatment of persons training to become psychoanalysts, as opposed to the therapeutic analysis of patients.

TRANCE   State of DISSOCIATION occurring in patients under HYPNOSIS and in mediums when they are purporting to be in touch with the spirit world. Trance-like states occur in HYSTERIA, though these are usually called spells, seizures, or dream-states; and in childhood, in the form of sleep-walking. The feature common to all these is that some part of the EGO (or SELF) is out of action, so that the subject either surrenders his WILL to another or acts on wishes and PHANTASIES that are otherwise inhibited (see INHIBITION).

TRANSITIONAL OBJECT See OBJECT, TRANSITIONAL.

TRANSFERENCE 1. The process by which a patient displaces on to his analyst feelings, ideas, etc., which derive from previous figures in his life (see DISPLACEMENT); by which he relates to his analyst as though he were some former object in his life; by which he projects on to his analyst OBJECT-REPRESENTATIONS acquired by earlier INTROJECTIONS (see PROJECTION); by which he endows the analyst with the significance of another, usually prior, object. 2. The state of mind produced by 1 in the patient. 3. Loosely, the patient's emotional attitude towards his analyst.

In the early days of psychoanalysis transference was regarded as a regrettable phenomenon which interfered with the recovery of repressed memories and disturbed the patient's objectivity. By 1912, however, Freud had come to see it as an essential part of the therapeutic process: 'finally every conflict has to be fought out in the sphere of transference'. It is not, of course, assumed that the analyst is the only person on to whom individuals tend to transfer feelings derived from the past, but that the detachment of the analyst – his refusal to play along with the patient's preconceptions or to respond in accordance with his expectations – creates a novel situation in which it is possible to interpret to the patient that he is behaving *as though* the analyst were his father, mother, brother, sister, or whatever (see INTERPRETATION). Such explicit statements made by the analyst are *transference-interpretations*; the patient's emotional involvement with the analyst is the *transference-neurosis*. The patient's relationship to the analyst *qua* father, mother, etc., is the *transference-relationship*, as opposed to the *analytical relationship*, which is the totality of the relationship between analyst and patient, including the latter's recognition of the actual nature of the contract and transaction between them and of the analyst's actual personality. *Transference-resistance* is the use of transference as a RESISTANCE against either remembering the past or facing ANXIETY connected with the prospect of ending treatment and having to forego the (in fact largely illusory) sense of security provided by being in treatment. Transference may be paternal, maternal, OEDIPAL, PRE-OEDIPAL, PASSIVE, DEPENDENT, ORAL, etc., according to the object transferred and the stage of DEVELOPMENT being recapitulated; OBJECT or NARCISSISTIC (identificatory, see IDENTIFICATION), according as to whether the patient conceives his analyst as an external person on whom he is dependent, whom he hates, etc., or as a part of himself; *positive* or *negative*, according as to whether he conceives the analyst as a benign or malevolent figure.

Most accounts of transference include the idea that early OBJECT-RELATIONSHIPS which the patient cannot possibly remember as such can none the less be reconstructed from the patient's transference-reactions. Instead of remembering his infancy and his relationship to the BREAST, the patient re-enacts it 'in the transference'. The work of Fairbairn, Klein, and Winnicott is inexplicable unless one realizes that they believe(d) that their patients' responses to themselves are valid evidence on which to base theories about the origin of object-relations in infancy (see FAIRBAIRN'S REVISED PSYCHOPATHOLOGY; KLEINIAN). Most accounts also assume that the therapeutic effects of analysis are largely due to the opportunity provided by it to resolve 'within the transference' conflicts dating from childhood and infancy, and attach little importance to novel aspects of the analytical relationship, such as the encounter with a person who combines interest with non-possessiveness and whose insight into the patient is probably more articulate and possibly actually greater than that of the actual parents.

TRANSVEST(IT)ISM Sexual PERVERSION in which the subject claims to get sexual pleasure from dressing up in the clothes of the opposite sex. The operative word in this definition is *sexual*; simply enjoying dressing up in or preferring to wear clothes of the opposite sex is not included in the term. It is virtually confined to men, is not in itself an indication of HOMOSEXUALITY, and is compatible with HETEROSEXUAL activity. According to Fenichel (1954), the transvestite believes (unconsciously) that putting on women's clothes enhances his virility by enabling him to identify with a PHALLIC WOMAN.

TRAUMA, TRAUMATA 1. In general medicine, structural damage to the body caused by the impact of some object or substance. The term includes wounds, fractures, burns, etc. 2. In

PSYCHIATRY and PSYCHOANALYSIS, any totally unexpected experience which the subject is unable to assimilate. The immediate response to a psychological trauma is SHOCK; the later effects are either spontaneous recovery (which is analogous to spontaneous healing of physical traumata) or the development of a TRAUMATIC NEUROSIS. 3. In psychoanalysis, by extension, any experience which is mastered by use of DEFENCES. Trauma, in this sense, produces ANXIETY, which is followed either by spontaneous recovery or the development of a PSYCHONEUROSIS. Traumatic theories of the origin of neurosis usually have the third, not the second, kind of trauma in mind. 4. Loosely, inaccurately, but frequently, any distressing or upsetting experience, regardless of whether it has lasting effects or not.

An *infantile trauma* is one which occurred in infancy or childhood and is inferred to have played a causative role in the development of the NEUROSIS under discussion. Infantile traumata may be either of type 2 or 3, and the term has come to include not only single, isolated experiences, such as sexual assaults, surgical operations without psychological preparation, or the sudden death or disappearance of a parent, but also long-term situations such as oral DEPRIVATION (see also ORAL), SEPARATION from parents, severe house-training, or even abnormal family relationships in childhood. The concept of trauma is a strictly causal one (see CAUSALITY). To label an event traumatic is to assert that it happened to the subject, without his in any way willing it or colluding in its occurrence (see WILL), and that its effects are causally determined consequences. As a result, proof that the neuroses are the result of traumata would justify Freud's assumption of the principle of psychic DETERMINISM.

According to Freud (1940), all neurotic illnesses are the result of infantile traumata: 'In every case the subsequent neurotic illness has this prelude in childhood as its point of departure. . . . We can easily account for this preference for the first period of childhood. Neuroses are, as we know, disorders of the EGO; and it is not to be wondered at that the ego, while it is weak, immature, and incapable of resistance, should fail in dealing with problems which it could later manage with the utmost ease. . . .' But, he goes on, 'No human individual is spared such traumatic experiences; none escapes the REPRESSIONS to which they give rise.' In the same passage, he also refers to instinctual demands from within as

'traumas', especially if they are met half-way by 'certain dispositions'. In other words, his theory of the traumatic origin of neurosis only holds if one assumes (a) that everyone is neurotic and
(b) that the susceptibility to being traumatized is affected by
'dispositions'. 'It is easy, as we can see, for a barbarian to be
healthy: for a civilized man the task is a hard one' – Freud (1940).
See also MEANING; AGENT.

TRAUMATIC NEUROSIS Psychiatric illness, the symptoms
of which (a) develop shortly after some unexpected, shocking experience (see SHOCK), (b) are not explicable as the physical result
of injury to the brain or any other part of the body, and (c) include either stereotyped actions or 'spells' in which parts of the
traumatic event are repeated and/or stereotyped dreams repeating
the experience. Traumatic neurosis differs from the other neuroses
in that its symptoms, including the traumatic DREAMS, are not
amenable to INTERPRETATION. In other words, traumatic neurosis
has no unconscious MEANING (see also UNCONSCIOUS). However, it
has a function, viz. that of enabling the patient to assimilate
retrospectively an unexpected experience by, as it were, getting
in front of it again and WORKING THROUGH it. Traumatic neuroses
either recover spontaneously, become chronic, or become transformed into PSYCHONEUROSES. The last is only likely to occur if the
symptoms prove advantageous, e.g. by making the patient eligible
for a pension or, if a soldier, unfit for active service.

TRAUMATOPHILIC Term sometimes used to describe
patients who seem to have a knack for collecting traumatic experiences (see TRAUMA).

TRUE AND FALSE Winnicott (1958) distinguishes between
a true and false self, the latter being a DEFENSIVE structure, a
'false' ADAPTATION to an ENVIRONMENT which has not met his
'true' self during the formative months of infancy. During psychoanalytical treatment, patients with a false self must regress to a
state of DEPENDENCE on the analyst during which the latter can
respond to his emergent true self. For a rather similar concept of
Balint's, see NEW BEGINNING and BASIC FAULT.

TRUST *v.* BASIC DISTRUST The first of Erikson's eight
STAGES OF MAN. It corresponds to the ORAL stage of CLASSICAL
THEORY. During it the infant either learns to feel at home in the

world and to believe in the existence of goodness in both others and himself, or develops a 'sense of evil and malevolence'. 'Mothers, I think, create a sense of trust in their children by that kind of administration which in its quality combines sensitive care of the baby's individual needs and a firm sense of personal trustworthiness within the trusted framework of their culture's style' – Erikson (1953).

TURNING AGAINST THE SELF One of the four instinctual (see INSTINCT) vicissitudes described by Freud (1915), the other three being REVERSAL into its opposite, REPRESSION, and SUBLIMATION, listed by Anna Freud (1937) as one of the mechanisms of DEFENCE. The concept seems to be used only to explain MORAL MASOCHISM, the phenomenon observed most clearly in OBSESSIONAL NEUROSIS in which the patient directs his SADISM against himself. 'The desire to torture has turned into self-torture and self-punishment' – Freud (1915).

U

UNCONSCIOUS 1. Adj. referring to mental processes of which the subject is not aware. 'It is generally agreed [that] conscious processes do not form unbroken series which are complete in themselves' – Freud (1940); and psychoanalysis assumes that those processes which fill in the gaps can be designated 'mental', in contrast to those theories which maintain that the idea of unconscious mental processes is self-contradictory and that the intervening 'completing' processes are physical ones only. In other words, it assumes that mental processes can differ in quality, some being CONSCIOUS, others unconscious. It also assumes that unconscious processes are of two kinds: those which become conscious easily, and those which are subject to REPRESSION. The former are *descriptively unconscious* or *preconscious* (see PRECONSCIOUS), the latter are *dynamically unconscious*. MEMORIES, information, skills, etc., which can be recalled when needed are descriptively unconscious; memories, PHANTASIES, wishes, etc., the existence of which can only be inferred, or which only become conscious after the removal of some RESISTANCE, are dynamically unconscious. Dynamically unconscious processes conform to the primary processes of thought, while preconscious and conscious processes conform to the secondary processes (see PROCESSES, PRIMARY AND SECONDARY).

2. N. The *Unconscious* or the *System Unconscious* is that part of the mind in which mental processes are dynamically unconscious; in contrast to the CONSCIOUS. In the 1920s Freud renamed the Unconscious the ID, and the Conscious, the EGO. When used loosely, the unconscious is a metaphorical, almost anthropomorphic concept, an entity influencing the SELF unbeknownst to itself. When used precisely, it is a structure with specific characteristics. 'To sum up: exemption from mutual contradiction, primary process (mobility of cathexes), timelessness, and replacement of external by psychical REALITY – these are the characteristics which we expect to find in processes belonging to the System Unconscious' – Freud (1915).

Although Freud's distinction between conscious and unconscious processes operating according to different laws, the primary and secondary processes, can be accounted one of his basic discoveries, it is one which lends itself to abuse in at least two ways. First, it can be and is used to obliterate a number of other distinctions, e.g. voluntary and involuntary, unwitting and deliberate, unself-conscious and self-aware. Secondly, it can be used to create states of sceptical confusion; if a person (patient) accepts the general proposition that he may have unconscious motives, he may then find himself unable to disagree with some particular statement made about himself, since the fact that it does not correspond to anything of which he is aware does not preclude the possibility that it correctly states something of which he is unaware. As a result he may formally agree to propositions (INTERPRETATIONS) without in fact assenting or subscribing to them. Patients with a speculative turn of mind may, if they have an unwary analyst, entertain an indefinite number of hypotheses about their unconscious motives without having any idea how to decide which of them are true.

UNCONSCIOUS, COLLECTIVE JUNGIAN term for that part of the Unconscious which contains ARCHETYPES and is therefore common to all men.

UNDOING (Germ.: *ungeschehenmachen* – to make something 'unhappen') DEFENCE-mechanism by which the subject makes as though some prior thought or action had not occurred. 'It is, as it were, negative magic, and endeavours . . . to "blow away" not merely the *consequences* of some event (or experience or impression) but the event itself. . . . In obsessional neurosis the technique . . . is first met with in the "diphasic" symptoms, in which one action is cancelled out by the second, so it is as though neither action had taken place, whereas, in reality, both have' – Freud (1926). Undoing occurs, typically, in obsessional rituals. See OBSESSIONAL NEUROSIS; OMNIPOTENCE; RITUAL.

UNPLEASURE This word, which is not a neologism, since it was used by Coleridge in 1814, is used to translate the German '*Unlust*', the PAIN or discomfort of instinctual TENSION, as opposed to '*Schmerz*', the sensation of pain. The PLEASURE PRINCIPLE is correctly the pleasure-unpleasure principle. See also CONSTANCY PRINCIPLE.

UNREALITY, FEELINGS OF See DEREALIZATION; DEPERSONALIZATION.

URETHRA The duct by which urine is voided from the bladder. Hence *urethral erotism*: pleasure associated with urination and PHANTASIES derived therefrom.

UTERUS The womb. Hence *uterine phantasy*: PHANTASY about what it was (would be) like in the womb. SLEEP is not uncommonly regarded as a uterine REGRESSION. 'Our relation to the world, into which we have come so unwillingly, seems to involve our not being able to tolerate it uninterruptedly. Thus from time to time we withdraw into the premundane state, into existence in the womb' – Freud (1916).

V

VAGINA (lit.: sheath) The female genital passage. No word exists bearing the same relation to vagina as PHALLUS does to

PENIS. Hence 'vagina' has to do for both the anatomical organ and the idea of it. Hence *vaginismus*: spasm of the vaginal muscles, usually a neurotic symptom.

VERBALIZATION   The process of putting into words. Usually gobbledegook for talking or formulating, but occasionally used to refer specifically to the transformation of visual imagery into words or to the conversion of primary process 'DREAM' thinking (see PROCESSES, PRIMARY AND SECONDARY) into the verbal thinking of CONSCIOUSNESS. Psychoanalysis constitutes an attempt to verbalize the unverbalizable, since its subject-matter, UNCONSCIOUS mental activity, is intrinsically non-verbal and is therefore distorted by verbal formulations. See WORD-PRESENTATION.

VIGILANCE   Neurological (see NEUROLOGY) and physiological term for the sustained state of alertness which enables organisms to notice changes in their ENVIRONMENT. A sentinel 'scanning' function which alerts the organism to the presence of danger or opportunities and prepares it for appropriate action. Vigilance can vary in intensity but is never totally in abeyance, even in sleep. SIGNAL-ANXIETY can be regarded as an in-turned form of vigilance, by which the subject is alerted to changes in its inner state. PHOBIC anxiety can be regarded as a perversion of vigilance, in as much as the patient reacts to his phobic object as though it were dangerous and then takes the avoiding action which would be appropriate if it were. See Rycroft (1968) for a discussion of the relation of apprehensiveness, concern, and expectancy to vigilance.

VOYEURISM   Sexual PERVERSION in which the subject's preferred form of sexual activity is looking at the sexual parts or activities of others. According to CLASSICAL THEORY, voyeurism is a derivative of infantile SCOPOPHILIA, one of the infantile COMPONENT INSTINCTS (see also INFANTILE). It also regards voyeurism and EXHIBITIONISM as paired opposites, the former being the ACTIVE version of the latter, and the latter the PASSIVE version of the former. OBJECT THEORY would emphasize the PHANTASY of control over the object viewed and the denial of exclusion from the relationship being spied on.

W

WELTANSCHAUUNG (Germ.)   World outlook; conception of reality; philosophy of life.

WHOLE AND PART OBJECTS   A whole OBJECT is a person to whom the subject relates in a way that takes cognizance of the fact that he (the object) is a person. A part object is either a bodily organ to whom the subject relates as though it existed solely to satisfy his needs, or a person whom he treats as though he were an organ existing solely to satisfy the subject's needs. 'The BREAST' is the part object *par excellence*.

WILL   Although Freud's early writings contain references to will and counter-will, particularly in connexion with HYSTERIA, the concept of will forms no part of psychoanalytical theory, being incompatible with the assumption of psychic DETERMINISM, and with the idea that MENTAL ILLNESSES are caused by unconscious processes to which the notion of will is obviously inapplicable. None the less PROGNOSES are often made on an assessment of the *will to recovery*, though this fact is often covered up by the use of phrases such as 'high motivation'. The usual psychiatric and psychoanalytic attitude towards will is summed up in the saying: 'The patient says he can't, his relatives say he won't, but the psychiatrist says he can't will.'

The notion of will is however too basic to human experience to be eliminated entirely, and it raises its head at at least three points in psychoanalytical theory: (a) The concept of NEGATIVISM is used to describe *wilfulness*, i.e. the assertion of willpower by refusal to follow the lead of others or to co-operate with others, even to the point of 'cutting off one's nose to spite one's face'. Negativistic behaviour can be regarded as the mode of expressing will, which arises in persons who experience agreement and co-operation with others as threats to their IDENTITY. (b) The term 'ACTIVE' is used to describe not merely the ability to perform actions, but also the willingness to initiate action, while 'PASSIVE' is used to describe not merely inactivity but also the willingness to be subject to the will of another. When Freud (1937) mentioned the ability to accept, when appropriate, a passive position as a criterion of health in men, he was referring to the ability to surrender one's will to another without feeling that one's identity is threatened. (c) The concept of motivation (see MOTIVE) can be used to bridge the gap between the idea of will and that of drive (INSTINCT). If a person is described as being highly motivated in some particular direction, this means he is prepared to expend time and energy in achieving his aim, but the formulation does not reveal whether this is because his instincts impel him strongly or because his will-power is great. See Leslie Farber's *The Ways of the Will* (1966) for a general discussion of the problem of will and for accounts of the pathology of will – and for the absurd consequences of trying to will sexual responsiveness. See ACTIVE AND PASSIVE.

WISH-FULFILMENT Freud's wish-fulfilment theory of DREAMS (Freud 1900, 1902) asserts that dreams express wishes as fulfilled. 'A thought expressed in the optative has been replaced by a representation in the present tense.' The theory assumes (a) that dreams have psychological MEANING, an assumption which was revolutionary in 1900; (b) that the hallucinatory quality of dreams (see HALLUCINATION) enables the dreamer to represent as fulfilled wishes which would otherwise have awakened him; and (c) that the wishes expressed are, in general, ones unacceptable to the sleeper's waking SELF, either because they are incompatible with his values (e.g. death wishes towards his nearest and dearest) or because they are INFANTILE and are therefore stated in a disguised, distorted manner. Assumption (c) is necessary because only a minority of dreams are manifestly wish-fulfilling. NIGHTMARES and ANXIETY dreams constitute failures in the dream-work which normally converts the unacceptable LATENT dream-wish into a 'harmless' MANIFEST dream. Traumatic dreams (see TRAUMA), in which the traumatic experience is simply repeated, are admitted exceptions to the theory.

Since manifestly wish-fulfilling dreams are a rarity (the usual examples given are children's dreams and 'dreams of convenience', i.e. those obviously provoked by sexual tension, a full bladder, or other physical discomfort), Freud's insistence on the theory is puzzling unless one realizes that his interest in dreams was not on their own account but because he believed that they exemplified a general psychic tendency towards wish-fulfilling thought. In other words, he held that there were two kinds of mental activity, the primary and secondary PROCESSES – the former being UN-CONSCIOUS and wish-fulfilling, the latter CONSCIOUS and realistic – and that dreams were a normal phenomenon familiar to everyone in which the primary processes manifested themselves. In fact, the distinction between primary, wish-fulfilling processes and second-ary, realistic processes was based on the study of neurotic SYMP-TOMS and only transferred later to the INTERPRETATION of dreams. Dreams, on this theory, resemble symptoms in being COMPROMISE FORMATIONS, the wish-fulfilling elements coming from the re-pressed (see REPRESSION) and the distorting dream-work coming from the repressing parts of the mind.

In one respect, Freud's formulation is fairly certainly wrong. Recent physiological research suggests that we do not dream in order to preserve SLEEP, but that, on the contrary, we sleep in order to dream.

WOLF-MAN Soubriquet given in the analytical literature to the patient described by Freud in his *From the History of an Infantile Neurosis* (1918).

WORD-PRESENTATION The mental image of a word. According to Freud (1915, 1923) the essential difference between UNCONSCIOUS mental processes and those which are PRECONSCIOUS or CONSCIOUS is that the latter have been brought into connexion with word-presentations; that an unconscious idea is a represen-tation of the object itself, a *thing-presentation*, whereas a conscious idea has attached to it a verbal image, this verbal image having been acquired (learned) from others. This notion is only explicable if one remembers that Freud believed that the human psyche starts as a structureless ID, part of which differentiates to form the EGO as a result of the impact of the ENVIRONMENT. 'The ego is that part of the id which has been modified by the direct influence of the external world.' The attachment of word-presentations to mental processes is evidence that they *have* been modified by the direct influence of the external world. It is not clear whether Freud believed that, when conscious, we always think with words, or whether he thought that non-verbal conscious thinking (as occurs in dreaming, daydreaming, reveries, etc.) is an irruption of the unconscious into consciousness.

Word-presentations play a part in Freud's views on schizophrenic THINKING. He held that in SCHIZOPHRENIA, the patient withdraws CATHEXIS from thing-representations (i.e. divests them of significance) and then treats word-representations as though they were things, constructing a delusional world on the basis of words not objects (see DELUSION). In schizophrenic thinking words are subject to primary PROCESS thinking, i.e. they are treated as normal people treat visual images in dreams.

WORK   Serious activity, usually contrasted either with PLAY or LOVE. In the early days of psychoanalysis, recovery of the capacity to love and work was regarded as the criterion of successful analytical treatment.

WORKING THROUGH   Originally, the process by which a patient in analysis discovers piecemeal over an extended period of time the full implications of some INTERPRETATION or INSIGHT. Hence, by extension, the process of getting used to a new state of affairs or of getting over a loss or painful experience. In this extended sense, MOURNING is an example of working through, since it involves the piecemeal recognition that the lost object is no longer available in a host of contexts in which he was previously a familiar figure.

WORLD   When internal (inner) and external (outer) world are used antithetically, *internal world* is synonymous with internal REALITY, psychical reality, *external world* is synonymous with ENVIRONMENT, external reality. *World-catastrophe* is the idea that the world has come to an end or has been destroyed, often a part of schizophrenic DELUSIONS (see SCHIZOPHRENIA).

Y

YAVIS SYNDROME   According to Schofield (1964), young male American psychiatrists tend to select for PSYCHOTHERAPY female patients who display the 'YAVIS' SYNDROME, being Young

Attractive, Verbally fluent, Intelligent and Successful, and having the same social background and aspirations as themselves. This ironic comment on the American psychiatric and psychoanalytic scene is part of a general attack on the tendency to expend professional time and skill on patients who are not ill in any clinical sense at the expense of research on the major psychiatric disorders.

Z

ZOOPHILIA   Bestiality. Excessive love of animals.

Bibliography

ABRAHAM, K., *Selected Papers*, Hogarth Press, London, 1927; Basic Books, New York, 1953.

ALEXANDER, F. 'The Neurotic Character', *Int. J. Psycho-Anal.* (1930), **11**, pp. 292–311.

BALINT, M., *Primary Love and Psycho-Analytic Technique*, Liveright Pub. Co., New York, 1952.

BATESON, G., *et al.*, 'Toward a Theory of Schizophrenia', *Behavioral Science*, (1965), **1**, pp. 251–64.

BENNET, E. A., *What Jung Really Said*, E. P. Dutton & Co. Inc., New York, 1966.

BERES, D., 'Communication in Psychoanalysis and in the Creative Process: a Parallel', *J. Amer. Psychoanal. Ass.* (1957), **5**, pp. 408–23.

BETTELHEIM, B., *The Empty Fortress*, Free Press of Glencoe, New York, 1967.

BOWLBY, J., *Maternal Care and Mental Health*, 2nd edition, World Health Organization, Geneva, 1952.

BOWLBY, J., 'Processes of Mourning', *Int. J. Psycho-Anal.* (1961), **42**, pp. 317-40.

BOYER, L. B., 'A Hypothesis regarding the Time of Appearance of the Dream Screen', *Int. J. Psycho-Anal.* (1960), **41**, pp. 114–22.

BRANDT, L. W., 'Some Notes on English Freudian Terminology', *J. Amer. Psychoanal. Ass.* (1961), **9**, pp. 331–9.

BRIERLEY, MARJORIE, *Trends in Psycho-Analysis*, Hogarth Press, London, 1951.

BROWN, J. A. C., *Freud and the Post-Freudians*, Penguin Books, Harmondsworth, 1961.

CANNON, W. B. *The Wisdom of the Body*, W. W. Norton, New York, 1932.

CARSTAIRS, G. M., *This Island Now*, Basic Books, New York, 1963.

Concise Oxford Dictionary, 4th edition, Clarendon Press, Oxford, 1951.

CRISP, A. J., ' "Transference", "Symptom Emergence" and

"Social Repercussion" in Behaviour Therapy', *Brit. J. Med. Psychol.* (1966), **39**, pp. 179–96.

DEUTSCH, F., 'Analysis of Postural Behaviour', *Psychoanal. Quart.* (1947), **16**, pp. 195–213.

DEUTSCH, HELENE, *The Psychology of Women*, 2 vols., Research Books, London, 1946; Grune & Stratton, New York, 1945.

EHRENZWEIG, A., *The Hidden Order of Art*, Weidenfeld & Nicolson, London, 1967.

ERIKSON, E., *Childhood and Society*, 2nd edition, W. W. Norton, New York, 1963.

EVANS, W. N., 'The Passing of the Gentleman', *Psychoanal. Quart.* (1949), **18**, pp. 19–43.

EYSENCK, H. J., *Fact and Fiction in Psychology*, Penguin Books, Baltimore, 1965.

EYSENCK, H. J., and RACHMAN, S., *The Causes and Cures of Neurosis*, Routledge & Kegan Paul, London, 1965.

FAIRBAIRN, W. R. D., 'A Revised Psychopathology of the Psychoses and Psychoneuroses' (1941), see Fairbairn (1952).

FAIRBAIRN, W. R. D., *Psychoanalytic Studies of the Personality*, Tavistock Publications, London, 1952 (under the title *An Object-Relations Theory of the Personality*, Basic Books, New York, 1954).

FARBER, L. H., *The Ways of the Will*, Basic Books, New York, 1966.

FEDERN, P., *Ego Psychology and the Psychoses*, Basic Books, New York, 1952.

FENICHEL, O., *Problems of Psychoanalytic Technique*, Psychoanalytic Quarterly Inc., New York, 1941.

FENICHEL, O., *Collected Papers* (First Series), Routledge & Kegan Paul, London, 1954.

FERENCZI, S., 'Introjection and Transference' (1909), reprinted in *First Contributions to Psycho-Analysis*, Hogarth Press, London, 1952.

FOULKES, S. H., and ANTHONY, E. J., *Group Psychotherapy*, Penguin Books, Baltimore, 1957.

FOWLER, H. W., *A Dictionary of Modern English Usage*, 2nd edition, Clarendon Press, Oxford, 1965.

FREUD, ANNA, *The Ego and the Mechanisms of Defence*, Hogarth Press, London, 1937; International Universities Press, New York, 1957.

FREUD, ANNA, *The Psychoanalytical Treatment of Children*, Hogarth Press, London, 1959; International Universities Press, New York, 1960.

FREUD, S., *On the Grounds for Detaching a Particular Syndrome from Neurasthenia under the Description 'Anxiety Neurosis'* (1894): Standard Edition, Vol. 3, Hogarth Press, London, 1962.

FREUD, S., *Project for a Scientific Psychology* (1895): Standard Edition, Vol. 1, Hogarth Press, London, 1966.

FREUD, S., *Further Remarks on the Defence Neuro-Psychoses* (1896): Standard Edition, Vol. 3, Hogarth Press, London, 1962.

FREUD, S., *The Interpretation of Dreams* (1900): Standard Edition, Vols. 4 and 5, Hogarth Press, London, 1953.

FREUD, S., *The Psychopathology of Everyday Life* (1901): Standard Edition, Vol. 6, Hogarth Press, London, 1960.

FREUD, S., *On Dreams* (1902): Standard Edition, Vol. 5, Hogarth Press, London, 1953.

FREUD, S., *Three Essays on the Theory of Sexuality* (1905): Standard Edition, Vol. 7, Hogarth Press, London, 1953.

FREUD, S., *Obsessive Actions and Religious Practices* (1907): Standard Edition, Vol. 9, Hogarth Press, London, 1959.

FREUD, S., *Creative Writers and Day-Dreaming* (1908): Standard Edition, Vol. 9, Hogarth Press, London, 1959.

FREUD, S., *Notes Upon a Case of Obsessional Neurosis* (1909): Standard Edition, Vol. 10, Hogarth Press, London, 1955.

FREUD, S., *Leonardo da Vinci and a Memory of his Childhood* (1910): Standard Edition, Vol. 11, Hogarth Press, London, 1957.

FREUD, S., *Formulations on the Two Principles of Mental Functioning* (1911): Standard Edition, Vol. 12, Hogarth Press, London, 1958.

FREUD, S., *Psycho-Analytic Notes on an Autobiographical Account of a Case of Paranoia (Dementia Paranoides)* (1911): Standard Edition, Vol. 12, Hogarth Press, London, 1958.

FREUD, S., *Fausse Reconnaissance (Déjà Raconte) in Psycho-Analytic Treatment* (1914): Standard Edition, Vol. 12, Hogarth Press, London, 1958.

FREUD, S., *Totem and Taboo* (1913): Standard Edition, Vol. 13, Hogarth Press, London, 1955.

BIBLIOGRAPHY

FREUD, S., *On Narcissism* (1914): Standard Edition, Vol. 14, Hogarth Press, London, 1957.

FREUD, S., *Observations on Transference Love* (1915): Standard Edition, Vol. 12, Hogarth Press, London, 1958.

FREUD, S., *Instincts and Their Vicissitudes* (1915): Standard Edition, Vol. 14, Hogarth Press, London, 1957.

FREUD S., *Papers on Metapsychology* (1915): Standard Edition, Vol. 14, Hogarth Press, London, 1957.

FREUD, S., *Introductory Lectures on Psycho-Analysis* (1916): Standard Edition, Vols. 15 and 16, Hogarth Press, London, 1963.

FREUD, S., *Mourning and Melancholia* (1917): Standard Edition, Vol. 14, Hogarth Press, London, 1957.

FREUD, S., *Lines of Advance in Psycho-Analytic Therapy* (1919): Standard Edition, Vol. 17, Hogarth Press, London, 1955.

FREUD, S., *Beyond the Pleasure Principle* (1920): Standard Edition, Vol. 18, Hogarth Press, London, 1955.

FREUD, S., *The Ego and the Id* (1923): Standard Edition, Vol. 19, Hogarth Press, London, 1961.

FREUD, S., *Inhibitions, Symptoms and Anxiety* (1926): Standard Edition, Vol. 20, Hogarth Press, London, 1959.

FREUD, S., *The Future of an Illusion* (1927): Standard Edition, Vol. 21, Hogarth Press, London, 1961.

FREUD, S., *Fetishism* (1927): Standard Edition, Vol. 21, Hogarth Press, London, 1961.

FREUD, S., *Civilization and Its Discontents* (1930): Standard Edition, Vol. 21, Hogarth Press, London, 1961.

FREUD S., *New Introductory Lectures on Psycho-Analysis* (1933): Standard Edition, Vol. 22, Hogarth Press, London, 1964.

FREUD, S., *Analysis Terminable and Interminable* (1937): Standard Edition, Vol. 23, Hogarth Press, London, 1964.

FREUD, S., *Splitting of the Ego in the Defensive Process* (1938): Standard Edition, Vol. 23, Hogarth Press, London, 1964.

FREUD S., *Moses and Monotheism* (1939): Standard Edition, Vol. 23, Hogarth Press, London, 1964.

FREUD, S., *An Outline of Psycho-Analysis* (1940): Standard Edition, Vol. 23, Hogarth Press, London, 1964.

FREUD, S., and BREUER, J., *Studies on Hysteria* (1893–5): Standard Edition, Vol. 2, Hogarth Press, London, 1955.

FREUD, S., and BULLITT, W. C., *Thomas Woodrow Wilson*, Houghton Mifflin, Boston, 1967.

FREUD, S., and PFISTER, O., *Psychoanalysis and Faith*, Basic Books, New York, 1963.

FUCHS, S. H., 'On Introjection', *Int. J. Psycho-Anal.* (1937), **18**, pp. 269–93.

GITELSON, M., 'The Emotional Position of the Analyst in the Psycho-Analytic Situation', *Int. J. Psycho-Anal.* (1952), **33**, pp. 1–10.

GLOVER, E., *Psycho-Analysis*, Staples Press, London, 1939.

GLOVER, E., 'The Psycho-Analysis of Affects', *Int. J. Psycho-Anal.* (1939), **20**, pp. 299–307.

GLOVER, E., 'Examination of the Klein System of Child Psychology', *Psychoanal. Study of the Child* (1945), **1**, pp. 75–118.

GORER, G., 'Cultural Community and Cultural Diversity', in *The Danger of Equality*, Cresset Press, London, 1966.

GORER, G., 'Psychoanalysis in the World', in Rycroft (1966).

GREENACRE, PHYLLIS, 'Penis Awe and its Relation to Penis Envy', in R. M. Loewenstein (ed.), *Drives, Affects and Behavior*, International Universities Press, New York, 1953.

GREENACRE, PHYLLIS, 'The Childhood of the Artist', *Psychoanal. Study of the Child* (1957), **12**, pp. 47–72.

GREENSON, R. R., 'The Psychology of Apathy', *Psychoanal. Quart.* (1949), **18**, pp. 290–302.

GROSSMAN, C. M. and S., *The Wild Analyst*, George Braziller, Inc., New York, 1965.

GUNTRIP, H., *Personality Structure and Human Interaction*, Hogarth Press, London, 1961; International Universities Press, New York, 1964.

HARTLAND, J., *Medical and Dental Hypnosis and its Clinical Applications*, Williams & Wilkins, Baltimore, 1966.

HARTMANN, H., *Ego Psychology and the Problem of Adaptation*, Imago, London, 1958; Williams & Wilkins, Baltimore, 1966.

HARTMANN, H., *Essays on Ego Psychology*, International Universities Press, New York, 1964.

HEIMANN, P., 'On Counter-Transference', *Int. J. Psycho-Anal.* (1950), **31**, pp. 81–4.

HERMANN, I., 'The Use of the Term "Active" in the Definition of Masculinity', *Int. J. Psycho-Anal.* (1935), **16**, pp. 219–22.

BIBLIOGRAPHY

HOCH, P., and ZUBIN, J. (eds.), *Anxiety*, Grune & Stratton, New York, 1950.

HOME, H. J., 'The Concept of Mind', *Int. J. Psycho-Anal.* (1966), **47**, pp. 43–9.

HORNEY, KAREN, 'The Flight from Womanhood', *Int. J. Psycho-Anal.* (1926), **7**, pp. 324–39.

ISAKOWER, O., 'A Contribution to the Patho-Psychology of Phenomena Associated with Falling Asleep', *Int. J. Psycho-Anal.* (1938), **19**, pp. 331–45.

JONES, E., 'The Theory of Symbolism' (1916), in Jones (1948).

JONES, E., *The Nightmare*, Hogarth Press, London, 1931; Liveright Pub. Co., New York, 1951.

JONES, E., *Papers on Psycho-Analysis*, Baillière, Williams & Wilkins, Baltimore, 1948.

JONES, E., *The Life and Work of Sigmund Freud*, Vol. 1: *The Formative Years and the Great Discoveries, 1856–1900*, Basic Books, New York, 1953; Vol. 2: *Years of Maturity, 1901–1919*, Basic Books, New York, 1955; Vol. 3: *The Last Phase, 1919–1939*, Basic Books, New York, 1957.

JUNG, C. G., *Psychological Types*, Kegan Paul, Trench, Trubner, London, 1923.

KLEIN, MELANIE, *The Psycho-Analysis of Children*, Hogarth Press, London, 1932.

KLEIN, MELANIE, *Contributions to Psycho-Analysis*, Hogarth Press, London, 1948.

KOFF, R. H., 'A Definition of Identification', *Int. J. Psycho-Anal.* (1961), **42**, pp. 362–70.

KUBIE, L. S., *Neurotic Distortion of the Creative Process*, University of Kansas Press, 1958.

LAING, R. D., *The Divided Self*, Tavistock Publications, London, 1960; Barnes & Noble, New York, 1960.

LAING, R. D., *The Self and Others*, Tavistock Publications, London, 1961; Barnes & Noble, New York, 1961.

LAING, R. D., *The Politics of Experience*, Penguin Books, Harmondsworth, 1967.

LANGER, SUSANNE K., *Philosophy in a New Key*, Harvard University Press, 1951.

LAPLANCHE, J., and PONTALIS, J.-B., *Vocabulaire de la Psychanalyse*, Presses Universitaires de Paris, 1967.

Larousse Encyclopedia of Mythology, Batchworth, London, 1959.

LEVEY, H. B., 'A Critique of the Theory of Sublimation', *Psychiatry* (1939), **2**, pp. 239–70.

LEWIN, B. D., 'Sleep, the Mouth and the Dream Screen', *Psychoanal. Quart.* (1946), **15**, pp. 419–34.

LEWIN, B. D., *The Psychoanalysis of Elation*, Hogarth Press, London, 1951.

LIDZ, T., *The Family and Human Adaptation*, Hogarth Press, London, 1964; International Universities Press, New York, 1963.

LITTLE, MARGARET, 'Counter-Transference and the Patient's Response to It', *Int. J. Psycho-Anal.* (1951), **32**, pp. 32–40.

LOMAS, P., 'Psychoanalysis—Freudian or Existential', in Rycroft (1966), pp. 119–48.

LORENZ, K., *On Aggression*, Harcourt Brace & World, Inc., New York, 1966.

LORENZ, MARIA, 'Language as Expressive Behaviour', *Arch. Neurol. Psychiat.* (1953), **70**, pp. 277–85.

LORENZ, MARIA, and COBB, S., 'Language Behaviour in Psychoneurotic Patients', *Arch, Neurol. Psychiat.* (1953), **69**, pp. 684–94.

LYND, HELEN MERRELL, *On Shame and the Search for Identity*, Harcourt Brace & World, Inc., New York, 1958.

MCDOUGALL, W., *An Introduction to Social Psychology* (1908). 22nd edition, Methuen, London, 1931; Barnes & Noble, New York, 1950.

MALAN, D. H., *A Study of Brief Psychotherapy*, J. B. Lippincott, Philadelphia, 1963.

MARTIN, D. V., *Adventure in Psychiatry*, Cassirer, Oxford, 1962.

MAY, R., *Psychology and the Human Dilemma*, Van Nostrand, Princeton, N.J., 1967.

MEAD, MARGARET, *Male and Female*, Gollancz, London, 1950; William Morrow & Co., New York, 1949.

MEAD, MARGARET, *Sex and Temperament in Three Primitive Societies*, Routledge & Kegan Paul, London, 1935.

'MEDICA' [JOAN MALLESON] *Any Wife or Any Husband*, 2nd edition, Heinemann, London, 1955.

MOHR, J. W., TURNER, R. E., and JERRY, M. R., 'Pedophilia and Exhibitionism', Toronto University Press, 1964.

OSWALD, I., *Sleep*, Penguin Books, Baltimore, 1966.

BIBLIOGRAPHY

Oxford English Dictionary, Clarendon Press, Oxford, 1933.

PAYNE, SYLVIA, 'A Conception of Femininity', *Brit. J. Med. Psych.* (1953), **15**, pp. 18–33.

PIERS, G., and SINGER, M., *Shame and Guilt*, C. C. Thomas, Springfield, Ill., 1953.

RADO, S., 'The Psychoanalysis of Pharmacothymia', *Psychoanal. Quart.* (1933), **2**, pp. 1–23.

RANK, O., *The Trauma of Birth* (1924), English translation, Kegan Paul, London, 1929; Basic Books, New York, 1952.

RAPAPORT, D., *Organization and Pathology of Thought*, Columbia University Press. 1951.

RAPAPORT, D., 'On the Psycho-Analytic Theory of Affects', *Int. J. Psycho-Anal.* (1953), **34**, pp. 177–98.

ROSEN, J., *Direct Analysis*, Grune & Stratton, New York, 1953.

ROSENBERG, ELIZABETH, 'Anxiety and the Capacity to Bear It', *Int. J. Psycho-Anal.* (1949), **30**, pp. 1–12.

RYCROFT, C., 'A Contribution to the Study of the Dream Screen' (1951), in *Imagination and Reality*, Hogarth Press, London, 1968.

RYCROFT, C., 'On Idealization, Illusion and Catastrophic Disillusion' (1955), in *Imagination and Reality*, Hogarth Press, London, 1968.

RYCROFT, C., 'Symbolism and Its Relation to the Primary and Secondary Processes' (1956), in *Imagination and Reality*, Hogarth Press, London, 1968.

RYCROFT, C., 'The Function of Words in the Psychoanalytical Situation' (1958), in *Imagination and Reality*, Hogarth Press, London, 1968.

RYCROFT, C., 'Beyond the Reality Principle', in *Imagination and Reality*, Hogarth Press, London, 1968.

RYCROFT, C. (ed.), *Psychoanalysis Observed*, Constable, London, 1966, Coward-McCann, Inc., New York, 1967.

RYCROFT, C., *Anxiety and Neurosis*, Allen Lane, the Penguin Press, London.

SARTRE, J.-P., *Being and Nothingness*, Philosophical Library, New York, 1956.

SCHOFIELD, W., *Psychotherapy: The Purchase of Friendship*, Prentice-Hall, Englewood Cliffs, N.J., 1964.

SEARLES, H., *The Non-Human Environment in Schizophrenia*, International Universities Press, New York, 1960.

SEARLES, H., *Collected Papers on Schizophrenia*, Hogarth Press, London, 1965; International Universities Press, New York, 1965.

SEGAL, HANNA, 'Notes on Symbol Formation', *Int. J. Psycho-Anal.* (1957), **38**, pp. 391–7.

SEGAL, HANNA, *Introduction to the Work of Melanie Klein*, Basic Books, New York, 1964.

SHARPE, ELLA, *Dream Analysis*, Hogarth Press, London, 1937.

SHARPE, ELLA, *Collected Papers on Psycho-Analysis*, Hogarth Press, London, 1950.

SPITZ, R., 'Anaclitic Depression', *Psychoanal. Study of the Child* (1946), **2**, pp. 313–42.

SPITZ, R., *A Genetic Field Theory of Ego Formation*, International Universities Press, New York, 1959.

STENGEL, E., *Suicide and Attempted Suicide*, Penguin Books, Harmondsworth, 1964; Hillary House, New York, 1964.

STERBA, R., 'The Fate of the Ego in Analytic Therapy', *Int. J. Psycho-Anal.* (1934), **15**, pp. 117–26.

STORR, A., *The Integrity of the Personality*, Atheneum, New York, 1960.

STRACHEY, J., 'The Nature of the Therapeutic Action of Psycho-Analysis', *Int. J. Psycho-Anal.* (1934), **15**, pp. 127–59.

SUTTIE, I. D., *The Origins of Love and Hate* (1935), Julian Press, New York, 1960.

SZASZ, T., *The Myth of Mental Illness*, Secker & Warburg, London, 1962; Harper & Row, New York, 1961.

TINBERGEN, N., *The Study of Instinct*, Oxford, New York, 1951.

VEIT, ILZA, *Hysteria: The History of a Disease*, University of Chicago Press, 1965.

WHEELIS, A., *The Quest for Identity*, Gollancz, London, 1959; W. W. Norton, New York, 1958.

WHITROW, G. J., *The Natural Philosophy of Time*, Nelson, London, 1961.

WINNICOTT, D. W., *Collected Papers*, Tavistock Publications, London, 1958; Basic Books, New York, 1957.

WISDOM, J. O., 'A Methodological Approach to the Problem of Hysteria', *Int. J. Psycho-Anal.* (1961), **43**, pp. 224–37.

WYNNE, L. C., *et al.*, 'Pseudo-Mutuality in the Family Relations of Schizophrenics', *Psychiatry* (1958), **21**, pp. 205–20.